Agent
Bishop

Mike McPheters is that pleasant neighbor next door whom you might never expect to be an FBI agent. Then you discover that his life has been as full of adventure as Jack Bauer's. The difference is, he does moonlight as a minister who rescues marriages that are unraveling and youth who are on a slippery slope to immorality. One day, he holds an automatic pistol in his hand. The next evening, he may lay his hands on the head of an ailing Church member to invoke the power of his priesthood As you read this book, you will experience the profound balance this man achieved as he weeded out the bad and nurtured the good in people from all walks of life. You will have great difficulty putting this book down.

—**Darby Checketts,** Author of *The New American Prosperity*

[Mike McPheters] has led two fascinating lives that he has woven into a real-life and interesting story. When we first met, I then suspected he had a "rendezvous with destiny" that many strive for, but few attain. His sharing of personal experiences that crisscrossed over the years will enlighten the reader with his humble presentation. Mike's specificity of detail never falters, regardless of whatever facet of his story that he relates. He made me proud of him years ago—he has done it again.

—**Edwin J. Sharp,** Assistant Director, FBI (retired).

It's difficult, if not impossible, to express what a fine book has been authored by former FBI agent of thirty years, Mike McPheters. I was a supervisor with Mike on my squad until I retired in 1976. I worked with many agents in my twenty-five years and none could compare with Mike. Readers of his stories will agree it's a fine and interesting book.

—**Robert G. Strong,** Supervisory Special Agent, FBI (retired)

Agent Bishop

True Stories from an **FBI Agent**
Moonlighting as a
Mormon Bishop

MIKE MCPHETERS

CFI
Springville, Utah

ISBN 13: 978-1-59955-317-7

Published by CFI, an imprint of Cedar Fort, Inc., 2373 W. 700 S., Springville, UT 84663
Distributed by Cedar Fort, Inc., www.cedarfort.com

LIBRARY OF CONGRESS CATALOGING-IN-PUBLICATION DATA
McPheters, Mike, 1943-
  Agent bishop / Mike McPheters.
    p. cm.
  ISBN 978-1-59955-317-7 (acid-free paper)
  1. McPheters, Mike, 1943- 2. United States. Federal Bureau of
Investigation--Biography. 3. Government investigators--United
States--Biography. 4. Church of Jesus Christ of Latter-day
Saints--Bishops--Biography. 5. Mormons--United States--Biography. I.
Title.

  HV7911.M3885A3 2009
  363.25092--dc22
  [B]

2009010071

Cover design by Jen Boss
Cover design © 2009 by Lyle Mortimer

Printed in the United States of America

10 9 8 7 6 5 4 3 2

Printed on acid-free paper

Dedication

Many people, both inside and outside The Church of Jesus Christ of Latter-Day Saints (LDS or Mormons), have asked me how I balanced the need for aggression and toughness, along with the "24-7" time commitment mandated by the Federal Bureau of Investigation (FBI), with the compassion, empathy, and dedication necessary to serve as the bishop of LDS congregations four times during a thirty year career with the Bureau.

Since I was not home much of the time during my "agent bishop" years, others inquire as to how I kept my own marriage intact and raised five children who excelled in their endeavors, finished college, and raised their families in the Church.

The answer: Rising up early in the morning and having a superwoman for a wife, a wife who was there for the kids when I couldn't be, and one who always had a hot meal ready and a shoulder to lean on when I needed it.

Being the wife of an FBI agent and a Mormon bishop simultaneously is another story for another book. Judy learned to be ready for anything, from giving me a good-bye kiss at 4:00 AM when I strapped on a pistol and walked out the door, to watching in amazement in church, as I rushed off the stand where I was presiding over a sacrament meeting to chase down a thief who was stealing tools from a pickup belonging to a member of my congregation.

The pages of this book are dedicated to the light of my life: my wife, Judy.

CONTENTS

acknowledgments
★ ★ ★ ★ ★

Like all first time authors, I have many people to thank for inspiring me to write. I could mention Chloe Winston whose writing seminar I attended aboard a cruise ship years ago, or Darby Checketts, a great motivational writer who encouraged me to "get the music out." It was my wife, Judy, however, that has always wanted me to write, and I am thankful to her.

When I undertook this writing, I asked several individuals to read and critique the chapters as I wrote them. Some were writers. Some were not. Some were acquaintances. Some I didn't even know. Some were members of my church. Others were not. It was this cross section of folks with different input that gave a healthy balance, and hopefully, adequate objectivity to my writing.

For the above generosity, I wholeheartedly thank Leah Bowen, Fred Rhodes, Kathy Houk, Myra Creviston, Joe Frechette, Lee Ann Fairbanks, and Bill Hayes.

I'm also indebted to the following individuals for their insights and encouragement: Myrna Houston, Frank Duffin, Leon Fish, Dave Callan, June Strickler, Irv Bruce, Ed Sharp, Bill "Cop" Kelly, Dave Jellison, Bob Strong, Charles Southerland.

Special thanks to Ed Sharp, retired Assistant Director of the FBI, who "greased the skids" for me by putting me in touch with the pertinent individuals at FBI Headquarters in Washington D. C. who granted me publishing authority.

Without the help of Darcy Creviston and Fred Rhodes, who did much of the pre-editing before my book went to the publisher, the grammar would have been a little ragged and creative insights would have been lost in thin air.

With very few exceptions, the characters' true names are used. The dialogue is essentially paraphrasing what I remember and in some instances is word for word. Where that is not the case, I created the dialogue to fit the situations based upon my intimate knowledge of the characters.

Last, but certainly not least, I thank my fellow FBI agents for their fidelity, bravery, and integrity and those who exhibited those same characteristics in serving with me in four bishoprics.

prologue

★ ★ ★ ★ ★

BECOMING THE AGENT BISHOP

August 1973

If a man desire the office of a bishop, he desireth a good work. A bishop then must be blameless, the husband of one wife, vigilant, sober, of good behaviour, given to hospitality, apt to teach. Not given to wine, no striker, not greedy or of filthy lucre; but patient, not a brawler, not covetous. One that ruleth well his own house, having his children in subjection with all gravity. (1 Timothy 3:1–4)

Throughout my life I have always looked up to and admired the bishops of my church, but never really planned to be one. Later in life, when my callings as bishop overlapped four times with my career as a special agent with the FBI, my wife asked me when I would finally "get it right." My response was that I was a slow learner.

Many people have asked how I was able to be successful in both my roles—the agent and the bishop. During the day, I dealt with the dregs of our society. During the evening, I counseled youths to be morally clean and parents to hold their marriages together. I fought crime and Satan with a pistol in one hand and the scriptures in the other.

My grandfather, Samuel Worthington, was a bishop in Boise, Idaho, and served that city at the same time as its mayor and city councilor. During that period, he also ran a huge coal company, so I knew it was possible to be busy and still devote time to the Lord.

Usually, the calling of a bishop comes as a surprise. It was not so in my case. I arrived at the Miami FBI office early one morning and walked over to my desk in the bull pen area.

What's that on my desk? I wondered, eyeing the thick binder that sat on the scratched metal surface, recalling that I had left it cleared the night before.

It was the Official Handbook of Instructions for The Church of Jesus Christ of Latter-day Saints. Special Agent Leon Fish, who had been transferred to Puerto Rico, had left it there. He was bishop of our ward, the Miami Third Ward, and I had been serving as his counselor for the previous two years.

Lee was not there with an explanation.

A light went on in my mind, and I figured it out. I stood there with a lump in my throat, contemplating the depth of ecclesiastical responsibility I would be taking on a few days later, when I was officially sustained as the next bishop. Other agents were settling in at the adjacent desks with their case files, noticing the expression of astonishment that had totally overtaken me. They must have thought I'd been transferred to a rotten squad detail or that I'd been notified I was behind on my mortgage.

I sat down, trying to get my breath and take inventory of my pulse and blood pressure. This was a monumental challenge that would have to be added to a ten hour work day as a G-man. I vaguely noticed a series of intermittent squeaking sounds, which jolted me out of my fixation on this new calling, and came to the strange realization that it was the sound of leather from my shoes, nervously scraping against the floor.

I quickly grabbed the manual and began thumbing through page after page without seeing any of them, asking myself how I would find the time I needed for Judy and the kids, but knowing the Lord would never give me an assignment that I didn't have the ability to fulfill. There was not a doubt in my mind. Of course I would accept the call when it came "officially."

On August 23, 1973, I traveled with my family from Miami to Salt Lake City, Utah, where I was ordained and set apart by Bernard P. Brockbank, an Assistant to the Quorum of Twelve Apostles. I had been called to preside over our congregation by President Harold B. Lee.

My duties were to minister to the needs of the youth and to counsel, admonish, and motivate Church members to become better people. I was also to administer the Church's welfare program and to take charge of the tithes and offerings.

From that day on, I began a quest for spiritual and temporal balance in my life. What I wasn't yet aware of was the contrasting, yet fascinating, range of experiences I would enjoy while being both a Mormon bishop and an FBI agent.

I would perform a marriage one weekend and arrest a bridegroom at his wedding on another.

I would travel to Salt Lake City one weekend to be set apart as a bishop and would attend Catholic Mass in the Virgin Islands on a homicide case the next.

I would show up at a Church road show practice in camouflage and face paint from a SWAT exercise just in time to wipe the grease paint from my face before my part.

I would spend countless hours kicking in doors and arresting armed and dangerous fugitives in early morning raids and then praying with those who needed to confide their sins to me, as their bishop, in the late evenings.

I would nearly die in a bloody shoot-out, while taking another life to preserve my own.

$$\star \quad \star \quad \star \quad \star$$

The agent bishop dichotomy was tested in a host of different situations, some more dramatic than others, like the time I rushed from behind the pulpit during a Church meeting to pursue a thief.

We were worshipping inside the old Miami Third Ward chapel on Northwest Ninety-fifth Street. The neighborhood around the church was rapidly becoming a high-crime area. In a prior incident, Lucy Peele, an elderly widow, had had her purse snatched on the front steps, while ascending into the chapel.

In a subsequent incident, two rifle shots were fired into the building: one through the window of the Family History Center and another through the chapel, lodging in the curtains behind the pulpit.

This particular Sunday, however, I was seated on the stand, listening to the concluding speaker finish his talk. I looked up to see Luis Villareal, a friend and fellow member, running in from the foyer and waving frantically for me to come down. No one else seemed to notice him.

In full view of about two hundred and fifty astonished members, I rushed off the stand and down the center aisle. This didn't qualify as a normal occurrence.

Approaching Luis, I asked, "What's wrong?"

"They're stealing Frank Fager's tools!" he whispered urgently. "You better get out there!" He pointed out a black youth, who was helping himself to the power tools in Frank's pickup. Frank made his living as a carpenter.

I raced outside. When I reached the parking lot and searched quickly for Frank's pickup, I saw the young male in his twenties, loading himself up with Frank's tools: a circular saw, hammers, measuring tapes, a sander, and other items. He saw me coming and charged across the church parking lot into the surrounding residential area, straining under the weight of all the tools.

"Hey, you, drop those tools!" I yelled, but he just kept running.

"I'm a law enforcement officer! Stop!" I shouted, as I ran after him. I was thirty-three years old, and in a suit and tie. The thief was much younger, only about twenty, but he was packing a lot of dead weight, which definitely gave me an advantage.

We were both sprinting through a black neighborhood, occupied by curious residents who were being entertained with a footrace between a member of their community and a white man in a dark suit, with his tie flapping in the wind.

I began closing in, as we ran by house after house, and through yard after yard. The thief started dropping portions of his booty, as I closed the gap. First jettisoned off to the side were the circular saw and sander, then the smaller tools.

After running through North Miami neighborhoods for about a quarter mile, the young man decided it was in his best interests just to escape and leave everything behind. I was exhausted and relieved to see him drop the tools and jog slowly away . . . empty-handed.

When I returned with the tools, the service was over. I entered the foyer of the chapel saturated in sweat, with dust covering my wingtip shoes. I realized several members of the congregation were putting two and two together. They had to be thinking: this is in the job description for a bishop?

How did I become involved in the dual role of agent and bishop? It all began with a Western Union telegram from FBI headquarters.

1

★★★★★

The Appointment

July 15, 1968
SAMUEL M MCPHETERS
410 VILLAGE LANE
BOISE, IDAHO
343-0816

YOU ARE OFFERED PROBATIONARY APPOINTMENT SPECIAL AGENT GRADE GS TEN SALARY NINETY TWO HUNDRED NINETY SEVEN DOLLARS PER ANNUM FOLLOWING ASSIGNMENT TO FIELD OFFICE ADDITIONAL COMPENSATION OF TWENTY THREE HUNDRED TWENTY NINE DOLLARS AND SIXTY CENTS PER YEAR MAY BE EARNED FOR OVERTIME PERFORMANCE IN CONNECTION WITH OFFICIAL DUTIES PROVIDED CERTAIN REQUIREMENTS ARE MET REPORT NINE AM JULY TWENTY SECOND ROOM SIX TWO FIVE OLD POST OFFICE BUILDING TWELFTH STREET AND PENNSYLVANIA AVENUE NORTHWEST WASHINGTON DC NO PUBLICITY SHOULD BE GIVEN IF YOU HAVE BEEN PLACED ON NOTICE BY ANY ARMED SERVICE THAT YOU ARE ABOUT TO BE ORDERED TO ACTIVE DUTY PLEASE ADVISE THIS BUREAU SO THAT APPOINTMENT MAY BE CANCELLED ACCEPTANCE OF APPOINTMENT CONSTITUTES AGREEMENT TO REMAIN THREE YEARS IF WORK SATISFACTORY ADVISE IMMEDIATELY OF ACCEPTANCE APPOINTMENT SUBJECT TO CANCELLATION OR POSTPONEMENT PRIOR TO ENTRY ON DUTY LETTER FOLLOWS
JOHN EDGAR HOOVER DIRECTOR FEDERAL BUREAU OF INVESTIGATION

There it was. The long awaited appointment as a special agent with the FBI.

Many would call being a G-man one of the toughest, most prestigious jobs in the world. It seemed incredible to me that I was even considered for the appointment. I was from the rural reaches of Ketchum, Idaho, and had only worked mundane resort jobs at nearby Sun Valley, such as bell-hop, skeet loader at the gun club, pin-setter at the bowling alley, and golf caddy. You might agree that delivering snacks to movie stars like Robert Young, or running the elevator for Frankie Avalon and Lucille Ball was interesting, but certainly not prestigious.

On the other hand, that telegram from Washington, D. C. meant I would become a special agent with the Federal Bureau of Investigation . . . a G-man! If I could survive the fourteen weeks training, and find my niche, I could actually add the adjective "meaningful" to my life's work, and maybe bring down some bad guys as well.

The telegram changed my family forever.

I had a degree from Brigham Young University, but no employment. To keep the wolves away from our door, I commuted sixty miles each way from Boise, Idaho, to Ontario, Oregon, where I taught General Equivalency Diploma (GED) courses to Mexican migrants at Treasure Valley Community College. The concept of permanent and steady paychecks from the world's premier law enforcement agency was exciting, to say the least. The Bureau's offer of eleven thousand dollars a year was good money in 1968.

During the eight months it took the FBI to conduct my background investigation, I often daydreamed as I commuted to work, envisioning myself kicking in doors, solving bank robberies, saving hostages, and handcuffing fugitives. It never crossed my mind that I might also be doing boring work, like writing reports and attending file reviews.

The months it took the FBI to conduct my background clearance seemed to go on forever. I often doubted I would cut it. I worried that maybe I had inadvertently forgotten to list all my traffic tickets on my application. *What if I forgot one? Will they think I'm some kind of crook? Why has it taken so long to hear back?*

Eight months had passed since I submitted my application.

I envisioned an army of FBI agents, trodding through remote parts of Uruguay and Paraguay, where I served as a missionary, checking with old landlords and police departments, making sure I was squeaky clean.

I wondered what my home town sheriff, Les Jankow, had told the

G-Men. Did he remember the mischief? That could be painful! Les was an impressive figure, carved right out of the old west. He stood six feet two inches tall and weighed at least two hundred pounds. He always wore a western shirt, a big oval belt buckle, cowboy boots, and a ten-gallon hat. He toted a big revolver on his hip.

I remember as a youth seeing Les in Sun Valley, standing next to James Arness, who played Matt Dillon in the *Gunsmoke* television series. They were carbon copies of each other.

One would expect Les to ride through Ketchum on a horse, rather than in that maroon Pontiac with the blue lights. He always displayed an air of congeniality towards us boys, in spite of the shenanigans we played on him at Halloween. That was the time to deflate his tires, so we could have our way with our little town. The fact that the Bureau would have contacted Les and had probably turned over every leaf in my past made me more than a little nervous.

Especially troubling was the incident where my friends and I got our hands on some smoke canisters used to eradicate gophers from the Sun Valley golf course. One night we lit one on the doorstep of a mobile home about half a block from the Spur Theater, then knocked, and ran.

While walking backwards, so as to be able to observe the expressions on our victim's face when he opened the door to a cloud of smoke, I backed right up into none other than Sheriff Les.

I will not go into detail about the water balloons plummeting off the top of the Alpine Café onto the drunks exiting the door below, the cars that couldn't make it up the hills in the winter because of the hooky-bobbers they were pulling, or the outhouses that ended up in Ketchum's main intersection on Halloween. For now, I will just say that I will be eternally grateful for Les's selective short memory when the G-Men came calling.

★ ★ ★ ★ ★

The week I had to report was just enough time to round up a suit and some ties, to say good-byes to family and friends, and to figure out how to get from what is now Reagan National Airport to the Harrington Hotel in downtown Washington, D.C.

Once I checked into the Harrington on July 21, 1968, the first new agent trainee I met was John Munis from Montana. I knew we both probably had a few elk hunting stories we could share, but other than that, it seemed there was very little I could connect with in this strange new environment. I had

Mike's Training Class
New Agents Class Two: Mike is on the back row, fifth from the left

immersed myself in Latin American culture for two and a half years, and had attended both a Presbyterian college and a Mormon university, so I wasn't entirely naïve. In fact, I was beginning to feel a surge of confidence. Nevertheless, I had yet to find my niche in the FBI culture, starting with "New Agents Class Two."

The next day I reported to Room 625, in the Old Post Office building at Twelfth Street and Pennsylvania Avenue Northwest where I joined forty-nine new agent candidates from all over the country.

After a brief introduction to the FBI by some high-ranking Bureau officials, I raised my right arm to the square, was sworn in, and was charged with investigating violations of the laws of the United States.

My training as a Special Agent with the FBI had commenced.

After five weeks, Judy sold our Volkswagen in Boise and quit her job, so she and baby Marni could come out and join me. It was such a joy to pick them up at the airport and hold them both in my arms. We rented an apartment in Arlington, Virginia, where we attended the Arlington Ward. We had no car, so we took buses to visit the major sites in D.C. on my free time. One Saturday I volunteered to participate in building calf stalls in the Church's dairy farm in Maryland as a service assignment on one of the Church's welfare projects.

★ ★ ★ ★ ★

Coming from a religious background, with a taboo against drinking, smoking, carousing, or using profanity, my agent classmates considered me a little peculiar. Tipping a few brews in Quantico taverns, or a night of partying in downtown Washington D.C., was not on my agenda.

I was a little younger than most of my class, and certainly more naïve. I was surrounded by people who were already professionals in other fields and were in career transitions. Surely, in their eyes, I had yet to travel up the hill and over the pass.

Our group of fifty trainees included attorneys, teachers, college-educated police officers, a CIA agent, and others with experience in the corporate sector. My specialty was languages: Spanish and French. We were all of the white male, garden-variety type. Diversity hiring was still in the embryonic stage.

For fourteen weeks, Bureau instructors blitzed us with courses in conducting investigations, surveillance, fingerprinting, photography, report writing, interviewing techniques, and defensive tactics.

The major attraction was the firearms training in Quantico, Virginia. It was on the Marine Corps base, where to qualify we had to shoot a score of seventy out of a hundred, with a thirty-eight caliber handgun. I shot a ninety-six once.

Through weeks of intense range instruction, the commands "Ready on the left! Ready on the right! All ready on the line!" became our mantra.

"Hogan's Alley," as I knew it, no longer exists. In this course, the shooter moved rapidly from one target to the next, making split second decisions to shoot or not to shoot at simulated human targets sliding out from fake building fronts. There were a variety of scenarios. If we misjudged the scenario, and proceeded to shoot a duck hunter or a hostage, we failed the course. An FBI agent shoots Hogan's Alley only once in a lifetime.

New Agent Firearms Training

Left: Hogan's Alley   Center: Mike takes aim at a target
Right: Mike shoots from a seven-yard line at a silhouette cutout

At the end of each day of classroom work, we worked off our nervous energy in the gym. We paired off, strapped on boxing gloves, and went at it, but never at full speed.

Our instructor, Jim Gump, taught us disarming techniques. He sold us on the concept that action was faster than reaction. Gump showed us how to sweep a handgun out of our opponent's grasp before he could pull the trigger. I'm grateful I never had to pull that one off on the street.

Time flew during the firearms training and stood still during the instruction in writing communications and conducting interviews.

The instructor thought my FD-302s were a little too "flowery." The FD-302 is the gem of the investigative reports, the "bread and butter" document of the Bureau, utilized for recording information that could eventually be testified to in court. The instructors had mastered the art of unveiling journalistic mediocrity in their trainees.

We were told that only one out of thirty-five FBI applicants were accepted for training. Out of my group of fifty, forty-two made it through, which attests to the fact that the Bureau is very choosy about who they put out on the street with a gun and credentials.

NOVEMBER 1968

It was "Assignment Day." We were ready.

The only real street work we experienced as trainees was one week with an experienced agent mentoring us. I spent the week in Maryland, doing background reinvestigations of Atomic Energy Commission employees. I envied the trainees who got to work fugitives and bank robberies that week. Nevertheless, after three months in class, even background checking was a breath of fresh air.

Everyone was guessing on their transfers. Since I was fluent in Spanish, my hunch was San Antonio, Texas. Places like New York City and Newark also needed Spanish-speakers, but new agents were usually spared the big city assignments for their first office. Medium to small-sized cities were, in the Bureau's view, more learner-friendly and far less traumatic from both the financial and mental viewpoints.

One of my class counselors read off the assignments. "Special Agent McPheters: San Diego, California." Yes! Who wouldn't want to go there? Great climate, beautiful beaches, and eleven thousand dollars a year. The balmy November temperature would be frosting on the cake.

★ ★ ★ ★ ★

We arrived in California with Judy eight and a half months pregnant and without a car. We bought a Chevrolet Impala and rented a house in Claremont. It was a great place for folks on a budget, and only ten miles from downtown San Diego and the beaches.

Two weeks later, the stork dropped off Shad Michael, our second baby.

The exhilaration of having a revolver and FBI credentials was almost overwhelming. However, after hearing about the overexuberant agent trainee who discharged a bullet through a television screen while sighting his revolver in on screen images, I was able to keep my thirty-eight caliber revolver holstered.

My first Special Agent in Charge (SAC), Bob Evans, presented a picture of authority and an air of detachment as he strode through the office with a Havana cigar in his mouth the length of a three wood. Evans was the epitome of the Bureau tough boss, but never hurt anyone that I knew of. He loved to hunt desert sheep with a Mexican guide in the lower reaches of the Baja Peninsula.

At office conferences, Evans would ramble through a couple Bureau directives, throw in a few observations, and then relinquish the floor to a senior agent, who stressed the need to cut back on time spent in the office in order to present our best image for a forthcoming inspection.

Every two or three years, an inspection staff, who the street agents would jokingly refer to as "Snow White and the Seven Dwarfs," would strike fear into the hearts of the agents and our supervisors. Files would be scrutinized, judgment would be questioned, and more often than not, heads would roll. Their sojourn in the host office could never end soon enough.

★ ★ ★ ★ ★

During that first week in the San Diego office, I noticed a letter from Director J. Edgar Hoover posted in the hallway. It was a congratulatory message to the elderly mother of a Bureau legend: Special Agent Samuel P. Cowley. His mother resided in San Diego. To honor both her and her legendary son, a street was named Cowley Way. In the letter, Director Hoover congratulated the Inspector's mother and wrote, "Sam Cowley was one of the greatest examples of physical and moral courage I have ever known."

That comment inspired me.

Cowley was a young Mormon attorney from Utah, hired in 1929 as a special agent by what was then called the Bureau of Investigation. He was promoted to the rank of Inspector in 1934 and eventually worked in the

Kansas City, Cincinnati, and Chicago field offices.

Cowley was widely-known for his sharp mind and tireless work ethic. Director Hoover assigned him to supervise the crusade against the infamous gangsters of the 1930s. In 1934, he coordinated the arrests of Charles Arthur "Pretty Boy" Floyd and John Dillinger, Public Enemy Number One, who had killed eight law enforcement officers in a bloody crime spree.

On the evening of July 22, 1934, Cowley positioned agents outside the Biograph Theatre in Chicago. They had received a tip from an informant, Anna Sage, that Dillinger would accompany her and Polly Hamilton that evening to see the Clark Gable movie, *Manhattan Melodrama*. Anna would be dressed in red, resulting in her subsequent news media reference as "The Lady in Red."

At 10:30 PM, Dillinger exited the theater with Anna on one arm and Polly on the other. Waiting outside, Agent Melvin Purvis lit a cigar, signaling the other agents to close in. As Dillinger ran for the alley, he grabbed a pistol from his right pocket, but before he could discharge a round, he was hit by three FBI bullets, and died at 10:50 PM.

Four months later, on November 27, 1934, Inspector Cowley and Special Agent Herman E. Hollis responded to a lead that Lester Gillis "Baby Face" Nelson was in the Lake Como, Wisconsin, area. Nelson, his wife, and a cohort, John Paul Chase, were located in a car near Barrington, Illinois.

A gun battle erupted. Agents Cowley and Hollis disabled Gillis' vehicle, which he abandoned. However, as the agents closed in for the arrest, Gillis and Chase succeeded in gaining a tactical advantage and shot down both agents.

Cowley went down firing, hitting his target repeatedly. Nelson died the next day, riddled with seventeen bullets. Chase was subsequently apprehended and sentenced to life in prison.

We new agents needed examples. Sam Cowley's legend was there for me, but I found another living legend. He was my new bishop, Jordan Naylor, a relief supervisor in the San Diego office who had been involved in several Top Ten fugitive apprehensions. He was the "designated hitter" for running high profile cases. He was not only a respected agent, but a dedicated Church leader, totally devoted to his wife, Marian, and his ten children. He inspired me and whetted my appetite for meaningful achievement, both in the Bureau and in the Church.

2

WORKING DRAFT DODGERS
AND DESERTERS

JANUARY 1969

Every new agent in San Diego was assigned to investigate Selective Service violators, or draft dodgers, for the first six months of his probationary year. We made regular runs to the San Diego County Jail to question arrestees who were booked without their draft cards. Generally, admonishments were given, but most of those cases were not prosecuted.

I covered some leads on a draft dodger I will never forget: Daniel Ben Jordan, a killer and a prior disciple of Ervil LeBaron, who was the founder of "The Church of the Firstborn of the Lamb of God."

★ ★ ★ ★ ★

It was August 20, 1972. Fourteen-year-old Ivan waited outside the house. His sneakers softly stirred the ever-present dust in which he stood. The blistering sun, unmitigated by more friendly cloud cover, beat down on his bare neck. It was typical weather for that time of year in Ensenada, Mexico, where he lived.

Inside the house, Ivan's father, Joel LeBaron, was negotiating the delivery of a pickup. Joel was the anointed leader of The Church of The Firstborn.

Ivan shifted uncomfortably as he sat on the curb. Time had passed. Too much time. He'd been worried earlier, before the meeting, but his father had assured him, saying, "I'll be out in a few minutes. Just wait here."

Ivan craned his neck to turn and look back at the house. He was on edge and increasingly more apprehensive. The whole tenor and mood of the men who opened the door for his father had been far too eager and patronizing.

He thought, *Shouldn't father have been through by now?*

The voices inside the house began to escalate and become more aggressive, and Ivan sensed that something might have gone awry. A cadence of profane and angry accusations followed, and this time Ivan rose to his feet, fighting to stem his fears, as he began walking towards the house.

Suddenly, it occurred to Ivan why he had been left outside. His father had anticipated the chaos that was now erupting and wanted to spare Ivan from any part in it. As the angry voices rose to a fevered pitch, Ivan could no longer contain himself, and began running towards the house.

The command, "Kill him!" exploded from inside the house, followed by deafening gunshots. Overcome with turmoil, Ivan ran inside and found his father, lying face up in his own blood. One bullet had entered Joel LeBaron's head and another had pierced his throat.

Daniel Ben Jordan and another man, believed to be Gamaliel Rios, ran from the house, dove into a station wagon parked next to it, and sped away.

Ivan barely noticed, as the men who had killed his father disappeared. Instead, he sat on the floor in a motionless stupor, cradling his face in the palms of his hands and sobbing violently. Through glazed eyes he looked down and knew that his hopes of finding any sign of life in the limp and bloody shell of his father were in vain. He was dazed, bereft of the slightest ray of comprehension.

In Ivan's mind, his father was one of God's chosen, a charismatic religious leader, not a target for assassination. Little did he know that his father's life had been snuffed out by his own flesh and blood. Ervil LeBaron had ordered his own brother's murder and was waiting anxiously for confirmation that Joel was put to rest, and that his edict had been successfully carried out. Ervil detested his brother and envied Joel's popularity as the leader of The Church of the Firstborn of the Fullness of Times. Fratricide came easily to a man like Ervil, who had even ordered the death of his own seventeen-year-old pregnant daughter.

Ervil was certain that as a spiritual leader, he could do much better for Joel's followers. He had tired of being second to one who couldn't possibly possess those qualities of leadership and charisma that he fancied possessing in such abundance.

Ervil was born in 1925, the son of a polygamist exile who had failed to register for the World War II draft. His family of farmers had founded a Mexican colony in Colonia LeBaron. Alma LeBaron, Ervil and Joel's father, was a self-proclaimed minister who had relegated his claim to authority to Joel, who was his oldest son.

The decree issued by Ervil to kill Joel was the crowning achievement in a power play to take over and maintain control of the members of his father's church. His brother was only the first of many that Ervil would order exterminated.

Ervil was a womanizer and fancy dresser who loved to be admired. He had become exasperated with the soft-spoken, low profile of his brother, so he started his own church, "The Church of the Firstborn of the Lamb of God." He thereafter began having revelations, including the one that directed him to kill Joel. In Ervil's mind, Joel had sinned against Heaven for not allowing him, Ervil, to have his way with their father's church.

Eighteen more murders followed.

The discord that culminated in Joel's murder was preceded by attacks, violence, and bloodshed in the Mexican colonies. Daniel Ben Jordan was surely an ongoing participant in the chaos, but the pivotal status of his role in it never fully came to light until he killed Joel LeBaron. In addition to murdering Joel LeBaron and his role in the Mexican skirmishes, Daniel Ben Jordan was also suspect in the murder of a huge man referred to as "a giant" in National City, California, near the Mexican border.

The Ben Jordan matter became known in Bureau jargon as an "old dog" case, since he had run free with impunity for so many years.

★ ★ ★ ★ ★

I was assigned to investigate the Ben Jordan matter a second time in the early 1980s, when he was apprehended in the Portland, Oregon area, and subsequently incarcerated in the Multnomah County Jail on the Selective Service charges. The draft dodger charges had become somewhat irrelevant,

Fresh out of training! Mike points to the map of his first assignment: San Diego.

since Selective Service violators were no longer being prosecuted, and further in view of the fact Ben Jordan was suspect in two homicides that ranked higher in priority.

I will never forget the day I interviewed Ben Jordan subsequent to his appearance in federal court on the Selective Service charges.

While assigned to investigate violent Native American crimes on Indian reservations in Oregon and Utah, I smelled and observed death repeatedly. I once removed the body of a murdered Indian woman from her grave. I have witnessed autopsies and recovered body parts for evidence. I have arrested and interviewed organized crime subjects in Miami, drug traffickers in California and Florida, and have conducted dozens of interviews of child molesters. I've observed evil in all forms, both as an agent and as a bishop, but never have I seen evil such as I observed in the face of Daniel Ben Jordan.

"Mr. Ben Jordan, I'm Special Agent Mike McPheters, FBI," I said as we sat down across from each other in the bleak gray interrogation room of the Multnomah County Jail. "I'm here to visit with you regarding some outstanding Selective Service charges."

As I displayed my credentials, Ben Jordan maintained his silence with a penetrating, icy countenance. A hint of smile appeared, as he glared at me with a look that seemed to say, "Why should I talk to you when I've refused to say a word to anyone else?"

I continued. "I also want to discuss some murders in Mexico and California. But first I want to advise you of your rights."

The eyes narrowed, with even more hostility and contempt, and challenged me to look into a dark and ominous past. The silent glare, set in tandem with a clenched jaw, presented a trap, ready to spring. The mouth creased just enough at the edges to convince me that he was mocking me. With his thumbs solidly tucked inside clenched fists, he telegraphed the message that he would be saying nothing. Nevertheless, I proceeded with the Miranda warnings that the Bureau was meticulous in providing with subjects who were in custody.

As I delineated each of Ben Jordan's rights to counsel and the right to maintain silence, I was struck by his resolve not only to maintain silence in response to the charges against him, but also his refusal to even acknowledge my presence while I sat across from and directly in front of him.

Ben Jordan stood out from the many serial killers of the 1970s and 1980s that found sick satisfaction in discussing their homicidal exploits. Nor was he like murderers on the Indian reservations that killed in a drunken rage, and then remembered nothing the next day. Ben Jordan was so caught up in his evil web that he was overwhelmingly resolved not to shed light on even one drop of the blood he had spilled.

The interview terminated five minutes after it had started, without a word from Ben Jordan.

A couple days later, my office phone rang. The Assistant U.S. Attorney handling the Ben Jordan matter advised me all federal charges had been dismissed against him, and that he had walked out of the Multnomah County jail a free man. For reasons still unknown to me, the Mexican authorities had refused to extradite Ben Jordan for the murder of Joel LeBaron.

Ben Jordan's day of reckoning would soon come.

On October 9, 1987, while camping with family members in the Sanpete area of Utah, Ben Jordan was approached and shot repeatedly at close range. One round entered his head, execution style, much like the way he had killed Joel LeBaron fifteen years earlier. His death, like that of other cult defectors who had fallen out of favor with Ervil LeBaron, definitely bore ritualistic overtones.

Prior to his death, Ervil had compiled a hit list that he passed on to his children and his other sympathizers. Ben Jordan's name was only one of many that were on it. There are others living today, whose names are also on that list. Ervil eventually died in the Utah State Prison, where he had been sentenced for murdering Rulon Alred, a rival polygamist leader, who had refused to pay him tithes.

The fact that Ervil wound up in prison was comforting, but the hit list legacy he left behind was troubling. I couldn't help but wonder then, as I sometimes wonder now, who will be next?

May 1969

The Vietnam War, that commenced in 1959 and ended in 1975, cost fifty-eight thousand American lives. While the U.S. and its Western allies backed South Vietnam, the Soviet Union and the People's Republic of China supported the North Vietnamese. The end result was disastrous when South Vietnam lost and millions of Vietnamese and Cambodians were killed, along with Americans.

Prior to my assignment to San Diego, the United States had increased its troops from sixteen thousand military advisers in 1964, to more than five hundred and fifty three thousand servicemen in 1969. The grim possibility of dying in a tropical jungle was a prime catalyst for desertion from military service. At the height of the war, young recruits were going absent without official leave (AWOL) in droves from the Marine Corps Recruit Depot in San Diego and from the marine base at Camp Pendleton, California, while protestors were burning their draft cards.

I spent my second six months as a trainee investigating these deserters. The deserter squad was where I met Billy Musik, an older agent who was the expert on deserters. Billy was middle-aged and naturally not as fast on his feet as the young military runaways he pursued. Nevertheless, he always managed to bring them in. Some of the more experienced agents attributed much of Billy's success to a heavy, leather- covered "zapper" he carried with him that seemed to always find its mark.

Billy consumed saccharine tablets at the morning coffee breaks to help him comply with the insane Bureau weight requirements. In 1969, the Bureau's weight standards, which had to be met twice a year, were better fit for jockeys and ballet dancers than for FBI agents. Those standards offered no leniency for the big body type, no matter how athletic. Large-framed muscular agents could be in great physical shape, but were always over the prescribed weight. They could do little about it, except popping saccharine or grabbing the railing next to the scales to shift off some of the bulk during weigh-ins.

As FBI agents, we viewed deserters as emotional eighteen- to twenty-year-olds who couldn't cope with drill instructors screaming at them, a confining life style, and the rigors of basic training. We knew those challenges, coupled with the prospect of a premature death in Vietnam, were more than they could handle.

We younger agents were drawn to deserter cases. These guys would run, and we could chase them. They would hide, and we enjoyed searching for them, plucking them out of attics and from under beds, or grabbing them as they sprinted through back doors. Sometimes they fought, and we had to subdue them. The excitement and the adrenaline rush were great medicine for having been cooped up at the training academy for three and a half months, while learning to write reports.

The Marine Corps Recruit Depot in San Diego and locations in Camp Pendleton, an hour's drive north, such as Pulgas and Horno, became my daily haunts. I reviewed service record books, scrounged through abandoned duffel bags for contacts and addresses, and then set out leads throughout the country to locate and apprehend the deserters.

If the deserter was absent from service more than thirty days, his service branch would send a form to the Pentagon, advising he was unaccounted for. The Pentagon then requested the FBI to locate and apprehend him. The

Bureau sometimes looked bad when the service branch erroneously declared the serviceman a deserter, when in reality he was in Vietnam, earning a Purple Heart.

My first FBI arrest was a marine who had found refuge in a YMCA in downtown San Diego. He was sleeping in movie theaters and eating whatever he could scrounge. He was nineteen-years-old and had been gone for five months. I grabbed an experienced agent, Phil Austin, to assist me in my first apprehension.

As we ascended the staircase in the dilapidated YMCA building in downtown San Diego, I knew Austin could sense my excitement for my first "collar." With each step, the adrenaline pumped harder. I had visions from glamorous detective and police movies where law enforcement officers always successfully cornered their prey.

However, as I approached the subject's room, questions invaded my mind, as my pulse continued to quicken.

If he runs, will I be able to catch him? After all, this was my first arrest, and with an experienced agent looking on. Gotta do this right! What if he's carrying a gun? Will I draw on time?

I calmed down as I recalled the marine's physical description, which gave me a significant weight advantage of about fifteen pounds and a height advantage of three inches. *But still,* I thought, *this guy's a marine. It's been seven years since I played college football.*

Then I reassured myself. *It's okay, I've been working out.*

Upon reaching the door, I yelled, "FBI, open up!"

No response.

It finally occurred to me that I could open the door with the key the facility manager had provided. Austin and I quietly slipped into a meagerly-furnished room.

There he was . . . sound asleep. My fugitive deserter was naked as a jaybird, sawing logs, and frazzled.

I thought, almost disappointed, *It's not supposed to happen like this. No show of muscle or resistance. Where's the challenge?*

In five minutes we had the young marine dressed, handcuffed, and out the door.

"I'm ready to go back!" he yawned. "Sleeping in movies and not eating is not my idea of fun." He had a smile on his face, as if we had just invited him to go to dinner.

"Back to a warm cot and three squares a day," he exclaimed, happily.

Not exactly a headline arrest, but this guy was in the bag.

In another investigation, I contacted the parents of a youngster who absented himself from the Marine Corps Recruit Depot in San Diego. They swore they hadn't heard from their son in weeks, but there was a lingering doubt in my mind. Perhaps it was the tone of the father's voice, or the fleeting expression on the mother's face that told me otherwise.

With the parents' permission to search the house, I climbed into the attic with my flashlight. I spotted their son, nestled in the corner amid garage insulation, trembling, and with anxiety written all over his face. I gently motioned for him to come down to the floor level where I handcuffed and searched him.

Moments later, we were on our way.

There was a strict Bureau policy that an agent could not go after a fugitive alone or transport one without another agent or police officer present. While with another agent, we routinely strapped the handcuffed subject into the rear seat behind the front passenger area. While one agent drove, the other sat behind the driver, next to the arrestee.

In this circumstance, where I was alone, the wiser choice was seating the arrestee in the front passenger seat, strapped in and handcuffed. I went with that, picked up the radio, and called my signal into the office.

"This is M-17 [my code signal], with subject in custody. Approximate arrival time is forty-five minutes. Will need help upon arrival at the garage."

Since I had violated Bureau rules by arresting and transporting the subject by myself and could now be facing discipline, I began rationalizing. After all, I had just happened onto this guy. If I hadn't acted on my intuition and searched the attic, I wouldn't have found him. But when one violates a Bureau rule, mitigating circumstances don't always cut it. As a first office agent who had just made a solo arrest, I knew I was in for it and in a big way.

How long would this hold up my next raise? I asked myself. *Worse yet, would I get a letter of censure or do time on the bricks?*

Upon arriving at the office, I was met by another agent who helped me transport the deserter to the office booking area, where he was fingerprinted and photographed.

The same agent, with an "I feel sorry for you" look on his face, then accompanied me in returning the young man back to the marines. After turning him in to authorities at the Marine Corps Recruit Depot, we headed back to the office. I dreaded the thought of what I would hear from my new supervisor, Bill Curran.

I walked into the squad room with a sheepish look on my face and started explaining to Curran, thinking that if I just appeared with enough remorse, he would realize that I had successfully entered upon the threshold of repentance and rehabilitation.

Curran and I sat in his office, face-to-face. He spoke first.

"Well, Mac, you know the rules. Don't let it happen again! By the way, kid, nice job."

I thought, *You gotta be kidding!* What a relief! I felt as if five hundred pounds had just been lifted off each shoulder.

Deserters were normally not severely punished on the first offense. They were restricted to quarters for a few weeks, often given a temporary pay cut, and some less desirable work, but usually not more than that. Their fear upon being apprehended was always the possibility of having to serve hard time in a naval prison back east.

Occasionally that fear would translate into tragedy. When being arrested, some of these young servicemen became suicidal, and others, homicidal.

Agent John Munis, a classmate of mine during new agents' training, had a chilling experience in the Chicago division, while searching a home for a deserter. He entered the bathroom with his gun drawn. The subject, who was hiding behind the shower curtain, decided there was no way he was going back to the service or to Vietnam and was totally committed to a surprise attack.

As Munis searched, the subject slashed down at him with a knife. It was like the shower scene in the movie *Psycho*. With gun drawn, Munis was ready, but exercised unbelievable restraint in not pulling the trigger. Fortunately, the youth dropped his knife just in time, and lived.

There are moments like this in law enforcement when Providence intervenes, and the angels come out for both sides.

In September 1969, my probationary year ended. I had successfully worked my share of draft dodgers and military deserters. Bureau policy then was to serve one year almost to the day in your first office. You were then transferred to a larger office, where you would be assigned for several years. I was ready to shed the stigma of a first office agent, and move on to fry bigger fish.

Did I ever luck out!

3

ON TO MIAMI

September 22, 1969
Mr. Samuel M. McPheters
Federal Bureau of Investigation
San Diego, California

Dear Mr. McPheters:
Your headquarters are changed for official reasons from San
Diego, California, to Miami, Florida.
Very truly yours,
John Edgar Hoover,
Director

Big things were happening in South Florida. Tens of thousands of refugees from Cuba were fleeing Fidel Castro's dictatorial regime in boats, on rafts, inner tubes, and whatever they could cling onto that wouldn't sink, and making their way to the U.S. mainland where our government was granting Cuban refugees special immigrant status.

Refugees coming within view of Miami's Freedom Tower, after their long and perilous ordeal in shark-infested waters, were experiencing something truly emotional, similar to the feelings of relief, joy, and apprehension that Europe's immigrants must have felt when they first sighted the Statue of Liberty. They were in a new home, emancipated, and ready for payback. Fidel no longer dominated their lives or their vision.

In Miami, ships docked in American harbors that were actively trading with Cuba were either being bombed or sabotaged by these same refugees. Since Spanish-speaking agents were in demand, my stock had risen in South Florida.

The ever-increasing number of Cuban ex-patriots enjoyed celebrating their newly-found liberty by parading down Southwest Eighth street, through the "Little Havana" district, with Cuban flags and cannon.

These were not the dregs of Cuban society that had washed up on American shores. Fidel had taken great pains to divest himself of anyone who could rise up one day to oppose him. He was particularly wary of those with intellect and leadership who could attract a following. Many refugees were doctors, technicians, educators, poets, and journalists. Most still had families in Cuba whom they knew would suffer the Cuban dictator's wrath if they remained there and rose up against him.

The refugees knew their lot in life was tentative, but still wanted to take back their island. For them, that meant ousting the tyrant. Numerous clandestine operations by Cuban refugees translated into a plethora of violations of Federal statutes, including bombings, sabotage, and other activities aimed at destabilizing and eroding Castro's support in the U.S. For the next several years, my future as an investigator would be intertwined with many of those Cuban refugees.

★　★　★　★　★

After making short stops in Blackfoot and Ketchum, Idaho, for family visits, Judy and I stashed Marni Jo and Shad Michael into our car and headed for Miami, with our GS-10 salary increase to twelve thousand dollars a year. Driving east to Omaha, then southeast to New Orleans, we began heading along the Gulf toward Mobile, Alabama.

We were not prepared for what we saw.

On the night of August 17, 1969, Hurricane Camille, described by many as one of the most devastating hurricanes ever to make landfall in the United States, had ripped a path through the gulf states of Louisiana, Alabama, and Mississippi, killing 259 people. It had stormed in through the mouth of the Mississippi River, causing damages of epic proportions and unleashing winds of up to 190 miles per hour. The hurricane careened inland, causing more death and devastation, as it crossed the Appalachians into Virginia. Almost nine thousand people were injured. Folks lost their life savings, because they had failed to obtain wind storm insurance, which would have protected them from something ironically labeled an "Act of God."

Driving through the wake of the hurricane, we noticed nearly everything had been leveled. Multi-million dollar mansions were ripped from their foundations. Ocean liners were grounded and overturned. Pleasure boats were torpedoed into palatial homes like spears into a stump. Trucks, cars, and other conveyances had made "direct hits" into business establishments, as if shot from a cannon. Scavengers were sifting through the rubble while looking over their shoulders for the authorities. Whatever wasn't under surveillance by local authorities was being carried away.

Later, while investigating car theft rings in Miami, I investigated cases involving vehicles salvaged from the Camille disaster that had been under water for weeks. These cars were foisted off onto unwary purchasers by crooked car dealers who advertised them as being in mint condition. The salt water exposure on the surfaces eventually caused the metal to erode away, leaving the buyers with nothing but junk.

★ ★ ★ ★ ★

November 2, 1969

When we arrived in Miami, we headed for the Vagabond Motel, at that time the popular layover for Bureau transferees seeking permanent housing. Situated just thirty blocks north of the FBI office, it became our temporary abode for thirty-two days, prior to renting a house in Carol City.

I had just reported to the Miami office and had entered the squad area, when a voice from the past rang out. A tall, athletic-appearing fellow, with an ear-to-ear smile, was closing in on me.

"Che Vos!" It was the Uruguayan greeting for "Good Buddy!"

Special Agent Leon Fish, a former Uruguayan missionary friend, grabbed me in a bear hug. Fish, who was from St. George, Utah, stood six feet two inches, and had played football and ran track at Dixie College in Southern Utah.

As Mormon missionaries, we had been a different lot: energetic nineteen-year-olds still warding off pimples, working twelve-hour days, six days a week, with no monetary compensation, and no dating for two and a half years. There was the inexorable wake-up call at 6:00 AM each morning for scripture study, some push-ups and sit-ups, a scanty breakfast of whatever was available, and out the door.

Local residents would often slam their doors in our faces. Fish and I joked about that as being a good way to toughen up for hostile FBI interviews. It was the camaraderie of guys like Lee Fish, the special feeling of making a difference, and that occasional smattering of success that motivated me while in the mission field.

Eventually the Bureau's recognition of its need to satisfy their foreign language requirements opened the door into the FBI for many of us who had become proficient in Spanish while serving the Church. Harold Burgess "Burke" Smith, another agent that I knew from the Uruguayan mission, was also in Miami for his second office. Smith had that genteel look about him, capped off by blonde hair covering a well-sculptured face. Burke was well-organized and kept a low profile, not a bad idea for a newer agent.

Since Fish, Smith, and I had lived for years in the Latin-American culture, we blended well into South Florida. We had traded in our scriptures and missionary badges for revolvers and government credentials, and were sometimes referred to by fellow agents as "The Mormon Mafia."

Assistant Special Agent In Charge (ASAC) Fred Fox supervised Squad Two, my first assignment in Miami. The squad handled bank robberies, extortions, interstate stolen car rings, and kidnappings. The stolen car cases, referred to in court as "Interstate Transportation of Stolen Motor Vehicle" cases, or Dyer Act violations, along with bank robberies and extortions, were Squad Two's bread and butter.

The Squad Two guys were as varied in character as the kinds of cases they handled. ASAC Fox was a dapper type, articulate, and by accent obviously a Northeasterner. He was ready to retire and duly concerned with anyone making waves. He was equally eager for meaningful statistics, like arrests, grand jury indictments, convictions, and stolen car recoveries, which produced numbers that were the panacea for passing Bureau headquarters inspections unscathed.

Prior to eliminating the height requirement, so that the FBI could begin hiring female investigators, an agent had to stand five feet and eight inches tall. Special Agent Irvin B. Bruce, whose father was a former chief of police in Colorado, stood a little under that requirement. He had an oblique way of reminding us he had out-foxed the applicant recruiters. Bruce might make five foot seven on a good day . . . maybe.

Bruce was okay with being short and, on a regular basis, would saunter up to me, bury his nose in my chest, and remind me that I had lint in my navel. After I became a member of Miami's first Special Weapons and Tactics (SWAT) team, Bruce would swagger up to me, give me a light slap on the chops, and say, "McPheters, it's been two weeks since I beat up a SWAT guy!"

Bruce was a trickster. Ed Brandeis, the bank robbery coordinator, towered over him. Brandeis had a stone serious "Don't mess with me" look that promised revenge. He greeted each day with his morning ritual of grabbing a fresh copy of the *Miami Herald* and heading off to the men's room for his morning constitutional. Bruce had it timed and would invariably have Brandeis paged at what Bruce imagined would be the height of his "business."

The day finally arrived when Brandeis' ritual had been compromised one too many times. This time when Bruce had him paged, Brandeis somehow figured out who had been setting him up. He stormed out of the men's' room in a rage, looking for the perpetrator. Bruce was suddenly unavailable.

Special Agent Lawrence Coutre, also known as Scooter, had a staccato-type laugh that resembled intermittent bursts from a Gatlin gun. He had a fun-loving disposition that could be fired up easily and on short notice. Scooter, a short, stocky type who was a former All-American football player at Notre Dame and held the school record for running back kickoffs, was recruited by the Baltimore Colts after playing for the Irish. Scooter's specialty was car thefts, and he was interested in working very little else. You couple Irv Bruce's mumbling out loud while reviewing reports with Coutre's bullet-burst type laughter, and you would think you were in either a Las Vegas casino or a mental ward.

During a car theft investigation shortly after I arrived in Miami, Scooter and I had a stolen car raised up on a hydraulic jack, so we could check the vehicle identification number (VIN), in order to determine if the car was stolen. I was still no more than a seasoned rookie. After reviewing the National Automobile Theft Bureau manuals, I decided I knew exactly where to look for the number, and began directing Coutre to the right spot. This was a bad mistake for the "new kid on the block." The Scooter wasn't happy with me. I had about seven inches and thirty pounds size advantage on Coutre but he could have cared less, as he informed me in a very direct way where I could get off. Once he got that out, it was like nothing had happened.

Special Agent Joe Saint-Pierre knew everything going on and filled in as relief supervisor when ASAC Fox was unavailable. Saint-Pierre would basically do whatever he wanted, without getting overly animated about anything at work. He saved his energy for when he got home, where he had ten kids waiting for him. The name "Saint" seemed very appropriate.

Special Agent Ed Putz, a Polish guy, who had kind of a broken-nose look and a big body to go with it, could scare the daylights out of you. He was a hard charger with a no-nonsense air about him, yet loved having fun. He and Agent Gene Flynn always volunteered to cook for Bureau get-togethers, and Putz made killer chili that was to die for.

Putz was the bank robbery guru and knew how to write a good letter of commendation for anyone solving one. ASAC Fox, and subsequently Bureau headquarters, would willingly sign off on Putz's recommendations. When monetary incentive awards were involved, Putz, the pen man, was even more appreciated.

As I was assimilated into Squad Two that first day, I was excited. ASAC Fox's squad was a mix of good humored professionals that formed an elite team in the Miami office . . . one that was highly regarded.

The Squad Two agent whose path would soon join mine and who would become my mentor was a former retailer from Indiana who sold Westinghouse washing machines and dryers: the indefatigable Special Agent James P. Hufford, who held the self-designated title of the "White Knight."

The Knight stood five feet ten inches tall and weighed one hundred and eighty-five pounds. He had a slender build with the beginnings of a paunch, common to a man in his early forties. He was dark-complected with brown, hawkish eyes. His stern appearance was often betrayed by an ear-to-ear smile, as he emitted muffled laughter from deep within.

The Knight had that Ernest Borgnine space between his front teeth that served him well, following an incident in a parking lot when he absorbed a smashing punch to the head that splintered his jaw. The melee occurred on an Easter eve when he and his daughter went shopping to buy his wife, Margie, a lily. Hufford ended up pulling off a chivalrous act that reinforced his knightly nickname. While pulling into the flower shop, he noticed a couple of characters taunting a woman, preventing her from backing out of her parking space. The Knight ordered the aggressors to move their car. Instead, they both approached the Knight simultaneously, with his daughter looking on, and one of them delivered a sucker-punch from behind.

When I visited him in the hospital the next day, the Knight was beyond recognition, due to the swelling. That space between his teeth allowed him to drain milkshakes for the next three weeks, while his jaws were wired shut.

The Knight was both meticulous and methodical. Back in those days, agents summoned stenographers to their desks for dictating reports. The time spent with those young ladies usually included some light visiting and was the best part of the day for a lot of agents.

The Knight would have nothing to do with it. He would rough draft every memorandum and every report. He knew that if he rough drafted his work, it would be correct, and then only he could be held responsible for error. By maintaining copies of rough drafts in case files, he knew he always had the original to rely on if his reporting was ever held in question.

The Knight was the epitome of the hard-working, relentless, and un-tiring Bureau servant. He was the master stolen car sleuth on Squad Two and could have written the book on the subject. He taught me how to identify hot cars through a complicated, painstaking process of searching for VINs or working to find the stolen reports through the National Auto Theft Bureau (NATB), which works in conjunction with vehicle manufacturers.

The Knight and I shared similar values. He sampled wine occasionally, but other than that, drank very little. He believed drinking, smoking, and chasing skirts were activities relegated to mere mortals. Everyone liked and respected the White Knight. There were few, however, that shared his inner sense of "mission" for the work. Eventually I did, but it took time to catch on.

Indeed, the White Knight had already become a legend among car ring investigators and had amassed a number of car thief convictions and stolen car recoveries before I came along. The only drawback for Hufford was his lack of proficiency in Spanish. He hadn't been able to penetrate the Spanish-speaking market, where he knew the real potential lay.

For the Knight's crusade against South Florida's stolen car ring opera-tions, he needed a Spanish-speaking standard-bearer, and I qualified. He designated me the "Holy Crusader," and we officially became a team. Huf-ford and I worked together right up to the time he transferred to Minnesota three years later. We reeled in scores of hot cars and submitted more car recovery reports than the division had ever seen.

Through our informants and interviews, we located and identified the hot cars, linked them to a suspect, and courted the interests of Assistant U.S. Attorneys (AUSAs) who prosecuted our subjects. We presented volumes of evidence to federal grand juries for the soul-satisfying reward of their "true bills," or indictments. We became regular court room fixtures, while assist-ing the federal prosecutors in trial presentations.

The Knight and I experienced great satisfaction from crossing swords with defense attorneys who tried to badger us on the stand. They gave up

The White Knight (Jim Hufford) and his family

on us. We never furnished them more information than necessary, although they always tried to get us to divulge information helpful to their cause, and even some knowledge they didn't need, such as the locations of the confidential numbers on the recovered vehicles, known only to the NATB and to law enforcement.

At the end of each day, the White Knight and the Holy Crusader rode home together, planning which dragon to slay the next day.

Some days we recovered as many as six stolen luxury vehicles from "innocent" purchasers who bought their late-model Cadillacs and Lincolns for as little as eight hundred dollars.

The Knight and I had our own way of meting out retribution, even prior to trial. We'd simply summon the purchasers to the office in their bargain basement trophy and verify the vehicle's stolen status while it was parked in the Bureau parking lot. Once confirming the car was stolen, we would keep it and direct the purchaser to the nearest bus stop.

Did we get some satisfaction out of that? You bet we did, since the federal attorneys would seldom prosecute the purchasers, who were buying stolen cars knowingly and with impunity.

The first major car ring Jim Hufford and I took on was the Cesar Enrique Acosta case.

4

★★★★★

CAR RINGS AND SHYLOCKS

JANUARY 1970

I had just recovered a stolen Cadillac Sedan de Ville, registered to one Armando Garcia on Northwest Second Avenue in Miami. In comparing notes with another Squad Two agent, I discovered that he had recovered another stolen Cadillac at that same address, registered to a Ruben Garcia. A group of Cuban car thieves, formerly refugees, were using the address on Northwest Second Avenue as a mail drop for license tags and phony registrations for stolen luxury cars, all registered to a Garcia with various first names. No one lived at the address.

The phony documents were spawned off titles from legitimate junked cars. The thieves only bought the VIN plates with the accompanying titles off wrecked cars from crooked junkyard dealers who knew what the thieves were up to. The phony VINS were swapped out from the junkers to the stolen cars, giving them an air of legitimacy. As a final step, the thieves obtained legitimate registrations and license plates with the junk titles and sent them on to the Northwest Second Avenue mail drop, all under the last name of Garcia.

The agent who recovered the other Cadillac registered at the mail drop didn't speak Spanish, so he was happy to transfer the case over to me. Since there were now two stolen luxury cars registered to the same address, we had the start of a car ring.

When the White Knight caught wind of this, he was fired up, recognizing my discovery as a link to something big . . . very big.

What Hufford and I didn't know at the time was that connecting these recoveries to the Northwest Second Avenue mail drop was the first step in infiltrating and shattering a stolen car operation that would go down as one of the biggest car theft rings in the history of the Miami Division.

Hufford and I continued to identify Cadillacs: Sedan De Villes, Fleetwoods, El Dorados, and Broughams, along with Lincoln Continental Mark IIIs, and Ford Mustangs, all of which had plates registered to the mail drop, under the last name Garcia, with first names of Fernando, Jose, Hector, Carlos, Carmen, Miguel, and so forth.

The cars were stolen in New York, New Jersey, and other locations on the eastern seaboard. Since the mail drop apartment had neither furniture nor utilities, it was used only to receive the license tags and phony documents. A federal grand jury indictment eventually charged renting the mail drop as an "overt act" in a conspiracy.

Cesar Enrique Acosta, his brothers, and a few other street thieves, hung out in a part of the Bronx in New York City where the life of a late model Cadillac was approximately thirty minutes before it was either stolen or stripped.

Luxury cars were stolen off the streets easily, using a "dent puller," the tool body and fender mechanics use to straighten out dents in cars with smashed-in fenders. The point of the tool fit nicely into the ignition once the door was opened (via a broken window or a clothes hanger put to good use). Once the ignition was extracted, the car could be efficiently hot-wired.

The Acosta gang took their stolen cars to sleazy garage owners in New York City who would give them a new birth with a fresh coat of paint. Once they placed the phony VINs on the door frame, the stolen car had a new identity, making it necessary for investigators like Hufford and I to find the confidential VINs in order to identify them as stolen.

After stealing the cars and changing their identity, the Acosta gang would place temporary license tags on the vehicles and transport them to South Florida with little fear of detection. Upon arriving in Miami, they would send a runner to pick up the legitimate license tags and registrations at the mail drop on Northwest Second Avenue and swap out the license plates and registrations.

Numerous days of surveillance at the mail drop proved unfruitful, but other avenues opened up for us.

The day came when I asked the Knight, "Jim, did you see the police report on that caddy the police picked up the other day? It bore a license plate for a compact." Upon hearing my question, the White Knight jerked to attention.

"You've got to be joking, McPheters. Our boys?" Hufford smirked.

He continued. "These guys go to all lengths to repaint, replace the VINs, and phony up the registrations, and they don't know about the Florida tags?"

"Apparently not. That's all to our advantage. Let's ask the cops what the driver had to say," I replied.

In Florida, cars were registered according to weight. The Cadillacs and other bigger cars had a designation of "I-WW" on the license plate, followed by the plate number. Cars a little lighter would carry the "I-W" designation. And even lighter, compact cars, would just have an "I" designation, followed by a number. A sure "giveaway" for a stolen car would be someone driving a Lincoln Continental or Cadillac Brougham down the road with an "I" designation.

Florida no longer uses that system, but at the time it was great for detecting out-of-state car thieves, like the Acostas, who didn't understand the system, and were prone to throwing on any old tag they had available.

A call to the Miami Police Department confirmed my suspicions. The driver had purchased a late-model Cadillac El Dorado, with a license tag for a compact car, from someone with the last name Garcia. He bought it for twelve hundred dollars cash and had no idea how to contact the seller. The purchaser had only a bill of sale for an Alberto Garcia, allegedly residing at the Northwest Second Avenue address in Miami.

We had found a chink in the Acosta gang's armor.

The Acosta gang's demise was also helped along by its purchasers. When The Knight and I interviewed them in their native tongue, we were relentless, always holding a fine edge so as not to violate their rights and always giving the appropriate Miranda warnings. The buyers knew they had a huge problem explaining how they could purchase vehicles worth five to eight thousand dollars for under a thousand.

At that time, federal prosecutors were not leveling charges against those who purchased the stolen cars, but the purchasers never knew they would not go to jail for knowingly purchasing stolen property. The Knight and I milked that for all it was worth. One of the greatest assets we have in law enforcement is what the suspect thinks we can do that we can't. It was this kind of interrogation that led us, step by step, suspect by suspect, to the resolution.

The purchasers began caving in, dropping a name here and a name there. During the course of our interviews, the Knight knew zip about Spanish, but wore a scowl that could draw water out of a rock. With the Knight's intimidating glare, some great informants, and my reasonably good command of the Spanish language, we were in the driver's seat. The thieves, the garage owners who knowingly repainted the cars, and the crooked salvage lot owners who provided the phony VINs, sensed that the sky was caving in, and suddenly wanted to deal.

Near the end of March 1970, Assistant U.S. Attorney Jose Martinez introduced the Knight and I to a federal grand jury convened in Miami, where we had the distinct pleasure of presenting our affidavit smiles and cold steel-blue eyes, along with a plethora of evidence, falling in the category of "overwhelming," to the jury.

We indicted seventeen subjects on an eighteen-count indictment that was returned to U.S. District Judge C. Clyde Atkins.

Two days later, we enlisted the assistance of the New York and Newark FBI field offices to coordinate the arrests of all the car thieves except two, who became federal fugitives. Eventually, we caught and convicted them all under the Dyer Act for the Interstate Transportation of Stolen Motor Vehicles, with specific conspiracy charges.

We recovered scores of luxury cars and nabbed seventeen conspirators who faced five years imprisonment and/or $5,000 in fines on each charge.

The Miami News quoted FBI Director, J. Edgar Hoover, who referred to the Acosta operation, as "an elaborate automobile theft ring operating along the eastern seaboard."

A few days later, on April 13, 1970, my twenty-seventh birthday, the excitement and satisfaction of solving my first major FBI case was eclipsed by something far more special and far-reaching. Our stake president, Stanley Clyde Johnson, placed his hands upon my head and ordained me a high priest in the Melchizedek Priesthood, and simultaneously set me apart as second counselor in the bishopric of the Miami Third Ward, to Bishop Anton Kuhlman.

★　★　★　★　★

May 1970

Our successes in recovering stolen cars and sending the thieves away to prison generated a lot of attention in the Miami Division and helped give birth to a new stolen car squad: Squad Eight.

The newly-designated supervisor was Ed Sharp, a cigar-smoking tactician,

The Miami Car Theft Squad

Working on Ed Sharp's car theft squad in Miami. Mike is in the back on the right. Ed Sharp is in the center on the left. Also pictured: the White Knight (3rd from left), Larry "Scooter" Coutre (4th from left), Bob Strong (5th from left), Irv Bruce (4th from right), and Mike Dooher (far right)

who was "on the rise" administratively, and eventually became an Assistant Director. He always remained a friend and confidant of the street agent, a somewhat tricky balancing act. Sharp was great to work for. He turned guys like the Knight and I loose and then got out of our way. He also had a keen sense of humor.

One day I was sitting at my desk, just outside Sharp's office, in the bull pen. In those days there were no wall separators or personal offices. The desks were butted up against one another, so you would be looking at another agent right across from you. It was very, very cozy. In close quarters like this, a good idea was to be friendly with everyone, and leave your attitude at home.

I had just calculated how many days it would take me to drive my family from Miami to Idaho, vacation and visit our families for about a month, and drive back. I'd hoarded my annual leave, so I was able to put in for five weeks. I sent Sharp a routing slip with my request. He immediately sent me a response. As I picked it up and began reading it, Sharp sat back in his office, puffing on a cigar, observing my response. There was my request, with the word DENIED written over it in red ink! Taken back, I immediately looked up at Sharp, who was laughing so hard, I thought he'd flipped out.

Sharp knew what the Knight and I could do for his squad, as far as meaningful accomplishments were involved, such as convictions, arrests, recoveries, federal grand jury indictments, and informant statistics. Were we prima donnas? Probably not. Did he cut us a lot of slack? Undoubtedly. He scratched our back wherever he could, because we were scratching his big time, and we carried out his expectations. We could not take the credit for his rise to prominence in the Bureau, because he had a lot going for him, but we may have helped move him along.

Our success in the Acosta case was the first of a healthy string of meaningful statistics on Squad Eight. We apprehended car thieves involved in a host of federal violations, including some shylocking activities, officially known as extortionate credit transactions, where the crooks loaned sums of money to folks who couldn't get credit anywhere else. The money was loaned out at extremely high rates of interest, called "vigorish." The muscle-heads working for the loaners would come after you in a heartbeat if you didn't pay up when the note came due and would not hesitate to break arms and legs, until they got their dues.

One Shylock in particular, Gary Bowdach, was making loans out of a used car lot in Miami, owned by Sonny Brock, and collecting them with the usual display of muscle, murder, and extortion. That is, until we arrested him, not for shylocking, assault, or homicide, but for a stolen motor vehicle that showed up in his car lot.

This case involved extenuating circumstances, where the U.S. Attorney prosecuted Bowdach for possession of the hot car, based upon his shy-locking activities and propensities to maim and kill. One witness testified how Bowdach laughed, as he shot him repeatedly. Convicting Bowdach for possession of a stolen car transported interstate was much easier than convicting him of murder. He could potentially serve five years on the car case while the homicide and assault cases were being proven.

Subsequent to Bowdach's arrest, a hearing took place in the U.S. District Court in Miami before U.S. Court Commissioner Edward Swan to determine whether there was probable cause to proceed to trial. The Knight sat next to me, across the table from Bowdach, glaring at him. Bowdach's record of violence and general wise guy demeanor really aggravated the White Knight.

While seated next to Hufford, I felt him brushing up against me a little, as he extended his leg straight out and under the table. He was thrashing around with his feet. Bowdach's head suddenly snapped up, as his face took on a slight grimace. His eyes began to redden as he gazed directly at the Knight, who was acting as if nothing was happening. Hufford and I were the only ones that noticed the sudden transition in the master extortionist and shylock's demeanor, as he squirmed and fidgeted across from us.

Suddenly I figured it out. As I glanced down toward the apparent commotion under the table, I realized Hufford was stepping all over Bowdach's white suede shoes, marking them in black with the outer soles of his oxfords. Bowdach continued sitting there, seeing red, perplexed, and unable to do anything, knowing that no one would believe that an FBI agent would do such a thing.

But this wasn't just any FBI agent. This was the White Knight. The issue regarding the damage to Bowdach's white suede shoes was never raised.

Bowdach made bond and went back to extorting and killing people.

Eventually, Bowdach's past caught up with him, and he went to prison. After serving several years on pending charges, he "saw the light," and appeared before a Senate sub-committee, where he testified about the impact of organized crime in South Florida, buying whatever consideration he could receive, in exchange for his testimony.

5

★ ★ ★ ★ ★

PLANE PIRATES

JUNE 1970

The Miami office received a telephone call early in the afternoon from the Opa-Locka Airport, advising that a Cessna aircraft had been tied down by its pilot and abandoned, just an hour earlier. Local airport security personnel had determined it had been stolen and subsequently flown from a neighboring state. The pilot's identity was still in question.

Irv Bruce and I, along with a few other agents, responded to the tarmac at the airport and found the aircraft, secured with tie downs and with its doors secured. We reconfirmed the stolen status by running the plane's serial numbers through the National Crime Information Center (NCIC).

Next, I disabled the plane by deflating the tires and detaching some spark plug wires.

We then positioned our bureau cars at discreet locations where we could maintain a vigil, and hopefully identify and arrest the phantom pilot. We initiated the surveillance at about 3:30 PM.

Opa-Locka was a different community, with its Arabic name and designs on many of the city buildings. Even the streets in some areas carried Arabesque titles and connotations. It seemed a strange motif for a city on the southern edge of the United States.

"Did we get any idea at all when this guy might return?" I asked Bruce.

"We have no clue. He parked it and walked away. We only know we need to jump on him when he comes back, see who he is, and hit him with a warrant." Bruce was as much in the dark for facts on this case, as I was.

Hours passed. No one came near the Cessna. Except for a little chit chat over our radios, everything was at a standstill.

Night fell. Still, no one approached. One of the agents left on a sandwich run. That usually meant Burger King or McDonald's.

A couple other agents broke off from the inner perimeter of the surveillance, which covered about a one hundred and fifty foot radius out from the plane, and drove slowly around the airport, looking for anyone fitting the pilot's description: Hispanic appearance, dark complexion, early thirties, slim, weighing about 165 pounds.

I didn't budge from my position next to some trees, about a hundred feet away, and just off the fringe of the tarmac. Bruce didn't move either. No way were we taking our eyes off that plane.

As I thought about a nice, hot meal at home with the family, and the fact I was going to miss some important bishop commitments, counseling some youth, I was starting to dislike the plane thief.

When this guy came back, I definitely wanted to be there for a piece of the action.

Burgers, fries, and sodas were delivered and downed, within minutes. It had been a long time since lunch. Ten o'clock was fast approaching, and the sultry, cooler air of Opa-Locka permeated the atmosphere.

The agents who had done a moving grid search of the airport's premises returned, not having seen any trace of our subject. Everyone's attention was again focused on the abandoned Cessna.

My mind was swimming with questions.

Why would this fellow just walk away from the plane after stealing it and bringing it this far? He wasn't observed carrying a briefcase or container away, so it must not have been a drug deal. And why the Opa-Locka Airport? Who would he know here? Surely he'll be back.

Midnight arrived, then 1:00 AM, 2:00 AM. At 3:15 AM a police car driven by a portly, older officer in his forties came screaming out onto the tarmac. It passed the Cessna and streaked on down the runway, with blue lights churning circles, and rubber peeling out black imprints along the way.

Suddenly, we were all on high alert.

"What was that all about?" came a voice over the radio, from someone apparently only half-awake.

Bruce answered first.

"Obviously, the officer had to relieve himself. The men's restroom is down at the other end of the runway."

It was a vintage Bruce commentary, but the audience was way too tired to laugh, and by now, was really put out with this jerk who liked to steal airplanes and keep grown men awake all night.

As I noticed the sun starting to come up on the horizon, my memory focused in on a prior surveillance, two weeks before, when Special Agent Paul Hudson and I set up on a fugitive's house in Miami.

We were parked just a half block from the subject's house, when at about 2:00 AM, we both drifted off into "Never Never Land." The car windows were rolled down.

A couple hours later, we were awakened by the sound of a police officer tapping on the car door with his flashlight, asking who we were. With sheepish grins on our faces, which were now covered with mosquito bites, we smiled half-wittedly at the officer and presented him our credentials, trying to remember what we were doing there.

Our current situation at the Opa-Locka Airport had not deteriorated to that point yet, but we were beginning to doubt as to whether our subject would show.

My mind started searching for answers. "Was the guy on to us? Were the two agents identified, driving around the airport?"

We continued the surveillance another couple hours. At approximately 6:30 AM, I heard Mother Nature calling, advised Bruce I was going to be unavailable for fifteen minutes, and headed for the men's room.

I was intent in doing what I needed to do in record time, to be sure I would not miss the return of the prodigal pilot. I made it back in less than ten minutes

"He's right over here, Mac!"

It was Bruce. He and the other agents were standing by the plane, with the subject in custody.

I could not believe it! I had left my post for ten minutes, after fifteen hours of surveillance, and missed my bust.

A few days after embarrassing myself by missing my opportunity to arrest the plane pirate, I found myself in an animated discussion with Bishop Kuhlman and his other counselor, Special Agent Leon Fish, regarding the manner of administering sports programs in our ward. As a counselor, I felt it was incumbent upon me to counsel. When I had strong feelings about a course we should adhere to, or avoid, I let my feelings be known. However, in the end, I accepted the bishop's final decisions and supported them.

All three of us in the bishopric were highly competitive, with sports backgrounds, and I had observed in one of our stake baseball playoffs that certain team members were not being given the opportunity to participate because of the coach's desire, as well as our own, to play only the best players, in order to win the tournament. I could see the disappointment in those who were playing less and who had been faithful in attending practice. I feared that denying them playing time could become a stumbling block in their Church activity. I emphasized that Church sports are designed for full participation, and that players should never be asked to choose between "playing just to play" and "playing to win."

I counseled whole-heartedly that as members of the bishopric, we distance ourselves from any coaching or refereeing assignments where we would be placed in a position to judge members of our ward in the physical arena, when we were already tasked with making judgments regarding their performance in spiritual pursuits. I stated that the bishopric was assuming an unhealthy burden in openly judging the physical qualifications of our ward members. I advised we actively seek out good coaches and referees for our athletic programs and support their decisions, rather than be involved ourselves.

As I listened to Bishop Kuhlman, I learned how wonderfully open-minded he was to my counsel and how willing he was to work with me and my recommendations. I took careful note of that characteristic of a good bishop and tried to apply it in my future bishoping. In addition, I realized how that same principal of leadership could be, and often is, successfully applied to the Bureau's supervisory process.

★ ★ ★ ★ ★

Through the early 1970s, I continued working airplane thefts of another kind: skyjackings.

During that time period, the entire Miami office was called out frequently, to respond to the Miami International Airport to debrief hijacked passengers, returning from Cuba.

Before the U.S. Marshall's Service began placing Sky Marshals on major flight routes, hijacking planes was commonplace. Planes were boarded by characters with all kinds of agendas. Huge sums of money were extorted for the release of passengers.

Some skyjackings were carried out by demented individuals, with non-specific motives, or no motives at all. These subjects would try to pull off copycat skyjackings and would end up getting shot, before anyone was aware how mentally unstable they actually were.

As skyjackings became more frequent, the FBI began detailed investigations into how to counteract them. We learned a great deal about ballistic considerations in disabling large aircraft like 747s, before they could get off the ground. Our Special Weapons And Tactics (SWAT) teams practiced rushing the planes and clearing them, while preserving the safety of hostages

This was extremely difficult and very risky.

One of my supervisors, Bob Strong, quickly discovered that our standard issue thirty-eight caliber rounds would not penetrate the tires on the larger aircraft, when he attempted to do just that on a Boeing 747, nicknamed the "Jumbo Jet," during a skyjacking in Miami. This incident helped us realize that the FBI's garden-variety type weapons, even our 12 gauge shotguns and sniper rifles, could not always deflate the tires on the big planes.

Soon, we turned to other mechanical means to stop the aircraft, and eventually discovered the answers we needed. Over the past couple of decades, skyjackings in the United States have been very rare.

★ ★ ★ ★ ★

On December 29, 1972, a very dark night just after Christmas, the Miami office was involved in another major aircraft case, but it involved neither aircraft theft nor skyjackings.

A Lockheed L1011, Eastern Flight 401, which was loaded with passengers, crashed into the Florida everglades, just outside of Miami. People who survived the crash began dying from exposure to the elements and the poisoning effects of the Florida swamp water that was contaminated with fuel from the crashed aircraft. There was no criminal mischief involved. The Bureau was tasked with identifying victims.

All that occurred in those Everglades that fateful night following the crash can only be conjured up in the gristliest nightmare of one's imagination. Dozens of human beings, half alive, were floating around in water rampant with noxious chemicals, human decay, and alligators. All possible efforts were made to salvage lives.

It's best left at that.

6

★★★★★

"THE DIRECTOR"

JULY 1970

All right. One last inventory: Shined shoes? Check!

Suit pants pressed? Uhhh . . . so-so.

The breath? Not fatal.

The palms? I'd read accounts about Mr. Hoover paying particular attention to the handshake, and how he found sweaty palms so distasteful, associating them with lack of confidence, or having something to hide. So far . . . dry.

The hair? Good, and a lot of it. The barber college students liked practicing on my outcrop, and for a dollar and twenty-five cents a cut, I was all for it.

My major concern kept coming back to that handshake and the possibility of sweaty palms. The Director can pick up on that! And if he does, it will be a question of trust. How many times had I heard that from other agents who had already run the gauntlet?

Why all the fuss?

I was back at Bureau headquarters, in Washington D.C. for a three week instructor course in "Firearms and Defensive Tactics."

Special Agent LeRoy Kusch, Miami's head firearms guy, thought I looked like instructor material, so he booked me as his next "trained killer." At six feet four inches, weighing two hundred and fifteen pounds, with a John Wayne voice inflection, at least I looked and sounded the part.

The truth was that my shooting skills were no more than average, and as a Church-going Mormon boy, my propensity for shooting someone was questionable. It would be years before I would develop that affidavit FBI smile and the cold, piercing eyes that you see on television. For now, all that was in the embryonic stage. I was still green behind the ears, and at best, a work in progress.

I was naïve. Evidence of that was apparent in the fact that I was the only one in the class that requested to meet the Man . . . the Legend, none other than J. Edgar Hoover.

Upon arriving in Washington D.C. a couple days earlier, and prior to joining thirty-five other trainees, I had inquired about the possibility of meeting Mr. Hoover. The secretary at the Department of Justice Building asked if I wanted anything, or desired just to meet the Director. Upon assuring her it was the latter, she advised me if an opening occurred, I would be notified, and called from class. A couple of days later the call came, and I was summoned.

My heart began racing as I mentally reviewed all the admonitions I had received. Upon discovering that I wanted to meet the Legend, my class peers looked at me like I was suicidal.

"You must look the Man right in the eye! Wipe your palms before shaking his hand. You better appear confident. You sure you want to do this?"

Compounding my anxiety were my own doubts.

Should I get a new suit? I have those two tears on the inside fabric. He could see those. And dang, I forgot about my shoes! Those craters on each sole will wear through in a couple more months anyway. Should I just buy a new pair now? No, that's forty bucks. I can get by. After all, he's not going to be down on the carpet, and I could sit up straight, with both feet on the ground.

Hey, all I want is to meet the Director. I'm not signing my own death warrant, nor am I putting my career on the line.

Or am I?

Suddenly that Popeye the Sailor Man thought cursed through my mind: I yam what I yam what I yam. Just go see him!

Making sure all the logistics of my personal appearance were covered, I again reran the inventory. Hair combed? Check. Pit stop? Check. Washed and thoroughly dried hands? Check.

One last glance into the mirror: Nothing hanging out of the nose. Good to go.

The elevator trip was easy, compared to the maze of doors that I negotiated to see Mr. Hoover. I finally made it to the outer chambers of his offices.

The agent posted at the desk outside of the Legend's office invited me to enter.

There he was! Well-groomed, poised, and alert. The world's major icon of law enforcement. Held in awe by his men, feared by his detractors, loved by America: J. Edgar Hoover.

This was the man that pioneered the foundation of the FBI and modern law enforcement as we know it today. Here was the champion of justice for all, and the major craftsman of the cutting edge of investigative technology.

I'm sure Mr. Hoover was curious about the hick from the sticks that had just invaded his space. Nevertheless, he immediately became cordial, inviting me to sit down in one of the eloquently appointed chairs that faced him. I was warmly welcomed.

I instantly became aware that the Man was sharp . . . very sharp. Born on New Year's Day in 1895, Mr. Hoover was now seventy-five years old, but still very much in control of his faculties and fiefdom.

The Director depicted Miami as one of the major anchor divisions in the Bureau.

"I hear a lot about what goes on in Miami, Mr. McPheters."

It was obvious Mr. Hoover was not only intimately familiar with the operations of the Miami Division, but the demographics of the community as well, and it's crime problems.

The Legend continued: "The phenomenon of the Cuban immigration is interesting."

Then, holding back a smile, he quipped, "The initial plan was for Fidel Castro's refugees to start off in Alaska."

For the first time, I became aware of this man's lusty, yet somewhat dry, sense of humor. Considering my precarious professional position at the time, that was like a breath of fresh air.

Yes, sir! I thought. *Keep smiling, Mr. Hoover. Just keep smiling.*

The chat continued . . . Wait! Did I say chat? Wasn't that a conversation between two people?

As the interview continued, I mused to myself, I'm really not talking much, but I'm sure a good listener. Yes, sir, Mr. Hoover!

The Legend resumed. "I'm gravely concerned about the light sentences being meted out by some of our judges here in the District. These are hardened criminals. Why, just the other day a judge ruled . . ."

The Director had galvanized my conviction that he had serious concerns regarding the trend turning to "slap on the wrist sentences" for hardened

J. Edgar Hoover

Mike received a personal
picture of J. Edgar Hoover,
first director of the FBI, after
visiting him. Hoover wrote
an inscription,

"To the McPheters,
Best Wishes,
J. Edgar Hoover
11.30.71"

recidivists, and the trend toward the softening of our society.

Then came the signal, about twenty minutes into the interview. The Director took a call, apparently from Attorney General John Mitchell. At that time, Mr. Mitchell was in the Director's good graces. He would not be convicted and incarcerated for his role in the Watergate scandal until three years after Mr. Hoover's death.

I heard the Director say, "Yes, John, one moment please."

He then turned to me, and kindly informed me, "Mr. McPheters, it has been nice meeting you, but I now have the Attorney General on the line."

I immediately arose, thanked the Director for his time, shook his hand (with dry palms even), and departed his office chambers.

A few days after returning to Miami, and subsequent to becoming a full-fledged George Zeis-trained firearms and defensive tactics instructor, I was called into my supervisor's office. While rolling a cigar around in his mouth, Ed Sharp casually tossed a memorandum down in front of me, and said, "Read this."

It was a memorandum to Clyde Tolson, Associate Director of the FBI, dated June 8, 1970. It read as follows:

Today I saw Special Agent Samuel M. McPheters of the Miami office, who is attending the Firearms and Defensive Tactics Instructors School. Mr. McPheters makes an excellent and mature personal appearance, and I would rate him above average. I think this agent has the potential for assuming additional responsibilities.

Very Truly Yours,

J.E.H. John Edgar Hoover, Director

Not one to mince words, Sharp came right to the point. "This means you'll pull relief supervisor duty on the car theft squad, Mac. Further down the road, you could advance up the line."

I pulled back a little. "I don't want it, Ed. I'm happy on the street, working car rings."

Sharp countered with the admonition that when the inspectors from D.C. rolled in for our next inspection, it wouldn't look good for me if I had refused the Director's promotion.

"Yes, sir, Ed. You got your boy."

I begin sharing duties on the desk.

Today, I guard that memorandum from Mr. Hoover very closely to the vest, realizing that even though he died less than a year after our visit, his example and influence in the Bureau will never be forgotten.

Near that memorandum, kept in my office, you'll find another treasured memorabilia: a framed picture of the Director, with the inscription, "To the McPheters. Best Wishes. J. Edgar Hoover. 11.30.71."

7

★ ★ ★ ★ ★

THE PILLO GANG

AUGUST 1970

Navigating my way around the streets of Miami, I learned there was a street code to decipher. Streets running north and south were given the CAP designation, for courts, avenues, and places. For east-west traffic, the code was STRL, for streets, terraces, roads, and lanes. Flagler Street divided the city, north from south, and Miami Avenue divided it, east from west.

Just eight blocks south of Flagler, and just west of Miami Avenue, was "Little Havana," running along Southwest Eighth Street. It was occupied mostly by the Cuban community and was a popular celebration center for refugees from Fidel Castro's dictatorship.

Once these refugees found freedom in America, they needed homes, bread, and butter. Many moved into residences that only limited funds could purchase, often in less prestigious areas and in deteriorated condition. Within weeks they would apply monumental energy in holding down two or three jobs, and would polish up and enhance these same homes to an immaculate standard. Most of their work was legitimate and honorable, but like all other communities, there were many who sought the fast track to wealth.

★ ★ ★ ★ ★

Cuban-born refugee Amado Leon, slender, approximately five feet ten inches tall, was light-complected, with a deep tan, and a receding hair line. From all outward appearances, the gas station he operated in Little Havana provided his sole source of income.

Laid back, with that carefree Latin charm, and a pleasing, contagious

43

personality, Leon had no major challenges in sustaining a thriving garage repair/gas pumping operation, located in the very heart of the Cuban community.

Few people were aware that the bottom line in Leon's budding prosperity was in the essence of his nickname, "Pillo," which, translated into English, meant "Bandit." Even fewer individuals, including Miami's local law enforcement community, were aware Amado Leon was the mastermind of a major east coast stolen car ring operation that would go down in history as the biggest ever . . . even eclipsing the Cesar Enrique Acosta operation. But this was all about to change.

The White Knight and I had been made aware of Pillo's activities and had spent relentless weeks surveilling him and his cohorts. Our work paid off. We had developed enough intelligence to conduct our first interview with him at his service station.

It was a sweltering day. As we approached, we watched him unobserved. The sweat poured from his tanned forehead from a receding hairline. He was well into his thirties. The furrows in his bronzed face tightened as he drained the last bit of rusty sediment from the oil pan before reinserting the drain plug, and lowering the car down with the hydraulic jack.

Ice cubes bobbed in a glass full of Squirt on his work bench, but even the chill of Pillo's beverage could not have eased the stifling heat wave, as he moved adroitly from the lube jobs to the gas pumps.

When we were close enough, I addressed Pillo in Spanish.

"How long have you been involved with the cars, Mr. Leon?" I asked, dangling out the hook. "What would happen if you did this in Cuba?"

"I don't know what you're talking about!" His expression reeked with contempt. It was that "You got nothing on me" kind of look. Pillo, now more fired up and emboldened, continued: "Don't you see I work hard for a living? I have a sick father. This is crazy, man!"

Pillo went back and forth with the Knight and me. He spoke a little English, but communicated mostly in Spanish.

On this first attempt at contacting Leon after so many weeks in the "just wait" mode, the Knight's patience was wearing thin. His eyes became catlike, narrowing more and more. Everything in his countenance was tightening, from his teeth to his buns.

I'd seen this kind of rigidity before in Hufford. A voice within me was saying, *Look out, Pillo! Look out! The mountain is ready to erupt!*

"Look, Pillo," I reasoned, "We know you're getting cars from up north.

New York. New Jersey. We know who's bringing them down for you. We know you're selling some here, and sending some south to the Caribbean. We even know who's doing your paperwork."

There it was again. That rock-hard "Sure you do" look. The Cuban just smirked.

"You guys don't know anything. I'm working hard for a living here. Why don't you leave?"

I detected a shimmer emanating from Hufford. The Knight didn't like being asked to leave.

I envisioned all the tires hanging from Pillo's garage wall being dispersed in volleys, all the way through Little Havana.

I continued dropping a few more names, a few more bits and pieces the informants had come up with, baiting the hook, with more and more sweet stuff.

I honed in on Pillo's fear factor. He was obviously struggling to determine what we really knew and didn't know. I was milking this strategy for all it was worth.

The Knight was beginning to froth at the mouth.

The dialogue went on. I would lay it out at Pillo's feet, and he'd keep stepping over it. This guy could bob and weave.

Suddenly, I sensed he was wavering a little. He was beginning to envision himself behind bars, missing generous rations of good Cuban cooking. I kept pounding the admonitions and "what-ifs" down his throat, throwing in everything I could muster up.

I sensed I had him on the brink of conversion. Yes, he was getting religion!

That's where it ended. That's when we were told whose garage we had to leave, who was not going to talk to us without an attorney present, and just how fast we were to disappear.

"All right, Leon. We're out of here." I yelled, "But believe me, we'll be back!"

"Yeah, punk! And it'll be with warrants and esposas," the Knight chimed in; hoping some of his rhetoric would sink in, even though it was in English.

I had taught Hufford that the Cuban word *esposas* meant handcuffs. Interestingly enough, the word also means "wives." It's a cultural thing.

As we sauntered off, with our tails between our legs, it was obvious the Knight was not pleased with the results of my interrogation techniques.

When I looked into his eyes, I no longer saw Jim Hufford. What I saw was a cougar, ravished with hunger, having the succulent buck deer trapped within his grasp, saliva running down his fangs, and suddenly having to freeze in motion, while watching the fresh meat walk away.

"Well, McPheters, we really didn't break him down, now, did we?"

He didn't have to say another word. I knew I'd fallen short. Somewhere, I'd missed a word, an admonition, a juicy morsel of evidence, that I could have thrown at Pillo . . . something that would have coaxed him over the edge.

What haunted me, deep down, was knowing the Knight could have pulled it off, had the interview been in English.

Even though I had experienced some success for a newer agent, the Knight was still the trainer. I had less than two years under my belt, and was continually getting feedback from working the street that humbled me. I knew it would take time, a lot of time, and lots of street work, to rise to the level of the White Knight.

To really interview effectively, you must keenly sense the direction the interview is going and perceive the exact moment to go in for the kill. Like the song of the gambler, "You need to know when to hold 'em, and know when to fold 'em." The Knight was a master at it, but I still had a ways to go.

Two days later, I was still kicking myself in the backside for not delivering Pillo and his gang. After our huge success with the Acosta car ring just eight months before, I thought I could score at random. But now, doubts were coming down like Idaho snowflakes.

Then my phone rang.

The call was for "Mack MacPater." My pulse quickened. It was Pillo! He wanted to talk. As the Knight overheard our conversation, he tensed up. He may have wet his pants. Within two minutes, he had me out of the office, strapped into a bureau vehicle, and onto Biscayne Boulevard, en route to Little Havana.

Pillo had set up the meet at a Cuban café fifteen minutes away from his garage and well out of the Little Havana area, where he would not be recognized. This place became the new rendezvous spot for our clandestine debriefings. Not only was it secure and isolated from the wrong kind of traffic, but the Cuban food there, as well as the chocolate cake, were to die for.

The Knight and I walked in with what must have been that "You knew we'd get ya" look.

Pillo was just finishing a tasty plate of pollo al horno (baked chicken), with the standard accompaniment of black beans and rice.

He invited us to sit down, suggesting we try the picadillo. We took his recommendation and dove into the sumptuous dish, laced with garlic, consisting of ground beef, onions, capers, and raisins, prepared in a tomato base. It was served with black beans and rice.

Pillo started the conversation with a little small talk, explaining that Cubans apply the term "Moors and Christians" to the black beans and rice. He advised the rice symbolized the Spanish Christians, and the black beans represented the Moors, or the traditional enemies of Spain, that occupied that country for several centuries.

After topping off the picadillo with a delicious piece of devil's food chocolate cake, Pillo was ready to talk shop.

We discovered, to our delight, that we had unknowingly scored on our interview with Pillo. Since our initial contact with him two days prior, he had been sweating bullets, wondering when he would be picked up. The axiom, "More nervous than a long-tailed cat in a room full of rocking chairs," would accurately define his state of mind, as beads of sweat appeared on his forehead.

Pillo was smarter than we thought, already having figured out the advantage of being the first to fold. In my years with the Bureau and as a private investigator, I've noted that while many perpetrators are as dumb as the bank robber in Portland, Oregon, who left his wallet on the teller counter after passing off the demand note, there are others whose lights brighten considerably when contemplating the advantages of embracing law enforcement from cap to coattails.

Pillo was spilling his guts. Why not?

For each stolen car count under the Dyer Act, which is used to prosecute individuals transporting, or causing vehicles to be transported in interstate commerce, one could be sentenced to ten years in prison and an unspecified fine. Pillo was involved in the theft, interstate transportation, fraudulent documentation, and illegal sale of most of the dozens of luxury vehicles we eventually recovered, either directly or indirectly.

He had the floor, and we were taking copious notes.

Over the next few days, Pillo continued singing. As he named his co-conspirators, many more successful interviews were generated with other potential defendants.

Not only did Pillo get religion, but he had made scores of converts, who subsequently revealed their roles to us. The choir seats began filling up, row by row, as the singing continued. The White Knight and I were the choristers. You might refer to it as "an outpouring of the Spirit." Everyone knew the word was out, and everyone was running for cover.

Two of Pillo's gang, Castor Martinez and Armando Navarro, in their early twenties, were members of a team calling themselves Los Cuervos, meaning The Vultures. They had been stealing cars left and right with impunity. After having "seen the light," and while waiting to testify in the confines of a witness waiting room in Miami's Federal Court, they presented me a neatly-penned document in Spanish.

The document read, "Tranquil place for the repentant; then forward to cooperate to the maximum with the Government!"

Miguel Buendia Mendoza and Enrique Jose Lopez were private detectives, skilled in repossessing automobiles, and had used their profession as cover for stealing in Pillo's operation.

Mendoza eventually made the front page of the Miami News, when he became the first of thirty conspirators to be led out of the Miami office building on Biscayne Boulevard in handcuffs.

Pillo and his cohorts had successfully involved numerous elements of the auto service industry in their operations in New York, New Jersey, South Florida, and the Caribbean. Like in the Cesar Enrique Acosta operation, the vehicles were stolen in the Northeast, transported to Florida, given false titles and vehicle identification numbers from salvage yard wrecks, and, by the time they hit Miami, passed off as legitimate.

The thieves endeavored to make it impossible to identify the vehicles as stolen, but the Knight and I knew where to look. It required some special techniques that I will never make public.

Assistant U.S. Attorney (AUSA) Jerome Ullman reported to the news media that "Easily one hundred cars were stolen, fixed up with false VINs, and shuttled for sale."

A federal grand jury was soon convened and duly exposed to four hours of testimony from the White Knight and the Holy Crusader. True bill indictments were issued for the arrest of forty conspirators throughout the eastern seaboard.

On August 9, 1971, we arrested forty people in a multi-state crackdown. Thirty arrests were consummated in the Miami area, and ten more would take place in New York; New Jersey; Jacksonville, Florida; and San Juan, Puerto Rico.

The sweep covered perpetrators running the gamut of occupations, including service station and garage operators, salvage yard owners, tow-service personnel, a comanager of a super market, a body and fender man, a vinyl roof installer, a car salesman, a school counselor, a construction worker, an auto parts dealer, two auto exporters, a route salesman for a soft drink company, and a junior college student.

Milt Sosin, a reporter for the *Miami News*, made this written comment concerning the Felix Aleman investigation: "In cases involving many principals, one defendant will sometimes request a trial by judge, while the rest of the defendants will ask for a jury trial. Veteran court officials believe that this case involves the greatest number to have been tried by a judge at the same time."

Subsequent to indicting and arresting Pillo's gang, AUSA Ullman met with the White Knight and I daily for several weeks running. We reviewed overwhelming evidence, consisting of numerous confessions, scores of stolen car recoveries, and mountains of corroborating incrimination.

The case was tried not by a jury, but by a federal judge, the Honorable U.S. District Court Judge Joe Eaton. Judge Eaton presided in the trial of fifteen of the defendants, all having their own individual counsel.

It was far from a fair fight. Prosecutor Ullman, the Knight, and I were lined up against fifteen defense attorneys. It was "dog eat dog" the whole way, as the trial became very messy.

Since Judge Eaton's goal was to have the case off his docket before the end of the year, we continued in trial night and day. During the six-week proceeding, only a miracle prevented the case from unraveling.

A federal judge, a prosecutor, two FBI agents, and fifteen defense attorneys and their clients constantly wore and tore on each other. Prosecutor Ullman took continuous heat on motions from the fifteen defense attorneys. In addition, he was constantly dodging criticisms from the bench that made him question whether his government grade and step in pay were really worth it.

In federal trials, Bureau agents are limited in assisting the prosecutor. The Knight and I acted as a resource for identifying incriminating evidence and bringing it to AUSA Ullman's attention. Corroborating the information we received from Pillo and others who admitted their participation was high priority. We spent countless hours pulling vital data out of voluminous files to help address each motion.

Every "burp" from the defense sent us scurrying. Many defense motions were designed only to put air in the case, or otherwise abort the facts, in order to buy time and the court's sympathy.

The Knight and I ran errands and made contacts for the prosecutor, in order to resolve issues arising out of the natural and spontaneous course of arbitration, issues needing to be resolved on a timely basis, to satisfy the judge and counsel. One thing we never wanted to witness was Prosecutor Ullman, looking surprised and gasping for breath, from not being adequately informed.

Never will I forget the night one of the coconspirators took the stand. It was about 10:00 PM , and everyone wanted to go home. The Knight and I were convinced this defendant knew the whereabouts of a fugitive we had indicted in the case and were still seeking.

I suggested to Ullman that he query the defendant as to the fugitive's whereabouts, since he had him on the stand and under oath. Ullman did so, and pandemonium broke out.

Judge Eaton read the intent and proceeded to go after me.

"McPheters! Boy! I know you put him up to that!"

In my mind, I was saying, *Up to what? What's wrong with that?*

Judge Eaton's eyes were reddening and spelling DEFENSE-ORI-ENTED, making it crystal clear that he found my influence in engineering this inquiry maddening.

What I did next brought me within a hair of being incarcerated for contempt.

I may be just an obscure guy from Idaho who doesn't wield much influence in many spheres, but I don't like being called "boy."

I threw my notepad across the table where the Knight, Ullman, and I were seated, in full view of His Honor, while clearly giving vent to pent-up frustration.

The Knight grimaced and shot me that "You dumb butt!" look.

As I envisioned spending that night in jail for contempt, I asked myself why I'd lost control. Too many one-sided decisions off the bench. Too many defense antics. Too much burning of the midnight oil, and, while eating at the same Cuban restaurant twice a day, too many black beans and rice.

Everyone went silent, gazing up toward the bench at a seething volcano that through some miracle never erupted.

Judge Eaton called time out at 10:30 PM, and recessed his court. However, prior to leaving, and after the courtroom was cleared of legal counsel, he approached the Knight and I.

"Mr. McPheters, sometimes I go home wondering why I say some things that I do. But in this case you have to realize that you, Mr. Hufford, and Mr. Ullman indicted forty people before a federal grand jury in only four hours of presenting evidence. I just worry about that being an abuse of the system."

I knew His Honor was awaiting my response.

"Judge Eaton, we presented the evidence late in the afternoon. The jurors seemed content that we had answered all their questions, and that we had presented ample evidence. The rest was in their hands."

The judge had no further response, bid us good-by, and left the courtroom.

The White Knight never could figure out how I got out of that one.

We endured the Pillo Gang trial. Most of the thieves were convicted. A few got off.

The Pillo Gang case drew very favorable write-ups from the *National Observer* and the *Miami Herald*, but the commendation that impressed the Knight and I the most was a note on a routing slip from our steno pool.

The note, which had a gold star pasted on it, read as follows:

> *For a splendid job by McPheters Raiders in catching the car thieves—because we wouldn't want our cars stolen.*
> *—Thanks from some taxpayers.*
> *Becky and Margaret, Steno Pool*

8

★ ★ ★ ★ ★

THE WEDDING BUST

FEBRUARY 1971

There was the name, CURTIS CRISEL, etched into the concrete sidewalk of the Surfside Police Department gun range.

I was conducting a police firearms training session for some local police departments with Special Agent Joe Frechette, the Miami office's head firearms instructor.

The name was haunting. This guy had been a police officer at Surfside, Florida, and we had just arrested him a few days before at his wedding.

The sea breeze blowing into the range from the Atlantic barely subdued the obnoxious odor from a nearby dump. It was an odor that reeked almost as much as Crisel's reputation. He had reportedly not been bashful about administering the "third degree" to obtain confessions or "cooperation" from subjects he arrested. He didn't last long in a department that had a stellar reputation for turning out good officers.

Crisel had also served as a probationary police officer on the Miami Beach Police Department from May 1968 to March 1969, but "did not quite meet the standards," and was allowed to resign, according to a spokesman from that department.

★ ★ ★ ★ ★

Two weeks before, Special Agent Jack Barrett was assigned to take a complaint at the front desk from two surly-appearing men, actually brothers, whose emotions were running off the charts. They were begging to be interviewed. Their description, transmitted from the clerk at the front desk, was "scared out of their wits!"

Barrett, who was assigned their case, wanted someone with him on the interview, so I got the nod.

"So, what's the story on this one?" I asked. "Where are these guys from?"

Barrett replied, "These two dudes, brothers, got hung up somewhere near Atlanta with a hot car. The cops caught on to them, so they ditched the car, and came home empty-handed. Whoever the cars were supposed to end up with lost money on the deal, and all hell broke loose. That's all the clerk out front knows. Why they would come to us, confessing they had possession of stolen cars, is the big question."

"Let's go find out what gives," I replied.

"These guys are acting like they've seen a ghost, Mac."

"Something is really weird here. Guys don't come in to see us who know they are on the brink of arrest. Makes no sense at all," I retorted.

Upon entering the interview room where big brother and little brother were wearing pallid expressions, it was painfully obvious that for them, our appearance was unsettling, yet a relief. The brothers regarded us with expressions that were both sheepish and apprehensive. We displayed our credentials.

Barrett led out: "Special Agent Jack Barrett. This is Special Agent Mike McPheters. What's up, gentlemen?"

It was apparent these guys had both been through a ringer.

James Wilson, the younger brother, spoke up first. "They gonna kill us! Sure as shootin.' They out to get us."

James moved ahead with their story, while William Wilson just sat there, dazed, about to drop from exhaustion.

"These two guys had us, Curtis Crisel, an ex-cop, and some guy Crisel said was his uncle, who paid out six hundred dollars for a hot Lincoln. They told us to take the car to Atlanta and hook up with some dudes who would take it off our hands and pay us some good money. We took off up there with the Lincoln, and next thing we know, the cops are all over us!"

"So, did the police take you down?" Barrett asked.

William Wilson finally came to life.

"No, we got away, but we had to dump the car, which the cops got their hands on. But when we got back to Miami empty-handed, the two dudes that sent us north with their money went ballistic."

The Wedding Bust
Left: James Wilson stands in the self-made grave that his would-be assassins forced him to dig.
Right: Special Agent Jack Barrett stands by grave.

James jumped back in and described how Crisel and his uncle, subsequently identified as Raymond Koon, had backed him and William up against a wall, grabbed them by their throats, and told them how they were about to die.

His voice began quivering, as he recounted being driven late at night in Crisel's car, to an area behind an outdoor drive-in movie theater in North Miami. His expression betrayed intense, pent-up trauma. He recounted how he and William were forced to dig their own graves at gunpoint. He explained how they were made to stand in the graves, up to their neck level, while their captors ranted and raved about how the dirt would be tamped in and covered with rock so firmly that they would never be discovered.

James, with quivering lips, stuttered, "We-we-we . . . we were standin' in those pits put-in-near twenty minutes when Crisel cocked a revolver, and stuck it to my head. I knew I was gonna die right there and then. The other guy did the same thing to William. But then cars drove in with their headlights on, probably some security guards or maintenance folks or someone, and done saved our bacon."

William re-entered. "Yeah, they thought someone would see 'em do us in, so they let us out o' them holes, and gave us two days to somehow come up with their twenty-five hundred dollars. That was last night, and that's why we're here."

James continued. "We couldn't go to the cops, because the one guy, Curtis Crisel, said he'd been a cop for awhile for the Surfside Police Department."

Barrett assured the Wilson brothers that their case would be presented to the U.S. Attorney for prosecution. We made it clear we couldn't guarantee them protection.

Two days later, Barrett and I were able to obtain warrants for Curtis Crisel and Raymond Koon, charging them with conspiracy for "Interstate Transportation of Stolen Motor Vehicles."

We coordinated with the police in Atlanta, Georgia, and with the Florida authorities to obtain the details of their investigations. We determined that Crisel and his uncle had set up the whole deal and had solicited and financed the Wilson's involvement so they could avoid being identified as the perpetrators.

We now had the warrants but had no idea where Crisel and Koon lived.

From the Wilsons, we learned Crisel was going to marry Barbara Duey in Bal Harbor, Florida's "Church by the Sea," the traditional scene of high society's weddings, located at the tip of the barrier island of Miami Beach, in South Florida. We verified that the wedding would take place the following Saturday, and the reception, later that afternoon, at the home of friends of the bride.

After cautioning the Wilson men to keep a low profile for the following few days, and to stay out of sight, we initiated surveillances on the Bal Harbor wedding site and the reception location.

The morning of the highly-anticipated event, Barrett and I were waiting at the wedding site two hours early, knowing the Church by the Sea was the one place we'd find Crisel.

The Reverend Charles H. Meeker was scheduled to officiate in the Saturday wedding. Once we arrived at his office, and explained that we were at the church to execute an arrest warrant on the prospective bridegroom, the reverend advised us to wait in a small office adjacent to his own, where the bridegroom and best man usually await the bride's arrival.

Crisel showed up early by himself. When he entered the waiting room approximately forty-five minutes before the wedding, Barrett and I grabbed him, handcuffed him, and read him his rights.

The next day, a newspaper article was headlined, "FBI Mutes Ex-Cops Wedding Bells." A subsequent article was published in the *Miami Herald* by Edna Buchanan, entitled "The FBI Takes This Man, Not to Love and Cherish." She quoted Reverend Meeker who declared, "When the groom came in, I showed him in . . . and they grabbed him."

The *Miami Herald* also stated the following in the aforementioned article: "Instead of honeymooning with a new bride today, a former policeman is still languishing in Dade County Jail. The click of handcuffs set the wedding march off key when the prospective bridegroom, Curtis Crisel, twenty-seven, found the FBI waiting at the church. The husky blue-eyed six-footer departed unwed and linked by steel manacles to a burly FBI man."

Shortly after arresting Crisel, the bridal party drove up. One of the agents we had stationed outside the church approached the bride and those accompanying her, and advised them the groom was sick, and the wedding would have to be postponed.

Once we turned Crisel over to other agents who transported him to jail, Barrett and I drove directly to the residence of a friend of the bride, which was set up for the reception, and waited with a warrant for Crisel's uncle, Raymond Koon.

Coincidentally, Koon had also just married, and was on his honeymoon. He had tied the knot shortly after sending the Wilson boys north with a hot car and was taking time off to pay respects to nephew Curtis. While Barrett and I surveilled the reception residence, the uncle pulled in with his new wife. Barrett and I closed in. I tagged him with handcuffs, while Barrett read him his rights.

As the wedding guests closed in around our Bureau car, where we had just stashed Koon, we became acutely aware how much family and friends resent having their wedding party messed up. Those were really unfriendly countenances that closed in around us.

I asked myself, "Are they going to block our exit and push over our car?"

Barrett was about to activate the siren and call for backup. Slowly, ever so slowly, the crowd began to disperse, and the driveway cleared. Within seconds we were out of there, barely avoiding the mob. Barrett was in the back seat with Koon, advising him of his Miranda warnings.

Barrett and I thought we had done the bride, Barbara Duey, a favor, keeping Crisel away from her. However, we were subsequently advised that she had mortgaged her home for sixty thousand dollars bail money for Crisel.

The week before Barrett and I arrested Crisel at his wedding, and broke up a marriage-to-be, I performed a marriage as a Mormon bishop at the Miami Third Ward chapel.

The agent bishop dichotomy was definitely in play.

9

★ ★ ★ ★ ★

BANK ROBBERS

JULY 22, 1971

For decades, bank robbery investigations have been a major FBI responsibility. That's because most bank losses are insured by the federal government through the Federal Deposit Insurance Corporation (FDIC), while savings and loans associations are insured by the Federal Savings and Loan Insurance Corporation (FSLIC).

FBI agents refer to bank robberies as "91's" or just "BR's."

There is a theory in police science stating that the perpetrator always takes something to the crime scene or leaves something there that will eventually incriminate him. In no violation is this made more evident than in bank robberies.

While assigned bank robbery details, I have covered some crazy ones. I worked one where an elderly perpetrator used a demand note, took the money, and walked a half-block down the street, where he bought drinks for his buddies until the authorities picked him up twenty minutes later.

In yet another instance, the subject robbed the bank and stuck a cocked revolver into his jeans while sprinting for the front door. The gun went off just outside the door and severed a major artery in his leg. He collapsed and bled to death within minutes.

In another BR, after the robber used a demand note, the teller gave him a dye pack. Dye packs are rectangular containers filled with red dye that can be electronically activated when the perpetrator exits the door of the bank. They are the size of a packet of bills with genuine twenty-dollar denominations attached on both sides. They give the appearance of a real money bundle. Once they are activated, they explode and stain the perpetrator's clothing. He can then be readily identified.

In this case, the robber stuck the dye pack into the inner pocket of his jacket and rushed out of the bank. As he passed by the front door, the bundle was electronically activated, and it exploded, igniting his clothing and dispersing the dye all over his clothing, starting with his jacket. Thanks to a stiff breeze, his pants became toast, as well as his shirt. Within seconds, he was in his underwear. In a state of panic, he flagged down a taxi. The cabbie immediately recognized what had happened and drove him to the police station, a short distance away, where he was arrested and booked.

★　★　★　★　★

Back in the sixties and seventies, before FBI offices became so huge and departmentalized, the entire office responded to bank robberies. We would all meet at the bank with the responding police departments and would begin interviewing tellers and witnesses. We would obtain the surveillance camera film, if there was any, and would secure all available information regarding the government insurance data.

On July 22, 1971, the day of my third anniversary with the FBI, the Citizens National Bank of Miami was robbed by two white males driving a white 1969 Pontiac, later identified as Harold Julian Grove and Robert Charles Boswell. One of them had previously fired a shot while escaping from a mental institution.

The entire office had cleared out in response to the robbery, except Bob Mills and I, who were still in the office doing paperwork. I began feeling those increasing pangs of guilt you experience when you know you should be somewhere that you're not.

I hollered, "Hey, Mills! Let's you and I go out and solve that BR."

Mills looked at me like, "Sure, new boy on the block. Why not? It's just that easy." He got up and followed me out the door, as we waived confidently to the support personnel and clerical staff who remained in control of the office, while the agents were looking for the bank robbers.

We drove into a middle-class residential area in North Miami, dotted with a lot of fast food stores. We had the robbers' descriptions and knew what kind of a car we were looking for. Both subjects had been wearing white T-shirts and Levi jeans.

Instead of driving directly to the bank, which was already swarming with agents and police officers, we begin canvassing the surrounding areas, looking for the getaway car.

A Dade County Sheriff's Office vehicle pulled into the parking lot of a fast food store, where we had parked to radio in our location. After realizing who we were, the deputy sheriff exited his patrol car, walked up to us, and furnished additional information on the robbers and their vehicle. He also had some interesting data that had not yet been distributed at the bank, regarding the subjects. For some time, his department had been aware Grove and Boswell were frequenting the area not far from the bank, robbing fast food stores while eluding the authorities.

We passed this new information on to our colleagues at the bank and then continued canvassing the areas within a mile of two away.

Approximately forty-five minutes had elapsed since the bank had been robbed.

Suddenly, just in front of us, we observed a white Pontiac slowly pulling into a gas station. I was ninety-nine percent sure it was our car. Mills pulled up to within one hundred feet.

The occupants, who fit the subjects' descriptions, sensed something was going down and remained in their car. They were looking in every direction, seemingly hesitant to do anything.

I yelled, "Let's go, Mills!" and within seconds, I was walking toward the suspect vehicle, grasping my revolver in my right hand, obscured slightly behind my back, just in case the one percent of uncertainty could cause me some real embarrassment.

The closer I got to the car, my pace quickened. I studied every movement in the front seat and every change of expression on the faces of the occupants. When I was fifty feet away with my eyes still glued on Grove and Boswell, I was sure we had them.

At twenty-five feet, I raised my gun to eye level and trained it on the suspects in the car. I committed myself to spraying the windshield full of semi-jacketed, hollow-point thirty-eight caliber rounds, if they brought a weapon into view.

Suddenly, a hollow feeling set in, as I glanced sideways and realized I was alone. Mills, the older, more experienced agent, was still at our vehicle, kneeling behind the open car door, driver's side, with the window rolled down for extra protection. Mills had gone by the book and had the car canted at an angle to the robbers, giving him the additional cover of the engine block and wheel well. And here I was, closing in, slowly but cautiously, with Grove and Boswell looking down the business end of my revolver.

When I was just ten feet away, another bureau car, loaded with agents rolled up behind the white Pontiac, with Special Agent Ed Gooderham at the wheel. Once Mills had hustled up behind me, and the Gooderham crew had jumped out to back me up, I was immediately emboldened.

I ripped open the front door of the Pontiac, and discovered a loaded .357 magnum revolver between the two subjects. I grabbed the driver, Boswell, by the hair and yanked him off his seat. As he spun out the door, his momentum caused him to collide with a fifty-five gallon drum filled with oil cans, which spewed forth, rolling in every direction down the incline of the gas station's approach, causing a din of epic proportions.

As Mills and I cuffed Boswell, Gooderham and crew followed up with Grove. We threw them both up against the station wall and patted them down for weapons and fruits of the crime. As I ran my hands over Boswell's jeans, I felt a huge bundle in his right pocket and dislodged it.

Thousands of dollars in denominations of hundreds, fifties, and twenties matched the amount of money taken in the robbery. That, along with the subject and vehicle descriptions, affirmed all suspicions. We had the right guys.

Once the agents at the bank were alerted that Mills and I, the last guys out of the office, had caught the bank robbers, we had plenty of company at the gas station.

Irv Bruce and "Scooter" Coutre transported Boswell and Grove back to the office, and interviewed them, while Mills and I started the paperwork.

After the interviews, I asked Bruce, "So, what did our boys have to report?"

Bruce looked at me somewhat seriously and said, "McPheters, this is your lucky day. When you walked up to their car, they had that gun between them in their front seat. Grove said, 'Well, there's the man. Shall we take him out or not?' They talked themselves out of it."

All's well that ends well. Besides, I couldn't be taken out yet. I still had more of the Good Lord's work to do. On October 23, 1971, I was set apart by Elder Boyd K. Packer of the Quorum of the Twelve Apostles, as first counselor to the new bishop, Special Agent Leon Fish, my good friend from the Uruguayan Mission. While placing his hands upon my head, Apostle Packer blessed me in my occupation as an FBI agent, that the Lord would watch over me and answer my prayers. That was better than a bullet-proof vest.

10

★★★★★

THE FOUNTAIN VALLEY MASSACRE

SEPTEMBER 1972

Wild mongooses scampered around the borders of a magnificent lake. The lake was shaded by palm trees and adjacent to a well-kept golf course at the Fountain Valley Country Club. Once part of a nineteenth century Danish colonial sugar plantation, the course's clubhouse was constructed on the side of a mountain that was over a thousand feet high.

The Virgin Islands setting at Christiansted, located on the "east end" of Saint Croix, was truly magnificent. The course was located on a mountain, above a beautiful valley landscape. Low-lying, verdant hills, dotted with flowering hibiscus and patches of red bougainvillea, encircled the greens.

St. Croix was first colonized in the 1700s. In 1917, the United States purchased the island from the Danes, who had dubbed the areas surrounding the golf course with names they felt worthy of their beauty, names like "Sweet Bottom," "Upper Love," and "Two Friends." Today the island is inhabited by about fifty thousand permanent residents.

Richard and Mattie Ruth Griffin and Charles and Joan Meisinger, from Miami, Florida, had enjoyed eighteen holes of golf at the scenic island's course, believed by many to be the Caribbean's finest. They had just lunched on cheeseburgers on the veranda of the clubhouse, while chatting with some other guests.

The two couples were benefiting from their employment with Eastern Airlines, where Richard worked as a machinist and Joan as a secretary. The airlines encouraged their employees to vacation during slack times, and had provided them free transportation to the islands.

The golfers were staying at the Estate Carlton, an old, upscale plantation hotel. They were living the vacationer's dream. After all, how many people got to vacation with free round-trip tickets to these islands, regarded as a tourist's paradise?

The Fountain Valley course, owned by David and Lawrence Rockefeller, was a seven thousand yard course with lakes and a meandering river. The ambiance they were enjoying, with giant orchids hanging from kapok trees, more than fulfilled their tastes for luxury and refreshment. They had hosted golf tournaments for other fellow Eastern Airline employees for years and were now taking some time to play lots of golf and to absorb an abundance of rays.

At 3:15 PM, they entered their rented Toyota, parked near the pro shop veranda, and were leaving the clubhouse. Suddenly, their rear door was opened by one of five men in their early to mid-twenties, each dressed in green fatigues and face masks.

These men were allegedly linked to a black power group, named "The United Caribbean Association." They had emerged from the shadows of the adjacent mountain undergrowth, near the clubhouse. Witnesses later advised that four or five of these men had rifles slung over their shoulders and walkie-talkies, which operated on the same wave length as the local police.

Both couples exited their car, and at gunpoint, returned to the veranda bar, without offering any resistance, where they were forced to kneel together, hoping, and praying for mercy. After handing over their billfolds, numerous gun blasts rang out, as all four tourists were summarily executed in cold blood.

The gunmen then proceeded to the cash register in the clubhouse and cleaned it out, obtaining only a few hundred dollars.

Next, they sprayed the dining area with bullets, killing three more white people and one black man. These included John Gulliver, a Massachusetts-born maintenance man and groundskeeper; Patricia Tarbert, a lady who was substituting in the pro shop and employed part-time as a model; Nick Beale, an electrician; and Alston Lowery, a light-skinned black man from West India, who was Beale's assistant. Gulliver and Tarbert were killed just twenty yards away from where the American tourists were executed. Beale died on a rear patio, and Lowery succumbed on the lawn, near the clubhouse.

Eight black witnesses survived, although four were wounded. They subsequently advised authorities that Lowery, the only black man killed, was promised by one of the gunmen, just prior to his execution, "Lie down, brother. You'll be all right. Nobody will hurt you."

Witnesses further stated that numerous rounds were fired from handguns, shotguns, and from a machine gun that was subsequently proven to be stolen from the local police.

One witness said the shots were continuous, "Like it went on for ten minutes."

★ ★ ★ ★ ★

Before I awoke, the phone rang several times at our Miami Lakes residence on Lake Lure Court. I lay there between the sheets, trying to ignore the shrill ringing that was ruining a good night's sleep. I wanted to just make it go away, as I rolled over, and tried to distance myself from the intrusion.

"What time is it?" Judy muttered, facing me with an expression of alarm. Her soft blonde locks tumbled down over a pretty face, fraught with apprehension. The alarm clock, reading 4:20 AM, was glaring at us, challenging us to come to our senses and answer the telephone, which was still ringing off the hook.

I picked it up. "Who is this? This better be good!" I mumbled angrily.

"It's the office, Mr. McPheters," the night clerk announced. "Eight people, including four American tourists, were murdered by terrorists yesterday in the Virgin Islands. It happened at a country club. The Bureau's been requested to assist the local police in Saint Croix, so Mr. Frechette's taking you and a few other agents over there with him. You need to saddle up and be ready to catch a Lear jet out of Fort Lauderdale in an hour and a half."

By this time, Judy was sitting straight up in bed, wide awake. She always came to her senses quicker than I did. It was those Idaho farm girl instincts. I told her what the call was about. She had that "You've got to be kidding me!" look written all over her face.

"This has got to be some kind of joke. You've got to call them back!" she insisted.

I picked up the phone and called the office. The night clerk answered.

"Hey, did you just call me?" I asked, sounding somewhat peeved, half-doubting and half-curious, while rubbing my eyes.

I went on. "Is this some kind of fantasy? Virgin Islands? Lear jets? Was that really you that called?"

"Sure was, Mr. McPheters. Joe Frechette, Frank Duffin, Leo McClairen, Joe Dawson, and John Walser are all gearing up. Mr. Frechette is counting on you. Fort Lauderdale Airport. 6:00 AM."

I had received confirmation. Blood had been spilled. It was the real deal, and I was needed.

"I'll be there!" I slammed down the phone and jumped out of bed.

"It's for real," I told Judy. "They said I was the sixth person they called and the third to call back to confirm it wasn't a hoax. I've got to go to Saint Croix to investigate some homicides."

Judy focused in on the reality of the situation, as she also bounded out of bed, asking, "How many days shall I pack you for?"

"The usual," was my response, which meant one suitcase with running gear, and several days of clothing for who knows how long.

The fact that Joe Frechette, our head firearms instructor, wanted me along on a case like that really hit my hot button. He and Frank Duffin, two World War II veterans, both office legends, would be on the St. Croix case. I knew I could learn from these guys.

We had been summoned, upon request of the governor of the U.S. Territory of the Virgin Islands, to become part of a team of one hundred law enforcement officers, including twenty-four FBI agents, fifteen U.S. Marshals, and sixty-one local law enforcement officials, assisted by a U.S. Coast Guard helicopter pilot and the owner of a private plane. We would conduct an island-wide manhunt for the killers. Our headquarters would be located at the Fountain Valley Country Club, where the crimes occurred. We would operate around the clock, until the perpetrators were apprehended.

As Judy packed my bags, she took serious note of our newly-born baby, Tylee. I wondered, *Would she have to raise her alone with the other two?* She knew I was walking into a dangerous assignment for an indefinite time period. She was trying to think positively.

Bureau wives are like that. They get used to having their man get up in the middle of the night, watching him strap on his weapon, and kissing him good-bye as he walks out into the night. It was part of the Bureau culture. The ladies knew they would get the details later, knowing then was not the time to ask questions, and trusting their spouse would make it back home.

As I immersed myself into a nice shower, Judy continued in her pensive mood while filling my suitcase, considering the length of time she would be alone again with the two youngsters, while still nursing a six-week-old baby. I could tell she was thinking of how many other times I had left like this and how many more times there would be just like it, when the calls came.

Judy had a degree in accounting. She had not yet used it and questioned whether she could support our growing family, if necessary. The day eventually came, following a hellacious gunfight that I narrowly survived, when she would prove herself, but that day was still distant, and at that moment, she had lingering doubts.

The irony was that even though there was some apprehension and fear, as she stuffed a suitcase with shirts, pants, and running gear, she was simultaneously and vicariously sharing with me the wonderment, thrill, and excitement that made this career so special.

Every early morning raid, every dangerous arrest, every opportunity I had to take drugs off the street, seemed to cause waves of excitement to cascade into our relationship. We both felt it and actually relished the feeling.

Spontaneous challenges like this, both in the Bureau and in my Church assignments, inspired feelings of awe and amazement in both of us. To us, these challenges were harbingers, signaling a unique and highly-desirable probability that I, with her support, could really make a difference somewhere in the world, while administering the long arm of the law and ministering to the needs of our congregation, as their bishop.

This FBI career was a team arrangement, just as my work as bishop was something we shared, in a very real sense. Judy did not have to be involved in the actual fray to vicariously experience what I experienced in both arenas.

We both knew that my work was now in the Virgin Islands. Packed and ready, I knelt with Judy in prayer and took a fleeting glance at our sleeping children. We embraced, shared a long kiss, and I was out the door.

As I sped towards the Fort Lauderdale Airport, I looked within myself. How would I contribute in Saint Croix? It was humbling to be part of Frechette's team.

I asked myself, "Why me?" There were so many agents in Miami with so much more experience. Frechette knew I would be loyal, that I would not turn away from anything, and that I would always have his back. I was big and strong, and I guess I looked and sounded enough like John Wayne, that he liked me.

We all rendezvoused at the airport, threw our bags and weapons into the storage compartment of a chartered Lear jet, and flew away.

As we swooped down on the tarmac of the St. Croix Airport, it was strikingly apparent that the Bureau and local police were in full control of the island. Agents from the San Juan, Puerto Rico Division of the FBI were everywhere, wearing body armor and strolling around, toting shoulder weapons. It was very obvious that whoever was responsible for the murders would have to find another way off the island, for they would never fly out of that airport unnoticed.

As we drove through Christiansted, and approached the crime scene at the Fountain Valley Country Club, blood was still splattered over the tile in front of the pro shop at the golf course.

During the weeks prior to the homicides, numerous assaults on tourists and other white residents of the island had occurred. The perpetrators were anarchists, totally out of control. The police could do nothing about it. They also had been intimidated by our subjects.

Under Joe Frechette's direction, our Miami contingent settled into a routine of patrolling the island in the areas adjacent to the country club. It was heavily wooded and steep, with jagged crags and narrow trails that were mostly overgrown.

A few days after the massacre, the local police captured two of the assailants. We made one of them, Meral Smith, lead us on searches for the other subjects. Frechette tethered a rope to Smith's waistband, and made him lead out front. We established a tacit understanding with Smith that if he led us into a trap or ambush, or if anyone in our single file procession was shot at, he would die immediately. This was more than an empty threat.

The trails were uphill and narrow, through thick brush. It was very dangerous and an ideal scenario for an ambush. More often than not, we were fully exposed to whoever might be in waiting. The only insurance we had was that explicit "understanding" with the guy on the end of our rope.

During one of our forays in the mountains in the mid-afternoon on a very hot day, we located what appeared to be one of the killers' camps, but we were not sure whether they were inside their tents. We could detect neither sound nor movement. The camp was set up on a grassy knoll that was slightly overgrown. We decided to charge in, full-throttle.

Special Agent Joe Dawson, a former Marine, went first, screaming at the top of his lungs. He jumped onto the first tent, crushing it down with both feet, while Frechette, Duffin, John Walser, and I followed, knocking down everything in sight, searching for evidence that proved our subjects had occupied the camp. No one was there.

Meral Smith, their accomplice on the end of the rope, had no explanation for it.

Each day we continued the jungle searches. Any new clues regarding the possible whereabouts of the fugitives were reported to the command post. The command post was also the eating area, where lunch often consisted of goat meat, rice, and beans, with a little armadillo thrown in. At night, we usually visited a rustic open-air diner, called "Captain Weeks," and ate conch chowder and Johnny cakes.

For an extra treat to top off the day, our Miami bunch would head for "The Golden Cow" in downtown Christiansted, and consume ice cream that was good beyond belief.

In the mornings, we would jump out of bed early, don our running gear, and log in a couple miles on cobblestone streets, bobbing and weaving around stores, through parks, and past the windmills constructed during the Dutch influence.

We jokingly referred to ourselves as "The Fountain Valley PTA."

On our eighth day in St. Croix, a local informant reported seeing the girlfriend of Israel LaBeet, one of our subjects, carrying trays of food into a rectangular building owned by a relative of Rafael Joseph, another subject, referred to by the locals as the "Long House." She was also observed bringing out empty trays. Another independent source confirmed that information. The house was located in Frederiksted, on the west end of the island.

This new information was announced just before lunchtime. After gulping down some fresh sandwiches, stew, and chips, we broke out some antique bullet-proof vests. They were so old, the straps were falling apart. They were black with grey stripes and a lapel vest pocket. They had the appearance of something way too fancy to be assault gear. It was obvious that when the Bureau purchased those vests, bullet-proof body armor was not a high priority.

Joe Frechette and Ken Rommel, the San Juan Division principal firearms instructor, laid out the game plan for the apprehensions. We caravanned to the west end of the island, arriving at Frederiksted at about 3:00 PM.

First, we cordoned off the area downtown, next to the Long House, and evacuated everyone within that area, which we referred to as the inner perimeter. People began gathering on the other side of the roped-off section, displaying intense curiosity, but with a pretty good idea through the grapevine of what was about to happen.

We worked our way in towards the Long House from all angles, clearing and securing all the buildings adjacent to it, one by one. As we closed in, Frank Duffin, personally and methodically, took it upon himself to make sure no stone was left unturned, until every building near the Long House was evacuated and secure.

Using a bullhorn, Frechette called out each of the subject's names, warning them to surrender immediately.

"Come out of there! You're completely surrounded. This is the FBI."

As the subjects continued to be called out, I noticed dozens of local residents converging around the ropes that cordoned off the inner perimeter, beginning to press in. That did not look good.

I thought, *We've got to get these guys, and get them soon, or we're going to have our hands full, with some of their relatives and sympathizers.*

These people were gripped with curiosity and resentful of the onslaught of law enforcement that had invaded their island.

On the other hand, there were many who were relieved to have their city back, to be able to walk down their streets again, and to live securely, without having to double lock their doors for fear of terrorists who did as they pleased with whom they pleased.

Studying the expressions and reactions on the faces of these throngs of onlookers, I guessed that at least one out of every three knew exactly who was in the Long House. The Bureau had been in town for a week and a half, and everyone knew what was going on as a consequence of the massacre at the country club.

Then, all at once, the five remaining fugitives filed out of the Long House with their hands above their heads, and without their weapons, which, I had to admit at the time, was smart thinking. They had beaten up some of the top brass of the local police, intensifying an already edgy situation. In addition, they had terrorized many of the local residents for over a month.

Any display of weapons by these murderers would surely have incited another massacre, this time by the police. Seeing the five subjects march out of hiding with their hands over their heads emboldened the local police. It was all they could do to control themselves.

The fugitives were taken into custody without incident, transported to the local jail, and processed. All the weapons from the country club massacre were located, except the machine gun. That mystery was solved during subsequent confessions and debriefings. The machine gun was buried in feces in the bottom of an outdoor privy. Special Agent Robert Mills was assigned the dubious honor of fishing it out, which he accomplished that same day.

Confessions were given voluntarily, linking all seven subjects to the tools of death. The subjects were tried in Federal District Court in Christiansted, and subsequently convicted in trial-by-jury, after eight days of jury deliberation.

In court, frustrated defense attorneys accused the Bureau of using all kinds of mischief to extract confessions, including a form of water boarding, using electrical impulses, and the use of cattle prods. The claims were outlandish and unfounded.

The attorney who was the most outspoken in these accusations was the famed and flamboyant New York defense attorney, Robert Kuntsler, who had formerly represented the "Chicago Seven," the group of defendants charged with conspiracy and inciting to riot during the 1968 Democratic National Convention.

Just like in the Chicago Seven trial, during this trial in St. Croix the defendants fought with the U.S. Marshals, and screamed and cursed at U.S. District Court Judge Warren Young. To prevent subsequent outbursts, the judge ordered the defendants chained around their waists and wrists, prior to being sentenced.

None of the antics staged by the defendants in court bore fruit, including their false allegations regarding the federal agents. They were all convicted and given eight consecutive life sentences each, to be served in the federal penitentiary in Atlanta.

That the killings occurred and the killers were punished were undisputed facts. Somewhat hazier, however, was the reason for the killings. Why did they take place? Just what were the motivations? There were mixed reviews.

Many authorities advised the massacre was racially motivated, since witnesses stated the attackers screamed anti-white insults during the killing and fled with only seven hundred and thirty-one dollars in cash. A witness heard one of the gunmen refer to one of the women as "a white bitch," before killing her.

Further strengthening the argument that the killings were based on white hate are the observations of Robert Ellison, a black former Saint Croix police commissioner: "Fountain Valley was a luxury mainland-owned resort, catering to white continentals. The selection of the target was racially motivated," said Ellison, "but once they (the killers) got there, everybody within range was going to get killed."

Even Ishmael LaBeet's younger brother, Francis LaBeet, stated many years later, "People were coming in and taking over. We Cruzans found ourselves oppressed and left in desperation. It was easy for people to relate what my brother did to fighting the white establishment."

The racial motives were also highlighted in articles by the *New York Times* and the *Miami Herald*. Because of the adverse publicity, branding Saint Croix as unsafe, many whites fled the islands and tourism dwindled for decades. Even though Saint Croix is a much bigger island (84 square miles)

The Fountain Valley PTA
Front Row (left to right): Agent Brown, Joe Frechette, Frank Duffin, Mike McPheters. Back Row (left to right): John Walser, Joe Dawson, Bob Mills, Leo McClairen

than St. Thomas (32 square miles) and St. John (19 square miles), it still only hosts a small number of tourists compared with the other two.

Differences of opinion regarding the motives for the killings were voiced by the attorney-general, Ronald Tompkin and his boss, Governor Melvin Evans, who swore the motive was strictly robbery, without racial overtones. However, these men were extremely concerned with the repercussions of losing one hundred million dollars in tourist revenue each year from visitors who loved to frequent their beautiful twenty-eight mile long island. They knew if people believed there was racial hostility on the island, the facts that it was surrounded by beautiful waters and framed in dense groves of orchards and exotic flora would be lost on wary travelers.

The five perpetrators were subsequently identified as Rafael Joseph, also known as "Raphie," Warren Ballantine, also known as "Tooms," Meral Smith, Beaumont Gereau, and Ishmael LaBeet.

Ishmael LaBeet had been a ringleader in the group of assassins. According to his father, Stanley LaBeet, Ishmael had come under the influence of Malcolm X, while spending a year in New York in the Bronx as a teenager. He had been kicked out of high school for hitting a white man with a rock and was thereafter imprisoned while serving in Vietnam for beating up a white officer. He was dishonorably discharged, but not before converting to Islam, and taking on the name "Ali."

On December 31, 1984, after having served eleven years in the federal penitentiary for the Saint Croix massacre, Ishmael hijacked an American

Airlines flight to Cuba and has never been recaptured. He remains the Virgin Island's most wanted fugitive.

Prior to our leaving St. Croix, a ballad was composed by an anonymous source. It describes the accomplishments of the Fountain Valley PTA and their fellow officers, and highlights the ridiculous and fabricated allegations made by the defense in the trial of the five murderers. It reads as follows:

THE SAGA OF FOUNTAIN VALLEY

They came from far off places
Miami, San Juan, New York
They ate ham, cheese, and chicken
And never used a fork
They paced the bloodied terrace
Where men had met their God
And every mother's son of them
Carried a Cattle Prod

They checked the caves and mountain paths
Old sugar mills likewise
Each deserted house and building
They swooped on by surprise
They carried shotguns and rifles
Wherever men had trod
And there are rumors I am told
Each carried a Cattle Prod

They walked the hills and valleys
With tired and aching feet
Thirsting, sweating, and cursing at
JOSEPH, BALLANTINE and LABEET
They were men from varied backgrounds
All different, none were clods
One thing they had in common
All used Cattle Prods

Some were short and others tall

Some clothes were old, some new
This mattered nothing—not at all
Every one of them was true blue
Some of them were city folks
And some, men of the sod
But they shared one resemblance
Each carried a Cattle Prod.

Some drank a bit—some not a drop
Though the price seemed to be right
They worked from morning early
Till far into the night
None of them were unbelievers
All present had faith in God
But that odd looking thing each carried
Was called a Cattle Prod

If it's water that they ask for
Don't put it in a bowl
Wrap a watered towel around their face
And watch each gasping soul
Go fetch another bucket!
We need another pail
I can't see how they didn't drown
Before they were put in jail

We saw them hit, the sound went s-p-l-a-t!
The blood went spurting wild
They fell, got up and fell again
Relax! This was only mild
No! Don't shoot! Rather use the boot
As all men gave a nod
They will not talk! Don't bet on it!
Bring on the Cattle Prod

They worked, laughed, joked by night and day
They were a motley crew

The Fountain Valley P.T.A.
They were referred to by a few
With hats and caps from you know where
Their apparel was not mod
But they used the same M.O. I'm told
Wet towel and Cattle Prod

It's over now, almost, that is
The subjects admit their guilt
Pack up! Go home! The job is done
You've had it to the hilt
And once again it's time for fun
Bid St. Croix a toodle-oo
But you will come back, you must return
Says Kunstler and the ACLU

ANON

11

★ ★ ★ ★ ★

LEO

JUNE 1973

Leo McClairen was one of two African-American FBI agents that had actually been "knighted" by J. Edgar Hoover, meaning they were so valuable to the Bureau for their community contacts and intimate knowledge of their environment (Miami, in Leo's case) that they were eligible to forego the academic requirements and the formal training at Quantico. Leo was hired by the FBI in 1952, long before black barriers began coming down with the civil rights movement.

Leo fought in the Korean War, while enrolled in the U.S. Army, and subsequently served at the Naval Air Station in Opa-Locka, Florida. He also served a stint with the U.S. Marine Corps. Once the Naval Air Station closed, he was employed by the government as an aircraft mechanic. When he applied for the clerk position with the Bureau, his goal was to get in his twenty years of government service.

At that time, no one would ever have anticipated the wide swath of accomplishment Leo McClairen would cut in the FBI, and the immeasurable value he would be to the Bureau.

Leo had been particularly close to Director Hoover, having been his chauffeur when the Director was in Miami, before and after he became a special agent. Due to this relationship, Leo was brought into close contact with six U.S. presidents, including Herbert Hoover, Calvin Coolidge, John F. Kennedy, Richard Nixon, Jimmy Carter, and Ronald Reagan.

Agent Joe Frechette, who knew Leo particularly well, having first met him in 1951, stated, "He was one of Hoover's favorite guys. The guy just knew everybody around and was a great hunter of fugitives because of the way he was respected by the local people. One Coconut Grove mother whose son was wanted for murder would turn him over only to McClairen, a guy whose word is good."

The story was that Leo had facilitated the apprehension of numerous fugitives on the FBI's "Top Ten" list of most-wanted criminals. He had a sterling reputation, not only for being the "go-to" guy for locating and apprehending fugitives of African-American descent, but also for treating all his fellow agents as royalty. He always exuded a special respect and admiration for those of us who had qualified academically and had received the official Special Agent training.

The truth was that Leo could accomplish more with his instincts and knowledge of the black community than we could with our academics. However, he was too humble to realize that.

From the day I arrived in the Miami Division, Leo made me feel like I was his equal, even though I was still a rookie agent. I was amazed at Leo's ties in the community and his ability to develop intelligence relating to the whereabouts of fugitive murderers and other high-profile subjects. There were few arrests that Leo could not broker through his informants, if we gave him a little lead time.

I once assisted Leo in a raid on the residence of an Unlawful Flight to Avoid Prosecution (UFAP) subject. It occurred in one of Miami's communities referred to in the 1970s as the "Central Negro District," or the CND.

Leo developed information that the fugitive, a young black man, was staying in a house occupied by several transient families. We hit the house with our warrant early one morning before daybreak.

In our searching, we discovered eighteen people residing there. Of course, none of them knew anything about Johnny Boy, our subject. Not where he was living, who he was with, nor when he had last been seen.

As we cleared the house, room by room, I was behind Leo. We entered a bedroom totally obscured by darkness. Suddenly, Leo drew his revolver. Just as he was about to squeeze the trigger, someone switched on a light, revealing Leo's reflection in a mirror, located directly in front of him. As I struggled to hold back laughter, I thought about the fallout of Leo's blowing away his own reflection in that mirror, while awakening the community of people still dozing away in that house. After clearing all the rooms, there was still no sign of "Johnny Boy."

Leo was not satisfied. He was intuitively drawn back to a bedroom that had already been searched by other agents. He noticed a slight protrusion in some bedding that had fallen down adjacent to the bed that immediately captured his attention. He gazed at that clump of blankets with a fascinating surge of curiosity, like an African lion smelling out his prey, prior to jumping on it and sinking fangs into its flesh.

The next thing I knew, Leo was jumping up and down on that clump of bedding with both feet, yelling at someone to come out with their hands up. The pile of bedding began shaking and rising, until it was fully animated, even gaining a voice. "Get off me! You're killing me! I give up."

The young man stood up and was immediately handcuffed by the man who had been pouncing on him. Leo had scored again! He had consummated an arrest in a house that had been "thoroughly searched and cleared," while the rest of us watched in amazement.

Leo's reputation for developing quality informants was without parallel. Not only did he maintain a bevy of excellent informants, but he knew how to work them. One of them was given the code name of "Cool Breeze." Once Cool Breeze was given a photograph and a name, the individual matching the description might just as well turn himself in, or get out of town, because Leo would be paying him a visit.

Leo had a fondness for a certain variety of rum imported from the Virgin Islands. In September 1971, I became especially endeared to him, when we worked together as part of the "Fountain Valley P.T.A." case in the Virgin Islands.

Upon our return to the States, Leo talked me into packing the maximum amount of rum through customs that one person could bring in duty-free. This enabled him to double his rum supply through the complicity of his non-drinking Mormon friend. I had gone the extra mile for Leo, packing in that extra booze from the Caribbean, and he never forgot it.

Leo and I, along with other agents, were involved in the investigation and apprehension of Amado Lopez, an escaped federal prisoner that had murdered the daughter of an FBI agent in Arizona.

In another investigation, I should have used Leo but did not. I stumbled unwittingly onto a black fugitive holed up in a ramshackle hotel room in downtown Miami. The run-down building was home to many African-American people of all persuasions, in transit. I had an unlawful flight warrant for a subject wanted in a homicide case that I suspected would be known to some of the local residents. I was directed to a corner apartment on the third floor with no more than a flimsy sheet of quarter-inch plywood for a door, with a chain fastener.

Accompanied by a back-up agent, I peeked inside. It was our guy, the murderer—sitting there calmly, watching television. And there we were: two white boys, about four years experience between us, in a building full of black folks, most of whom were probably wanted.

The thought immediately entered my mind, "How would Leo handle this? Wish he were here!"

With our guns drawn, I kicked the door as hard as I could near the most vulnerable spot, within a six inch radius of the handle. A normal door would have broken open with that kind of force. This one just sprang back and forth, as quarter-inch plywood secured by a thin chain will do. The subject, who we could clearly observe through the cracked-open entrance, just gazed toward us, piqued with curiosity.

I kicked the door repeatedly, but always with the same result, which was no result. The man inside continued to stare with astonishment at the two white men in suits and ties, trying to break down his door, with guns in their hands.

Finally, I did what I knew Leo would do. I stopped kicking the man's door, looked straight at him through the opening, and said, "Hey, sir. This is the FBI. Would you please come to the door and open it?"

The burly fugitive and murderer rose to his feet, walked to the door, opened it, and told us to come in. We advised him he was under arrest for murdering someone in another state. He extended his hands. We handcuffed him, escorted him out of the building without incident, and booked him into the Dade County Jail.

Leo McClairen's nice-guy approach always paid off.

In another case scenario, Leo, myself, and a few other agents were parked in an area on the outskirts of Miami, conducting a surveillance on a subject wanted for unlawful flight on aggravated assault charges.

Leo was wearing his grey utilities, dressed like a plumber. The rest of us were dressed casually in sports clothes. We were parked in two different vehicles.

Unexpectedly, about twenty feet behind us, a young African-American youth in his early twenties began scuffling with a Dade County uniformed deputy, who had approached him to ask some questions. It was obvious the deputy was way out of shape, and no match for the man he was interviewing. It was also obvious the officer was losing ground fast, as he tried to handcuff the guy. Within seconds, the subject pushed away from the deputy and was running past us. He was not who we were looking for, but the fact he had just resisted arrest made him fair game.

I exited our vehicle and began to chase him.

Leo, who had been driving our car, decided to circle the block and cut off the runner. The other car would do the same. The plan was for me to pursue on foot, and hopefully tag the runner before he passed the end of the block, then the other agents would provide backup.

Before long, I was leaping over fences with wire criss-crossing over the top. I was going full-throttle, just to keep the subject in sight. The runner continued jumping the fences like a high hurdler. I could not keep jumping that high and eventually had to grab the top of the fences to pull myself over, puncturing my hands in the process. Blood started oozing out.

Finally, the subject dove into a house and sat down on a couch in the living room, panting to get his breath. I followed him in and sat down beside him, gasping for air.

I summoned all the strength I could, and applied a half-nelson around the younger man's neck. That's when I felt his teeth sink into my left forearm. It was the first time I had been bitten by a human being. Within five minutes, the bitten area had swollen to the size of a golf ball.

Leo came storming in, with the two other agents and a half dozen Dade County officers. It was 4:00 PM, during shift changes.

There we were: Four feds, dressed like golfers and plumbers, and me with this guy's tooth marks in my arm, and blood dripping out of my hands and forearms, with a handcuffed subject.

"Yes, officers. We really are the FBI."

There was only one reason they believed us. They all knew Leo.

12

★★★★★

AS A MORMON BISHOP

AUGUST 1973

The Church of Jesus Christ of Latter-day Saints, more commonly referred to as "the LDS Church" or "the Mormon Church," has no paid ministry. It is administered by lay workers who are compensated only by their joy in serving.

The bishop serves as the head of each congregation, known as a "ward." The ward is part of a larger geographical and ecclesiastical unit called a "stake," presided over by a stake president, also an unpaid volunteer.

The bishop is expected to spend several hours a week working with the youth, counseling couples, presiding in various meetings, correlating the activity of the components of the Ward, including the Sunday School, a woman's organization known as the "Relief Society," several men's groups known as "Quorums," and youth and children's organizations.

If disciplinary councils are necessary to question activities of members, it is either the bishop or stake president that takes action. The bishop presides over, and conducts, the general worship meetings. He is also responsible for the financial management of the ward unit and fulfills the overall role of presiding high priest in the ward.

The question that has been posed by many who were aware of my time-consuming involvements, both in the Church and in the FBI, was "How could you possibly be keeping up with both of these very time-consuming challenges?"

I have asked myself the same question. Aside from being aware Higher Powers were (and continue to be) involved, I cannot fully answer that question.

What I do know is that while serving as bishop four times in Florida, Oregon, and Utah for over fifteen years, one amazing truth has been made evident to me. That is, that the more I focused my life on serving my Church, my friends, and my family, the more fulfilling were the FBI cases assigned to me, and the more interesting were my other Bureau responsibilities, including functioning as a firearms instructor, a SWAT team member and team leader, and a police instructor.

There were many moments, even in the first ten years of my career, when I paused to consider some of the engaging cases I worked, and I would think, I have already had more fascinating investigations than many agents enjoy in their entire career. In a very real way, I feel these opportunities with the FBI have evolved as a reward for striving to stay diligent in my faith.

In August of 1973, when I accepted my first calling as bishop, the prospect of fulfilling two sets of completely different duties (ecclesiastical and law enforcement oriented) was initially a bit daunting, but with all the variables in play, there were a few common denominators that I could rely on. I had developed some consistency and the tenacity of a bulldog. I was mission-oriented, bent on protecting society and bringing about the demise of the bad guy. I was a work horse, not always the most innovative, nor the most polished, but always ready to walk through a wall for the case. Following my probationary year in San Diego, I consistently led out in producing meaningful statistical accomplishments in each division that I was assigned to.

I felt the same zeal in my Church responsibilities. I could not stand the thought of a youth under my watch going astray who I might have influenced, or missing an interview with a depressed or distraught person who needed me, or with a couple struggling to keep their marriage together who were in need of my counsel. I was able to help one Miami couple stay together who named their son after me. That honor overwhelmed me.

Some of the most interesting people I knew while I was an agent, I actually met in Church circles. One was Bishop Anton Kuhlman, who I had formally served as his bishopric counselor, and who I knew as "Tony." A tattooed Navy veteran, who had gone from working on the south side of Chicago in meat-packing plants and gradually becoming a Chicago "hood," by his own admission, to becoming a Mormon bishop, presided over the first ward in Miami that my family attended. He was fortunate enough to have met a Mormon girl earlier in his life who straightened him out and turned him around.

As previously mentioned, Tony eventually asked for two FBI agents to serve as his counselors: Special Agent Leon Fish and yours truly. We both accepted, and I became amazed at how much we both learned about Christian service from a reformed Chicago hood.

After putting in my ten hour FBI workday, I would stop by the stone-faced chapel on Northwest Ninety-fifth Street to assist Tony with youth counseling and other assignments.

The "Hood-Turned-Saint" had two interesting sides. He had this magnetic, spiritually-sensitive personality, tempered with a deep affinity for competitive Church sports, like softball, touch football, and the infamous church slugfest that starts with a prayer, called Mormon basketball.

Bishop Tony, Agent Fish, and I were a little over-exuberant when it came to competitive sports. Fish and I would lure in our fellow FBI agents from all different faiths to share in our basketball "riots" in the Ninety-Fifth Street chapel gymnasium. Suit coats, firearms, handcuffs, and other Bureau attire would be stashed in the church dressing rooms while the FBI, the Mormons, and African-American kids from the surrounding neighborhood, would mix it up, shooting hoops during our lunch hour.

On one occasion, the famed golfer, Billy Casper, stayed at Fish's home for several days while playing in the National Airlines Open golf tournament. When Brother Casper spoke at a special fireside service the Sunday after the tournament at the Ninety-fifth Street chapel, the audience was infiltrated with Miami office FBI agents from all religious persuasions who were avid golf fans.

Bishop Tony even scheduled a couple basketball games for our Church men's team with some of the Miami Dolphin football players as a ward budget fund raiser. The result: Dolphin greats like Mercury Morris, Larry Seiple, Jim Kiick, and Larry Little socked it to us big time. In one game, I was high-point man for the Mormon team with only eight points. Does that tell the story?

Marcus McGinnis, a rotund, fun-loving air conditioner repairman and retired Army sergeant, was always seeking something to laugh about and someone to laugh with or at. Marcus loved his Pepsi-Cola, and between Church meetings on Sundays, he habitually indulged his cravings at the neighborhood 7-Eleven convenience store, located just a few blocks down the street.

Leon Fish and I always gave Marcus a hard time about going there on the Sabbath for his caffeine fix. "Water off a duck's back, guys! You can't change this old boy," was always his response.

In November 1971, during one of Marcus' "Pepsi breaks," he was standing in line at the 7-Eleven with a bottle of his preferred fluid in his hands, waiting to pay, when a black youth shoved a pistol into his belly and demanded his wallet. Marcus was convinced and willingly shelled it over.

Marcus's response to having been robbed was, "I can't get away with anything, with the FBI watching me on Sunday and the 7-Eleven robbers waiting for me down the street!"

Another rainy Sunday morning, Lee Fish and I picked Marcus up in Lee's car for an early Church meeting. Lee was bobbing and weaving around mud puddles. Marcus was seated behind me, and I was in the front passenger seat, with my window rolled down. We hit a monster hole in the road, filled with murky, black water. I had time to duck down, but not enough to roll up the window. As the muddy water cascaded into our car through the window, Marcus took the lion's share in his face and onto his brand new gray suit that he was wearing for the first time. He was thoroughly drenched.

Marcus's subsequent comment to the folks at Church was, "Lee and Mike were jabbering away with Mike's window down, not watching the road. I knew Mike was gonna get it, but he ducked. There went my new suit!"

Judy's life as the totally dedicated, energetic, yet fun-loving spouse of an FBI agent/bishop became increasingly interesting. One day she would be at an FBI wives' luncheon, being warned by other ladies who knew we did not drink that there was alcohol in the chocolate mousse. The next day, she would be packing my bags for another case she knew little about, or she would be fielding really strange phone calls from people in my congregation, like this one:

"Sister McPheters, is your husband going to marry my husband?"

The lady calling was recently divorced. As her bishop, I was scheduled to perform the marriage for her ex-husband, who had decided to remarry another lady in my ward.

"Excuse me?" Judy responded, truly amazed by the question. "Would you repeat that?" asking for a little more clarification.

"Well, this is Sister Hendricks. I need to know if Bishop McPheters is really going to perform Fred's marriage to Jean Wilcox!"

Judy responded, "Sister Hendricks, I'm not aware of all the details. Please call my husband."

Judy's answer was her normal response in these situations, and by far, the wisest.

Surprisingly enough, shortly after performing the marriage for Brother

Hendricks was when I broke up Curtis Crisel's wedding at an exclusive South Florida church.

Judy was always a great listener. Members of the Church loved to unload on her.

Brother Coates, an elderly life-long bachelor, who really needed a psychologist, but could not afford one, called regularly to ask when I would be available for a "very important interview."

"How soon will he be home, Sister McPheters?" he would ask.

Judy would respond, "Probably about forty-five minutes."

"Okay. I'll just visit with you until he gets there. Thanks." No way was he going to wait to call back.

"Brother Coates, I was just fixing dinner for the children," Judy responded.

"Oh, tell me about the children." Judy ended up talking until I got home, about an hour later. Then she handed me the phone, as she pulled a burnt roast out of the oven.

I was often not around when our accident-prone son, Shad, was taken to the emergency room by the designated driver, one of Judy's other jobs. Shad had been there so many times, the doctors and nurses knew him by name.

Nor was I home when Lillian Burleigh's baby was dying and Judy took her to the hospital, where she spent the day comforting her.

As a bishop, I became acutely aware that all people need faith, but it is very difficult for many to recognize that need. It is true that many folks are in church only three times in their lives: when they are "hatched," "matched," and "dispatched."

I am certain that being an FBI agent gave me extra credibility, and made it easy for members of the Church to confide in me, as their bishop. I am equally convinced that serving in that Church capacity facilitated my fellow agents' trusting in me as a team player. Several confided in me that their impressions of my church were based upon their observations of my behavior.

I was advised by some Bureau friends that I should distance myself from working organized crime cases, since immersing myself in investigations requiring interviewing underworld figures, and trying to empathize with and understand their culture, would be out of my league. I was further counseled that their way of life was so different from my church standards that it would surely be a futile effort.

I could understand those concerns, but nevertheless, felt highly rewarded with the results of the James Michael Capotorto case several months later, where I was successful in pursuing convictions against Capotorto and his henchmen, who were involved in taking over the major drug traffic in the Fort Lauderdale area. Neither my Church affiliation nor its philosophy prevented me from enjoying success in that effort, which constituted a major strike against organized crime in South Florida.

Time spent as shepherd of my congregation educated me in identifying very real dimensions of specific needs of human beings, which may have very little to do with what makes sense.

One evening, an older sister called me, complaining that her neighbor's dog was barking incessantly, and she couldn't sleep. Listening to her about a barking dog wasn't in my job description as bishop, but calling me took away her hurt, and that was awesome. I learned that pain suffered by one person would not even be felt by another. In every case, if the pain became too acute, whether it were physical, mental, or spiritual, talking to the bishop would help. For those reasons, just being there for people made it a great ride.

My first three years serving as bishop came to an end, upon receipt of a letter from the First Presidency of the Church dated July 22, 1976, a few months before being transferred to Portland, Oregon.

During my tenure as a bishop in Florida, I had the privilege of seeing broken souls mended, and spirits uplifted. I witnessed misguided youths find the right path, and observed many people walk from darkness into the light.

On my office wall, hangs a beautiful plaque, with the following inscription:

BISHOP SAMUEL M. MCPHETERS
In appreciation for the many wonderful
things you have done for us. We shall
always cherish having known you and
having had you as our bishop.
MIAMI THIRD WARD

What I did not know was that I would be called to serve as bishop three more times, and for twelve more years, before completing my tenure with the FBI.

13
★ ★ ★ ★ ★

Pioneering SWAT with the Unforgettables

September 1973

It was a hot, sultry day in Miami. I was in the Miami Police Department gymnasium where Agent Terry Nelson and I went for our workouts, basically because it was free, and we could "pump iron" there anytime we wanted.

Our SWAT team, the first one in the history of the Miami division, participated with the Miami Police Department SWAT team occasionally in joint training. Nelson and I had ingratiated ourselves sufficiently to Lieutenant Ken Harms, their SWAT coordinator, that we were granted full access to their weight training facilities.

On this particular day, Joe Frechette, our team leader, and agent Frank Duffin were demonstrating a "take down" drill. Both these guys were in their early fifties, but were in better shape, mentally and physically, than most of our agents in their thirties.

Frechette had just demonstrated the take down, making Duffin collapse to the mat, somewhat voluntarily. After all, this was only practice, at three-quarter speed. Once Duffin was down, Frechette, who we all referred to as "Jefe," Spanish for "boss," posed the question, "How should he [referring to Duffin] defend himself, once he is down on the ground?"

Suddenly, Duffin thrust out his left foot behind Frechette's right calf, then trapped it with his right foot over Frechette's right knee, and applied pressure.

Frechette went down instantly, not expecting Duffin's move, which bordered a little on the aggressive.

Now, both Frechette and Duffin were down and were more than just a little serious. Jefe insisted that the move on Duffin's part was not that ingenious . . . that there was a better way, while Duffin insisted that it was effective. After all, he had taken the instructor down.

Suddenly, the two men were at one another in a verbal dispute, both ready to demonstrate more moves at full speed right then and there. Neither was ready, or willing, to lose face.

Fortunately, the two World War II veterans realized that the police department was probably not the best venue for them to pound on each other, especially in a training exercise. They cooled down and lumbered off the mat, with Frechette announcing the training for the day was concluded.

No two agents in the division respected and even admired one another more than these two FBI legends: Joe Frechette and Frank Duffin. Nor were there any two men in the division that were more admired by their fellow agents.

During World War II, Frechette flew a B-17 bomber for the United States Army Air Force, at the tender age of seventeen. At eighteen, he was shot down over Germany. He and his navigator were the last two to bail out. They were flying so low when they jumped that their parachutes had just enough time to deploy before they caught a glimpse of several German farmers, running towards them with pitchforks and clubs.

A couple hundred feet behind the farmers were a detachment of German soldiers. Frechette prayed the soldiers would capture them before the guys with the clubs and pitchforks. Fortunately for Frechette, he was not beaten up that seriously, but there were some that had bailed out from his plane that were severely injured by the irate welcoming committee.

The Germans held El Jefe for six months in a prisoner of war (POW) camp, until the Russians finally liberated it, towards the end of the war.

Frechette never liked to talk much about those six months, but when he did, he only complained that there was never enough to eat. He likened the living situation to that in the movie *Stalag 17*.

After leaving the Air Force, El Jefe earned a business administration degree at Holy Cross, where he played baseball.

Frechette had the classical "gift of gab" and acted as master of ceremonies at all the retirement dinners. His "tell it as it is" style on these occasions would occasionally unveil the mediocrity of certain supervisors or anyone at all that was antagonistic towards the common street agent.

Since neither one of us drank, El Jefe's concluding remark was always, "McPheters and I will tend the bar."

One of Frechette's favorite New York sayings was, "It's spring! Da boid is on da wing. Don't be absoid! Da wing is on da boid."

During World War II, Frank Duffin fought in Italy, as a member of the U.S. Army's Tenth Mountain Division.

Duffin was one of the coziest guys you would ever meet. Totally low in profile, he would always come through . . . completely dependable and tough. He had a sterling record for never going "10-7," the radio communication term for "out of service," over the air.

With his Boston accent, Duffin had these peculiar one-liners that were characteristic of him and him only.

"Hey, Duff. These French fries are great! You want to try some?"

Duffin's response: "No, thanks. I just had a bar of soap."

"Duff, look at all those folks lined up at the ticket booth."

Duffin's response: "Yeah, there must be fifteen hundred to a tousand of 'em!"

"Come on, Duff. Hurry, we got to go!"

Duffin's response: "Just as soon as I peel this grape."

The indefatigable Duffin, who spoke not only in Bostonian English, but also in Spanish and French, was the true romanticist, the philosopher, who could quote any number of the immortals, word for word. He even made up some of his own, illuminated proclamations.

Years after he and Frechette retired, our original Miami SWAT Team traveled from all over the country, to meet in Oregon, where we ran white water rafts through the Hells Canyon between Oregon and Idaho, climbed Mt. Hood, and flew over Mt. St. Helens, not long after the volcano exploded. We each received a T-shirt, inscribed with a cowboy on a bucking bronco. Written underneath the cowboy was a Duffin original: "Every man, before he dies, should ride a wild horse into the sun."

Duffin had waxed poetic. It was his way of describing our great adventure.

Duffin had this line for the field marches we would do in training: "A loaf of bread and a pound of meat, and all the cheese that you can eat. Hot dog!" I added a ditty of my own, as a preface to Duffin's line: "When I'm old and I have to go, send my bones to Quantico."

Frechette and Duffin became two of my principal role models. Not because we were of the same religion. They were staunch Catholics, and I was Mormon. Not because we had similar backgrounds. They were Irish guys, raised in Connecticut and Massachusetts. I was from Idaho. Not because we

First Miami FBI SWAT team, 1973

Pioneering SWAT with the Unforgettables. Front (left
to right): Wendell Hall, Mike. Back (left to right): Frank
Duffin, Joe Frechette, and Terry Nelson.

were of the same generation. They were two decades my senior.

They became role models for me, because in them, I could see how life
could be interpreted in fun and humor without taking myself too seriously.
I learned from them how I could deal with anything urgent in low key and
put things in proper perspective.

I loved these two guys, because deep down, they made me feel special,
and convinced me they were glad I was part of their team. Duffin convinced
me I could have cut it in the Tenth Mountain Division and Frechette gave me
every impression I would have gotten along as a POW with him in a German
concentration camp.

Today, the Miami division of the FBI sponsors some of the finest SWAT
teams in the nation. Their training and state-of-the-art equipment are almost
without parallel. Their traditions are the finest, and their history is golden.

My place in that history started in mid-September 1973. Frechette
approached my desk. "McPheters, we're forming a Special Weapons and
Tactics Team, and the boss and I want you on it." This would be an ongoing assignment, fashioned after the Los Angeles Police Department model,
where five individuals, highly-trained in the use of sophisticated weaponry
and para-military techniques, combine brawn, intellect, and courage to neutralize gun-wielding subjects and to rescue hostages. Frechette was sure I
could handle it based upon my performance where I had helped him catch
the killers in the Fountain Valley Country Club case in the Virgin Islands.

I would be called on for the most dangerous of the FBI missions:
making dynamic entries into the homes of drug dealers, breaking down
doors, rushing in and clearing rooms where armed criminals were often

lurking. Eventually, I would serve on teams in both Miami and Portland, Oregon. The fact that both Frechette and SAC Kenneth Whittaker wanted me on their team, which would be the first to represent the Miami division, bolstered my confidence and self-esteem.

I did not want to let them down. "You got your man, Joe. Where do we saddle up?" I asked.

"We report to Quantico in mid-October. I'll give you more information later." Frechette was off to notify the other guys, including Terry Nelson and Wendell Hall. Frank Duffin was already in.

Wendell Hall was an older agent in his late forties, but an avid runner. Nelson was a former Vietnam veteran and, like me, had played college football.

The SWAT courses at the FBI Academy at Quantico, Virginia, were run at all hours, in different conditions of weather and environment.

James "Yogi" Harmon was our instructor/moderator. He pushed us to our limits, and personally demonstrated everything he asked us to do, inspiring confidence all along the way.

In the wrestling event, we started off sitting on a mat, about twenty feet by twenty feet, back-to-back against opponents from another team.

Houston was our first opponent. They had two fairly distinguished individuals, an older guy called "Swede," who had participated in the Olympics as a swimmer, and Gordy Smith, who had played tight end for the Minnesota Vikings.

I was lined up against Gordy.

Our game plan was for me to handle Gordy, and try to at least stay on the mat, until the other guys threw one Houston opponent off. Then the spare man left would come over and help me with Gordy.

It worked. Even though Gordy was all over me, he could not throw me off. I held fast long enough for Frechette and Wendell Hall to eject one of Houston's guys off the mat, and onto the floor. Then Hall and I together pushed Gordy off. Now it was five against three, and from that point, we won easily.

Our next challenge was Tampa. Once I cleared off their big guy, Ted Seamans, it was five to four, which led to a second victory.

Nelson and I won third and fifth spots in the two mile run, and as a team, we did great in pushups, the obstacle courses, and the other events.

Our team fared well at Quantico. We prevailed against excellent competition from the San Antonio, New Orleans, Houston, Jacksonville, and

Tampa teams. While wrestling, running, swimming, and negotiating the Marine double-obstacle courses, we eluded serious injury, and avoided banging up any middle-aged muscles. Although our team was the oldest, averaging forty-one, we won the overall competition. Houston, who had the second oldest team average at forty, came in second. We had set a high standard for future Miami division SWAT teams.

Throughout the following years, the SWAT concept evolved rapidly, and eventually became the standard for responding to armed and barricaded subjects, saving hostages, raiding drug houses, and conducting other dangerous assignments. We trained by going up in helicopters, looking for sharks to shoot: moving targets from a moving platform. We began training other local and state police SWAT teams from all over South Florida. We even trained Special Forces units from the U.S. military at the Homestead Air Force base. We'd teach rappelling techniques, building entry techniques, firearms, and whatever else we thought would keep them safe.

In 1975, two years after our Miami SWAT team's first training, we returned to the FBI Academy at Quantico, Virginia to fulfill a special assignment as part of a sixty-man contingent that could respond anywhere in the nation, but more specifically on a regional basis, to dangerous, high profile situations. The HELO-SWAT concept embodied ultra-fast techniques for inserting and extracting SWAT operatives with ropes from helicopters, and transporting them as teams of five, from one place to another. We hooked up at the end of a forty-foot rope, tied off with a figure eight knot, were lifted into the air, dangling from the end of that rope, and were whisked several hundred feet through the air from point A to point B. It was a blast!

We learned to rappel out of Huey helicopters, the kind they used to transport the president of the United States in for short distances. We'd rappel out of the helicopters from distances up to eighty feet, wearing air force crash helmets. This was before the FBI learned to implement the "fast-roping" techniques where the operatives would just slide down a thick rope out of a helicopter.

In the extraction process, the helicopter pilot would drop us twenty foot long nylon ropes, $7/16$ inches in width. We would tie off at the bottom of the rope with a figure eight knot, give the pilot a thumbs up, and go airborne over one hundred feet off the ground as a team of five guys literally at the end of their ropes.

This training was the forerunner of today's FBI Hostage Rescue Team (HRT).

Most of our SWAT training in Miami was done at the old U.S. Air Force base near Homestead, Florida, just off Quail Roost Road (Southwest 183rd Street), near where the Miami Zoo is currently located.

To rappel out of the helicopter, as our rappel master, it was my job to tie us off from what we called a "doughnut," or a set of ropes and carabiners on the center of the floor of the helicopter, then send off two team members from each side simultaneously, to maintain balance. We would be roughly eighty feet off the ground. I would be the last out, and we would all rappel to the ground.

The auxiliary equipment we had for that first Miami team was primitive by today's standards. Frechette had contacts to secure rappelling gear, camouflage, hats, boots, packs, and radio hook-ups, but that was about it. What we did have, and what is still used, are M-16 automatic rifles, M-P 6 assault rifles, .308 caliber sniper rifles, grenade launchers, and short-barreled 12 gauge assault shotguns. We each carried at least one sidearm as well, back then a .357 caliber revolver, soon to be replaced by semi-automatic pistols.

For me, the night before a SWAT raid was like Christmas Eve. I was always far too excited, far too stoked with enthusiasm, to be afraid or apprehensive.

Only on one occasion did I write Judy a special note, in case I did not come home. It was in Salt Lake City, Utah, the night before arresting the principal cocaine dealer in the Juan Renteria case. The agent making the buy from Renteria was to utter some key words, at the precise moment he wanted us to rush in from an adjacent hotel room and subdue Renteria, who we assumed would be armed. I was to be the first through the door and was assigned to tackle the drug dealer, before he had a chance to access his firearm.

The major problem was the fact that I had only two hands, and I needed one to open the door on the signal. Having the gun in my right hand meant only having one arm available to make my tackle. I had to go through that door with both hands free. Knowing I would have to charge into the hotel room of an armed drug dealer empty-handed, and tackle him before he could get to his gun, made me a little pensive; ergo, the note to Judy.

Things couldn't have gone better. When I heard the key words through the door, I burst through, and dropped Renteria in about two seconds. As luck would have it, he was unarmed.

There were several instances in our SWAT responses where timing meant everything, like when we apprehended the bad guys who were going for their guns just seconds before they could get to them.

We always planned our SWAT raids for early in the morning, when the subjects were still sleeping, and frequently in the company of some woman who enjoyed living on the edge with her bandit boyfriend.

We would customarily hit the door with a "key," which was a huge, lead pipe weighing about thirty pounds. Then we would rush in, two-by-two, clearing and securing rooms along the way.

Prior to our entry, wherever possible, we would toss in a "flash-bang" kind of grenade that would emit lots of smoke, and explode with a sound that was so loud, you would think the world was coming to an end. Usually, the bad guy and whoever he was with, would leap up out of bed stark naked, with both hands in the air, ready to be taken downtown and booked. There were some, however, that would try going for their guns, that is until they found themselves looking down the barrels of M-16 assault rifles and 12 gauge shotguns, and into the greased faces of SWAT G-Men.

While in Florida and Oregon, I loved being involved in SWAT responses and was usually the first or second man through the door. Being bilingual, I would be the first in to shout out orders in Spanish, and to announce our identities as *federales*.

Getting up at 4:00 AM, greasing down the face, slipping into camouflage with Kevlar bullet-proof vests, then looking into the gung-ho expressions of confidence and enthusiasm of your buddies, knowing you would take down the bad guys and walk away with their drugs and weapons that day, was a feeling that could not be duplicated, and one I will never forget.

Joe Frechette and Frank Duffin were prime movers in the early stages of FBI SWAT history that commenced in 1973. Wendell Hall, Terry Nelson, and I tried to follow their examples, wherever possible, and emulate their outlook and confidence, as did the other Miami teams that followed us.

Over the past thirty-five years, our Miami SWAT team has come together every few years to run the white water in Oregon and Idaho, to climb Mt. Hood, and to retell the stories of our past escapades. To this day, we enjoy drifting back to the "Little Havana" Cuban restaurant on Miami's Biscayne Boulevard, to continue bonding in those associations, and to keep each other honest.

Joe Frechette still conducts a "Firearms Training Steak Fry" in March of each year, just to keep track of us veterans (now in our sixties, seventies, and eighties), to make sure our powder is dry, and that we can still shoot straight.

14
★★★★★

OTHER MIAMI HAPPENINGS

1973–1975

Agent Terry Nelson and I, both thirty-three and vigorous, were faithful in our weightlifting and running at the Miami Police Department workout facility, even before we were recruited onto the first FBI SWAT team out of Miami. But after coming back from Quantico, we were even more determined to stay in shape and set a good example for future SWAT team candidates from our division. Three days a week, just before noon we took advantage of the workout allowance the Bureau provided for all agents to exercise an hour three times a week to maintain their health. By coupling that hour with our forty-five minute lunch break, we could do a short, heavy workout on the weights, cap it off with a two mile run across the Miami River, shower, and stop somewhere for a sandwich and some chips, before returning to work.

One day we caught Agent Frank Duffin at the police facility, doing dips off the parallel bars in his white shirt and tie. He was obviously enjoying it, while working up lather, exclaiming, "Where has this stuff been all my life?" He was making our twenty years age difference look like no difference at all. After visiting with "The Duff" for a few minutes, and finishing off a tuna sandwich and sour cream and onion chips with Terry, I headed over to the federal courthouse for a follow-up trial session in the Jesus Matthew Burch case. Burch, an African-American defendant, was being tried for the interstate transportation of a stolen car. The federal judge was U.S. District Court Judge Emmett Choate, who was in his eighties, and very conservative in dealing with criminals. The defendants appearing before Judge Choate would die a thousand deaths as they waited the full minute it would take him to shuttle from his chambers onto the bench, once court was called into session. The judge's reputation went before him, and soft sentences were not his bag.

As I was called to the witness stand and sworn in to testify on the Burch matter, I was asked specifically regarding my findings in the alleged car theft. I related to the court and jury how a particular car registration was determined to be fraudulent. I also testified to my interviews with Burch prior to, and after, I arrested him. The interviews had been congenial, because as a "bishop-in-embryo," I was learning how to respect people of all persuasions and ethnicities, trying to allow benefit of the doubt wherever possible.

In a follow-up letter of commendation written to my boss, SAC Kenneth Whittaker after Burch's conviction, Ms. Carol Anderson, the prosecutor who I had assisted, stated that I had exhibited "warmth and sincerity" in my contacts with defendant Burch. She stated, ". . . his diplomacy is best expressed by the words of the defendant himself, who while on the stand, said 'That agent tried to sweet talk me.' " Ms. Anderson kindly went on to characterize me as an "unusual and extraordinary" law enforcement officer, when I was only treating Matthew Burch as another child of God, convinced that Our Creator doesn't make junk. In my mind, there was nothing unusual or extraordinary about my performance. I believed that kind of interaction with people should just constitute the norm. But I supposed that was only in the perfect world.

A couple days later, Nelson and I were jogging across the drawbridge over the Miami River, where a very obese bridge tender with a huge paunch hanging over his belt, seemed to delight in drawing up the bridge just before we could cross, even when the river traffic hadn't even approached it. We always asked ourselves what he had against joggers, and were always coming up with different reasons. It made for an interesting run. Nelson and I pushed each other in the weight room and were delighted each time we could add on another five or ten pound plate for the ten repetitions in each set. Benching over three hundred pounds was a high mark which we celebrated with a double order of sour cream and onion chips at lunch, and it even got better. "Look out, bad guys, here we come!"

One afternoon, after the workout and lunch, I advised Terry I had a lead on a fugitive that I thought was in town, but I was just going by myself to check out a long-shot address. As luck would have it, the "long shot" part went by the wayside, when I drove up into the parking area by the guy's apartment and saw him standing by the door. In two minutes, the fugitive, wanted for unlawful flight to avoid prosecution, was in my car handcuffed and I was on my way to the office to interview him, prior to booking him in at the Dade County Jail. I was on the phone with Nelson.

"Hey, man! I got the guy with me I was telling you about. Can you come meet me?" We arranged to meet at the office in the basement, to avoid giving the appearance I had brought the subject in by myself. From the time I had put on the handcuffs, I had flashbacks of San Diego in my first office, when I had done that, violating Bureau policy about not making solo arrests, and had barely got away with it.

Nelson was cozy enough to keep a secret, and I never told him I'd done it once before.

There was always something going on in Miami, like the Christmas day raid when we raided the homes of all the bookmakers with sledge hammers and search warrants. The idea was to get in and grab the illegal bets for evidence before they could flush them. One good idea was for someone to go around the back where the bathroom window was slightly cracked and throw in a smoke or gas grenade prior to making entry.

It seemed like the more really meaningful cases I was involved in and the harder I worked, the more good things were happening on the bishop level. People who had been inactive in the ward were accepting callings, really getting into them, and never looking back. I observed the foundation being dug for a new chapel in Hialeah that had been in the planning stages for years. Top quality people were being baptized. We were up to eight full-time missionaries in our ward to cover all the work there was there to do. We were united as a congregation. I even got to teach a little karate at a Church youth conference.

With the SWAT background, my assignments took on a varied flavor. When President Richard Nixon dedicated the new Cedars of Lebanon hospital in Miami on February 15, 1974, several of our SWAT personnel were assigned to assist the U.S. Secret Service in protecting him. The concern was a huge construction project going up right across from the hospital, which would provide the perfect setting for a sniper or renegade fanatic. I positioned myself on the highest level of the hospital where I could train my eyes on the building project through the scope on a .308 sniper rifle, while visually searching for possible threats to the president. There were no incidents.

Two months later we apprehended several subjects at a Miami motel who were robbing banks all over the country and came to South Florida to spend their money. When two of the men left their room, climbed up on a trailer with their helmets on, and started the engines of a couple of road bikes they were taking out, they were tapped on the shoulder. As they looked up, it was into the barrels of our revolvers. The third subject of this gang, known as the Doyle Henderson gang, came out of the motel with a Bureau shotgun trained on him.

On February 10, 1975, I participated in arresting Earl Bernard Sutton Jr. and Brenda Evans for unlawful flight to avoid prosecution in an illegal confinement case. This was a new twist, in that I had not investigated any form of involuntary servitude or illegal confinement up to that point in my career.

On November 10, 1975, we arrested the murderer of the daughter of an FBI agent from Phoenix, Arizona. The subject was an escaped federal prisoner. As I drew down on this individual, contemplating how protective I was of my own daughters, and what he had done to the daughter of a fellow agent, I had my finger on the trigger, rather than the trigger guard. I learned a lesson I would never forget: the importance of self-discipline and objectivity, no matter how you feel toward the person you're arresting. I fear that at that moment, I may have come close to forgetting my religion.

Two months later, I participated in the arrest of Marvin Williams and Johnny Crochham, two local bank robbers.

Miami was a fun office. We had lots of office cookouts and parties, with special lunches for the Bureau wives. We had football games between the clerks and the agents. The chemistry was fantastic before the office became so huge and departmentalized. Key West was a beautiful drive to the south over the ocean causeways with the promise of super good fishing. I went on overnighters, boating with a commercial fisherman several miles out in the Gulf Stream, where we would routinely catch a couple hundred pounds of bottom fish: snapper, blue runner, grouper, cobia, catfish, and even shark, each time out.

There was never a dearth in good criminal work in South Florida for those of us that wanted those assignments, and the federal prosecutors were aggressive. United States Attorney Bob Rust, an ex-marine was totally "Gung-Ho," as were his departments' strike force attorneys.

I returned twice to work in Florida. Once in 1980 when President Jimmy Carter ordered sealifts and airlifts for Cuban refugees coming into the United States. Fidel Castro emptied his prisons and sent us some very questionable

Mike McPheters meets L. Patrick Grey, second FBI director in Miami.

Here, he greets Clarence Kelly, third FBI director in Miami.

characters. Being bilingual, my job was to interview the newcomers and try to ferret out the spies.

In 1982, I returned, again on a Spanish-speaking assignment to investigate the "Omega Seven," a small Cuban right-wing nationalist paramilitary terrorist group based in Florida and New York whose goal was to overthrow Castro. They were Bay of Pigs veterans, responsible for car bombings and murders of pro-Castro affiliates.

15

★ ★ ★ ★ ★

THE HIT MAN

JANUARY 23, 1974

At daybreak, the moisture was still hanging thick on the Florida Everglades. The sun was edging up over the horizon in the largest subtropical wilderness area in the United States. The Everglades was home to many endangered species, including the American crocodile, the Florida panther, the West Indian manatee, and, on that day, an escaped federal prisoner by the name of Roy Walker Lacey.

We were near Monroe Station, north of the Tamiami Trail, otherwise known as Highway 41, about sixty miles west of Miami.

There it was, just like the informant said. The white paper plate, tacked onto a wood post, a little above the level of the saw grass, and about ninety-five yards from the hunting cabin, where hopefully our fugitive would be located.

The agents who debriefed the informant had come through. The informant had advised them the first thing the escaped convict, Lacey, would do when he got up would be to grab a bolt-action Mauser carbine rifle, stroll outside, and fire off a few shots at the paper plate. By the well-configured group of holes in the plate, it was obvious the man was an excellent marksman.

The hunting cabins in the Everglades were few and far between. Situated almost anywhere you find a slight rise in the saw grass, the cabins were usually no more than a ramshackle hut, hastily constructed, ugly, and remote. This cabin, the second one we had stumbled upon that morning in our search for Lacey, was a perfect hideout for an escapee from the Lompoc Federal

Correctional Complex, near Los Angeles.

Lacey, who had a long record of criminal violence, had fled Lompoc's maximum security prison seven months earlier on June 22, 1973, where he was serving a ten-year sentence for the interstate transportation of stolen property.

During a mass prison breakout, he pretended to be hit by shots fired by guards, who were trying to quell the disturbance. When two officers checked him out, he leaped to his feet, overpowered them, and escaped. He then hitchhiked across the country to Miami, where he had been hiding and working out. At six feet one inch and a solid one hundred and ninety pounds, he enjoyed lifting heavy weights and posing for the muscle-head magazines.

Lacey went to work for Stan Harris, a Miami hit man, who would one day be found face down in a mud puddle, riddled with rounds from a hostile semi-automatic pistol.

While working for Harris, Lacey packed a sawed-off 12 gauge shotgun. The stock and barrel had been cut back and modified, so the weapon resembled a handgun. The trigger guard had been removed. Lacey had apparently tried out the weapon in that condition, because the web of his right hand was severely lacerated, probably from the weapon's recoil during one of his jobs.

Lacey's car had been spotted at the Mercy Hospital in Miami the night before the informant had handed over the details of his activities but had sped away in a green Camaro when approached by FBI agents with an arrest warrant on escaped federal prisoner charges. He had left the agents in a cloud of dust.

★   ★   ★   ★   ★

It was mid-afternoon, humid and sticky, when several agents riding in a swamp buggy pulled up onto the dirt road entering the saw grass that lead into an area in the Everglades where the manhunt for Lacey would commence.

First office agent Neal Herman and I were already at the place the Tamiami Trail crossed the primitive road spur leading into the Everglades to within hiking distance of the cabin where we had information Lacey was hiding out. We had begun off-loading some shoulder weapons and ammunition from our vehicle onto the ground to outfit the troops.

Suddenly Big Al Spuckler, Lacey's friend, and an unidentified female passenger squealed out of a spur leading into the saw grass and out onto the highway in a dark green Camaro, veering in and out of traffic. The Camaro's description matched that of the vehicle our agents had approached two nights before.

Thinking it was Lacey getting away, Herman and I quickly distributed the weapons to the surprised agents who had just driven up. There were several 12 gauge shotguns, loaded with double-ought buckshot, some .308 caliber rifles, bull horns, and other miscellaneous gear. We were definitely ready. We crammed as many people into the Ford as we could, and transported them back to their cars. Arms and heads were protruding from the windows of the Ford, like in a Keystone Cops movie. We dropped them off and began pursuing the Camaro, with Herman and me leading the chase.

It was show time for the big Ford. My bureau Ford, with the big engine, would be tested to full capacity. We flew after the Camaro on the two-lane portion of the Tamiami Trail, weaving in and out of cars full of passengers with puzzled expressions. I was at the wheel, with the siren screaming and blue light flashing, and Herman looking on, fully enjoying the change in pace. The scenario created an ambivalent sensation of both power and anticipation.

We strained to keep the Camaro in sight, as it flew on ahead. We radioed our location to the other units, requesting that Jim Neal, another agent in the area, set up a roadblock.

I had the pedal floored and the Ford pushed to maximum speed. The engine was groaning, and the floorboards were shaking as I pushed the big car in and out of traffic.

During moving surveillances, I had crashed through toll booths before, with only a foot clearance on both sides, and had negotiated some turn angles that would scare you silly, but I had never driven that fast. We flew by road markers that appeared as blurs. We couldn't even read them in order to report our location. Herman had his head tilted down in the "ready to crash" position.

"Get ready, Herman," I hollered. "And tell Neal where we are, so he can set up a road block and felony car stop!"

"You kidding me?" he retorted. "First, I gotta be able to read the markers!"

Herman radioed Agent Neal, and had him set up a road block at the intersection of Krome Avenue and the Tamiami Trail. Neal successfully commandeered a tractor-trailer into blocking the two lanes of traffic heading east.

The next thing we observed was Big Al and his female friend, swerving into the roadblock, where they faced four Florida Highway patrolmen, with the business end of their shotguns pointed at them.

Suddenly, I was also riding the brake and laying down rubber to keep from colliding with the roadblock.

Herman and I pulled up directly behind Big Al, who, at six foot three inches and two hundred and forty pounds, was in tears. He was shaking like a leaf as he exited the Camaro with the palms of his hands glued to his head.

The girl inside the Camaro, who we had not yet identified, was still in her teens. The frozen expression on her face made her appear catatonic. She didn't utter a word or move a muscle.

Bottom line: We determined Big Al Spuckler was not Roy Walker Lacey, but discovered he had been with Lacey the previous two days, and was driving the same car Lacey had used to escape from the agents at Mercy Hospital. In view of that information, we arrested Big Al for harboring a federal fugitive and did not release him until he confirmed Lacey's location in the sea of saw grass, nor until his father convinced us that Big Al really didn't know Lacey was a fugitive.

In Bureau parlance, Spuckler was "unarrested" once he assured us he had left Lacey that same day, provided information as to the approximate location of Lacey's cabin, and the fact that Lacey was still there.

That night we placed sentries on the dirt road leading into the saw grass, while we awaited the next morning's raid on Lacey's cabin.

Meanwhile, agents continued searching for our fugitive, carefully checking different camp sites along the edge of the Tamiami Trail.

The stage was set for a great early morning raid that commenced at 4:30 AM.

It was late January. The Everglades were mild and pleasant, bearing average temperatures from fifty-three to seventy-seven degrees Fahrenheit. The ever abundant sea of saw grass, though shrouded in darkness, was humming with the din of things awakening.

There were twelve of us, but only agent Terry Nelson and I had gone through SWAT training at Quantico. We'd learned the advantage of five officers, skilled in paramilitary techniques, with sophisticated weaponry, making a stealth raid on a barricaded subject. The idea of rushing Lacey's cabin with a wave of manpower, going in straight up like wooden soldiers, was nauseating.

The advantage the darkness provided would not compensate for sacrificing ourselves to open shots from a barricaded subject.

We drove two miles north into the Everglades on a dirt road. Then we proceeded on foot for about forty-five minutes, before arriving at the first cabin. It was foreboding and suspiciously quiet.

Leading the detail was Special Agent in Charge (SAC) Kenneth Whittaker, a take-charge kind of guy, who didn't back down. At about six foot three inches and two hundred and forty pounds, Whittaker could appear overwhelming. He was wearing his casual attire and street shoes.

"Well, why not?" he would say with a grin. "You never know when you will meet the press." Whittaker was not about to miss out on this case, which could become a headliner. Being street agents, we appreciated that he was involved and willing to take risks, even if he did relish meeting the press.

As we closed in on the cabin, we had no concealment cover. There were no rocky outcrops or tree stumps to hunker up against, if necessary.

An eerie impression sunk in. This is a crap shoot, I thought. A roll of the dice. Why don't we just shoot ourselves right now and get it over with?

We surrounded the cabin, forming the "L" to avoid crossfire. It was show time. The agent with the bullhorn sounded out the warning with that "I gotcha!" tone in his voice.

"Roy Walker Lacey. This is the FBI. You are surrounded. Come out with your hands up!"

A few long moments went by without a response. The agent sounded off again.

"Lacey, give it up! Come out. You're surrounded."

A third time. Same commands were given. Same response. No Lacey.

We rushed the cabin, only to find it vacant. As informants go, the information wasn't bad, but still severely lacking for vital detail. The informant had indicated a "probably" on the first cabin, but he was only ninety percent sure.

There was a second cabin, about an hour farther to the west that the informant had mentioned. We were convinced we had misread the directions the source had furnished, and that the second cabin was Lacey's residence.

We had lost the advantage of night cover, as we approached the second shack. The troops were sloshing away through the saw grass, fully visible from far off. I shivered at the thought of what could happen if the informant was right about Lacey coming out with his guns, and target practicing at the break of day each morning.

It would be like the Revolutionary War, with the British Redcoats marching into the long rifles of the patriots, hiding behind trees. In my imagination, I conjured up the roll of the drums. Lacey had most likely killed before and certainly wouldn't hesitate to kill again.

The sun was now fully risen. The Everglades had come to life. And there we were, fully exposed to the cabin, and standing next to a white paper plate, with a tight group of rifle prints carved into it.

Orders came down again to form the "L" around the cabin. We closed in and brought out the bullhorn.

"Roy Walker Lacey. This is the FBI. Come out with your hands up!"

The door opened, and there stood a hundred and ninety pounds of muscle in nothing but a pair of under shorts . . . defiant, scowling and cocky, but without a weapon.

Lacey responded lustily, "I ain't gonna do it!" He started to turn back inside.

SAC Whittaker didn't waste a second in his response. "You've got just thirty seconds."

At that point, Lacey's braggadocio began ebbing, as he walked slowly out from the cabin. He reluctantly obeyed an order to kneel.

As we closed in on him, he reached for the head of a sledgehammer, lying on the ground, well within his grasp.

SAC Whittaker had run out of patience.

With the shotgun aimed between Lacey's eyes, and with the frosty look of real intent, the boss warned, "If you pick that up, I'll blow your head off!"

Not one of us doubted he would do it.

We all had just about enough of Roy Walker Lacey. Although we had him surrounded and grossly outnumbered, he continued spitting out defiance.

As an agent stepped in to handcuff him, Lacey spun and knocked the handcuffs out of the agent's hands and onto the ground.

I was now beginning to take this personally. There were twelve of us, and Lacey was challenging us.

With my handcuffs extended out, I baited him, knowing he'd pull the same trick. The instant he went for my cuffs, I released them and slapped a choke hold on him, while Terry Nelson applied the leg irons and supervisory special agent Bob Strong handcuffed him.

We secured Lacey, extracted his rifle and handgun from the cabin, and headed towards Miami.

The Hit Man
Taking Roy Walker Lacey into custody. Left to right:
Paul Mallet, Mike Dooher, Roy Walker Lacey,
Mike McPheters.

We arrived in convoy at our office on Biscayne Boulevard. Although Lacey was securely shackled, I still felt an ominous sense of foreboding that I couldn't quite put my finger on. Something in Lacey's expression telegraphed the notion that he hadn't really, totally surrendered, and that sometime soon, he would again strike up the band.

My suspicions were soon justified. As we exited the transport vehicle in front of the office, the news media and a raft of photographers were waiting for every little crumb we would throw them. To avoid creating a scene and to facilitate transporting him, we removed Lacey's leg shackles.

That was a mistake.

There were at least a dozen reporters and television cameramen waiting to question us and get their first glimpse of the swamp man.

I snickered at the naiveté of one particular cameraman, who stuck his expensive camera into the big man's face for a close-up. I noticed Lacey squinting angrily at the photographer and shifting his weight towards him as the newsman brought his camera up to eye level.

Lacey's right leg shot up like a catapult, and suddenly the reporter was staring haplessly, watching his equipment soar about fifteen feet into the air.

Once his legs were freed up, it had only taken Lacey about two seconds to negotiate an NFL kick.

That action occurred after Lacey had spit on the hapless photographer.

Having sloshed through mud and water since 4:00 AM that morning, SAC Whittaker was now ready for the lights and cameras. He eagerly favored the ten o'clock news audience with some fine press. The photo highlight was a great shot of the craters in the bottoms of his oxfords, covered with swamp moss.

One thing was unforgettable about that day.

According to our informant, Lacey never missed target practice at sunrise. It was broad daylight by the time we reached that paper plate. We had lost the element of surprise, when we hit the wrong cabin at daybreak. Lacey's targets would have been plentiful, if he had followed his usual routine.

Surely, some guardian angels beat us to Lacey's cabin that morning.

16

★★★★★

WORKING THE JIMMY HOFFA CASE

JUNE 1974

It was just past 7:00 AM. The air was heavy . . . sultry. Nothing was moving at the upscale South Florida residence we had been surveilling for the past two weeks.

The subject's car was there now, and fresh information had filtered in from the case agent's sources that he had finally returned. We had a material witness warrant for the occupant.

I exited my vehicle, and approached the front door, accompanied by other agents. If we were not admitted into this residence voluntarily, I would assist in effecting what the FBI calls a "dynamic entry" into the residence. Such an entry could consist of kicking or smashing in the door and then launching smoke canisters.

In this instance, a maid immediately responded to the door, and with an expression of both fear and curiosity, allowed our entry. As I entered, I observed other agents, streaming in through the back door.

Why all the precautions?

This was no ordinary bust going down. The target here was Anthony Provenzano, also known in the underworld as "Tony Pro," the major suspect in the disappearance of the president of the International Brotherhood of Teamsters, Jimmy Hoffa.

★ ★ ★ ★ ★

Anthony Provenzano was a *capo* (captain) in the Genovese crime family, one of the five families constituting the Mafia in New York City.

106

Provenzano was a vice president of the Teamsters' organization under Hoffa, and was in control of the most corrupt unit of that organization: the Union City, New Jersey chapter, where he was skimming off union monies into his own pocket.

It was common procedure for union representatives, called shop stewards, to confront workers once each week on payday, who were loading and unloading trucks, and to solicit money for the "lottery." It was understood that the lottery collection had only one winner week after week, and that was Anthony Provenzano.

Hoffa was tight with Provenzano and other Mafia figures that used the Teamster locals to extort the money.

Eventually, both Hoffa and Provenzano were arrested and incarcerated for their illegal activities. While in prison, Tony Pro exercised his status as an underworld overlord to capture the loyalty of the other prisoners, and looked after Hoffa, who was subsequently pardoned by President Richard Nixon in 1971. In spite of that relationship, the two eventually had a falling out, and mutually opposed each others' affiliations with the Teamsters. It was Hoffa, the union hero, against Provenzano, the Mafia captain.

In 1972 Local 560 Secretary-Treasurer Anthony Castellito was killed by Salvatore "Sally Bugs" Briguglio, an upstate New York mob figure, who was involved in extortionate credit transactions (loan sharking). Later on, Briguglio, along with Provenzano and others had been named in Hoffa's disappearance.

★ ★ ★ ★ ★

This was the man whose door we had just walked through. Once inside Provenzano's luxury home, I noticed the door to his bedroom was ajar, opened slightly to the living room area. I approached the room with Irv Bruce, the assigned case agent, and observed Tony Pro lying in his bed, barely awake, appearing puzzled and confused.

"What's going on here?," he uttered, as Bruce and I drew near him, with our weapons still holstered but ready.

"Get up, Mr. Provenzano!" Bruce ordered. "We have a warrant for your arrest."

Tony Pro remained in supine position with an expression of shock and disbelief covering his face. He didn't budge.

I decided to weigh in. "Get up now! Right now! You heard him say you're under arrest."

Provenzano pulled himself, hesitatingly, to the edge of his bed, attired only in his underwear and looked up towards us with this pleading look in his eyes.

He pointed to a fifth of gin on the floor next to his bed. "You guys got to let me have a drink of this, or I'll never get my engine running."

None of us had ever had a request like that from someone we were taking into custody, but it was mutually agreed upon that an exception would be made, just so this guy could get out of bed and get dressed, without being pulled out.

Bruce, the lead agent, gave his approval. "Drink up, Mr. Provenzano, but make it fast."

Provenzano quickly heisted the bottle to his lips, and indulged himself in a long, obviously invigorating swig. He then put the bottle back down, wiped the liquid from his mouth and chin, and said, "Thanks."

As I studied this man, sucking down the welcomed liquor as though it were water in the desert, just to gain some mobility, I reflected upon my Mormon admonitions regarding the importance of staying alcohol-free. This scene, illustrating Tony Pro's unquestionable dependence on liquor, confirmed the wisdom of those teachings against alcohol abuse that emanated from the Lord through the Prophet Joseph Smith in the year 1833.

I reflected upon my own birth father, who I had not yet even met, largely because his life had become consumed with alcohol, eventually causing my mother to divorce him.

Having satisfied his thirst, Tony Pro clumsily put on his trousers, slowly managed to pull on a short-sleeved shirt, and stepped into his shoes. We handcuffed him, double-locking the restraining devices, and whisked him into a waiting transport vehicle.

Although the FBI was fairly certain it was Provenzano who ordered Hoffa's murder, we were never able to prove it beyond every reasonable doubt. However, there is credible evidence, including the fact Provenzano was observed in the car with Hoffa shortly before his death.

My assignments in the Hoffa case continued.

The Bureau's investigation of Provenzano produced evidence Hoffa may have been buried in a landfill in New Jersey, owned and operated by Phillip Moscato. I eventually interviewed Moscato in Miami in the presence of his attorney. It was one of those "fat chance" shots in the dark, against the overwhelming odds of Moscato giving up any information, and he didn't.

Upon the advice of legal counsel, he wouldn't talk. I obtained his full name, address and telephone number, but nothing else.

To this day, Anthony Provenzano's name is that most often mentioned in conjunction with the disappearance of Jimmy Hoffa, whose remains have yet to be discovered.

Tony Pro's illegal union operations were shut down by law enforcement. In 1978, he was convicted for the 1961 murder of Anthony Castellito, whose body was allegedly run through a tree shredder.

Provenzano died from a heart attack while in prison in 1988 at the age of seventy-one.

17

$\star\star\star\star\star$

Extortion in the Everglades

October 1974

The Squad Eight Supervisor, Bob Strong, approached my desk.

"Hey, McPheters, Squad Two has something they want you to do. This rich guy over in Miami Beach has been extorted for two hundred and fifty thousand dollars, which he's supposed to deliver somewhere out in the Everglades near the Tamiami Trail. It goes down tomorrow afternoon at 2:00 PM. There are no known suspects."

"Where do I fit in?" I asked.

"You look just like the guy who was extorted, so tomorrow you'll be driving his Cadillac out into the saw grass. There'll be plenty of agents there covering you, disguised as fishermen and tourists. No worries," Strong assured.

I reported to Squad Two for my briefing. I discovered there was still no suspect identified, so the plan was to follow the steps Strong had mentioned, basically the instructions ordered by the extortionist. They were going to stick me out there as bait and grab whoever showed up to collect the bag of cash that I would bury at a location in the Everglades, picked by the extortionist.

I was advised that even though the drop-off would be covered by several agents in disguise, I should still be prepared to respond, in the event I was taken hostage by the perpetrators. I was to carry a weapon on my person that could absolutely not be visually detected.

I would be driving the victim's 1974 Cadillac Sedan Deville and I would be by myself. A bank bag, bulging with shredded paper, would be lying next to me on the front seat. Upon arriving at the drop location, I was to exit the vehicle, take my time shoveling a hole into the saw grass, and deposit the cash bag. Then I would re-enter the Cadillac and drive back to the victim's house in Miami Beach. I was told exactly how to dress.

The Squad Two Supervisor then attempted to assure me, "Mac, you'll be under surveillance from the time you get into the guy's Cadillac to the time you get back. There should be no problem. We'll grab anybody that gets within one hundred feet of you."

I responded warily, "That's always good to know."

I apparently sounded more than just a little tentative.

The supervisor reiterated that I would be covered by agents at all times, but also added: "The bad guys will probably also be watching you. We don't know what their plan is. There's no guarantee they won't move in on you. Just make sure you've got a gun stashed."

Before leaving the office, I entered the firearms vault, and checked out a snub-nosed revolver with a two and a half-inch inch barrel. I also examined several different kinds of holsters. I spent my entire ride home contemplating the best way to carry the revolver, so that it could not be detected.

I concluded that it could not ride on my hip under a jacket, where I would normally carry it, nor could I wear any kind of shoulder holster.

Could I tuck it under my waistband? I asked myself.

No way. It would be found immediately, if I were searched.

Suddenly, I was struck with an idea that I thought was extremely innovative.

I could stick it between my buns, maybe? With the barrel out and handle in? Then I became aware of the fallacy in that idea, and uttered to myself, *The minute you relax your sphincter, the gun would drop out, dummy!*

I kept pounding my imagination all the way home and right up to the second I walked into the house.

Judy was immediately aware my head was in a cloud.

"What's the matter, honey? You look like you've been through a wringer." Judy could read me like a book.

I explained the whole scenario during dinner. I asked for her ideas on how to hide the gun. She covered the same ground I had been over. It was unusual for her not to come up with a viable solution.

Bedtime arrived. Judy dove under the covers, and was on her way to "La La Land." I was still straining my imagination. After going through contortions of all kinds in front of the mirror in the master bathroom, it finally hit me.

Zzzziiiipppp. Zzzziiiipppp. Zzzziiiippp. As the zipping sounds became more constant, Judy's eyes suddenly popped open.

"What's going on in that bathroom," she asked herself. She got up, realized I still was not in bed at 11:30 PM , and opened the bathroom door.

There I was, zipping open my fly, reaching in, and pulling out the snub-nose revolver.

I had the speed for the whole drill down to about two and a half seconds. I'd anchored an elastic band with a holster opening to the inside of my left thigh, and there my revolver had found its home.

"It's perfect, honey," I advised Judy. "If they do grab me, they'll never suspect anything when I tell them I've got to relieve myself. Instead of pulling out what they expect, I'll just treat 'em to a little surprise."

I was smiling at my own ingenuity.

Judy could not handle it. She just raised her eyebrows in non-belief and went back to bed.

I sprang out of bed the next morning with alacrity, animated about getting on with the case, and feeling fine about my creativity.

I was escorted to the rendezvous point in Miami Beach, where I drove off in the victim's Cadillac, and headed down the main thoroughfare, across the causeway and onto the Tamiami Trail, heading west.

Through the rearview mirror, several car lengths behind, I was comforted by the familiar sight of FBI cars that I knew had me under constant surveillance. As we entered the vicinity of the drop area, those cars backed off, but I noticed fishermen along the canal and near the drop vicinity that I recognized as G-men in disguise.

I pulled off onto a dirt side road, and into an alcove overgrown with saw grass.

I was within fifty feet of the designated drop site. I grabbed the bank bag with one hand and a shovel with the other. I glanced in several directions, but did not waste any more time in the Everglades than was necessary.

The thought raced through my mind, *Who's the extortionist and where is he? How many of them are there? How fast can my guys get to me if this whole thing suddenly goes to seed? The gun's riding fine on my thigh, but if I have to run, will it fall out?*

Just dig the hole, bury the bag, and get out of here! I ordered myself, firmly and decisively.

I breathed a sigh of relief as I drove away, again catching sight of the back-up surveillance vehicles.

Nothing happened. No one was sighted, and my role was fulfilled without an ounce of excitement.

Two days later, the entire story unfolded. The victim's son was taken into custody. It was the father' own flesh and blood that wanted a quarter of a million dollars so desperately that he concocted the entire plan for taking money from his father that he felt he could not have obtained otherwise.

I was never made aware whether the federal prosecutors followed up on the case, since it had turned into a family affair, but I had learned one thing: A sure fire remedy for hiding a gun where few people would ever expect.

18

★ ★ ★ ★ ★

BIG JIMMY'S GANG
GOES DOWN

NOVEMBER 1975

In 1975, Miami was referred to as the "Cocaine Capital of the World." Coca leaves grown in Bolivia were processed in Colombia into a white substance, commonly called *polvo del perico* in Spanish, or "parrot powder," making reference to addicts ingesting it through the nose. This product was then smuggled by small aircraft flying under the radar into South Florida and delivered at night to men armed with fully-automatic weapons who awaited its arrival at clandestine air strips.

More Latin American flights from Central and South America flew into Miami than into any Spanish-speaking city in Central or South America, and more cash sales were generated there than any other part of the country, except possibly Southern California, where comparable amounts of drug traffic filtered in through Mexico.

Cocaine use ran the gamut, from street addicts to social users at high brow parties put on by the socially elite. It was in vogue for the rich to furnish lines of "white magic" to party guests, and for couples to use it to enhance their sex drive.

Couples hooked on this mind-altering substance would sit in front of their TV sets for days, without ever turning them on, breathing the coveted powder through their noses, having no desire to eat or indulge in normal activities.

After days of sniffing cocaine, noses would become congested and glazed with the precious powder, but blowing one's nose, and thereby wasting it, was out of the question.

★ ★ ★ ★ ★

The drug culture in the North Miami, Hollywood, and Fort Lauderdale areas of South Florida especially catered to the highs produced by the white party powder. It was that susceptibility that provided the perfect environment for James Michael Capotorto, also known as "Big Jimmy," and his associates, to ply their trade.

Big Jimmy, known to local law enforcement as "a big time organized crime figure," and to the news media as "a reputed Mafia enforcer and leader of a clutch of interstate cocaine smugglers," was apparently operating on the fringe of the Mafia and with their blessing. His intention was to control all major narcotics trade in Broward County through extortion and other strong arm tactics.

His modus operandi was to identify and extort the lower-tier drug dealers, by forcing them to allow him and his cronies to be present at their buys from major dealers and then ripping off these suppliers for their drugs and cash. Like a barracuda working its way up through a line of bait, gobbling each worm off the hook at his leisure, Big Jimmy would eventually get to the guy at the top, work him over while holding him hostage for a few days, then would use him to move even further up the line.

It was a sweet gig for the Capotorto gang, who reveled in the easy money, all tax-free, knowing they had the backing of the Big Man, the man who was gutsy enough even to meet the press and discuss his exploits in some braggadocio detail. Big Jimmy's justification was that he was doing more than the cops by subjugating drug dealers to his advantage.

Capotorto's brash mentality was demonstrated in the following article, where he is quoted in the *Fort Lauderdale Sentinel* on November 4, 1975 in an article written by Ott Cefkin: "Maybe I do rob dope dealers. But it's more than the cops do to stop narcotics. How can they, when six or seven police cars pull me over to stop me just to give me a traffic ticket?"

These comments from Capotorto eventually came back to haunt him and his fellow thugs, as they continued ripping off drug dealers with impunity.

Big Jimmy's waterloo occurred the day he grabbed the Stanton brothers. It was the beginning of the end. John Stanton was an undercover officer for the Broward County Sheriff Office. His brother, David, was not an officer, but was helping him as an operative. Posing as big-time drug dealers, they made Capotorto's short list, and once they fell in his grasps, they were bullied and extorted, like all his other victims.

That is when word got out to the FBI, and I got involved.

I was given the green light to go after Capotorto under the auspices of the Racketeer Influenced Corrupt Organizations (RICO) statute, legislation passed on October 15, 1970. The RICO statutes charge individuals who engage in criminal enterprises affecting foreign and interstate commerce, conducting affairs knowingly and unlawfully through a pattern of racketeering activities. In this case, the activities included extortion, kidnapping, and robbery, in an effort to unlawfully obtain marijuana and cocaine.

Bill Eddy, the supervisor on our new Organized Crime Squad, advised me that Gene Flynn, one of the most gifted senior investigators in the Miami office, had volunteered to work with me on the Capotorto case, the first RICO investigation in the history of the Miami Division.

Flynn was an Irish guy with unbelievable instincts. He was not a classy dresser. In fact, he was a weird dresser who more often than not would show up in the office wearing green tennis shoes. He wore T-shirts of all kinds whenever he could get away with it. I think he slept in the office, because he was always there. In fact, when he retired, he never left. He was assigned to some kind of task force working with the Bureau, so he was allowed to keep the same desk for years after he retired from the FBI. He just kept showing up.

Flynn had lots of kids, a great wife who worked as a nurse at a local hospital, and was a devout Irish Catholic. He, Ed Putz, and Dan Long would do all the cooking at our office get-togethers. There was nothing Flynn would not do for you, if he liked you, but if you were a bad guy and Flynn was on your case, you were "dead meat."

I had never met anyone who would put in more time on a case than Gene Flynn, unless it was Jim Hufford, the White Knight. Since Hufford had transferred to Minneapolis, there was no one I would rather work the Capotorto case with. Big Jimmy was in real trouble!

Flynn and I had split up the first interviews of Capotorto's henchmen. One of Capotorto's cronies on my list was Vincent E. Lynch, aka "Vinny," age thirty-five, a tough guy who had physically picked up a fellow and thrown him across a pool table. This beer tavern event occurred just a few nights before Special Agent Michael P. Dooher and I first contacted Lynch. Dooher was a big red-headed fellow with a very deep, authoritative voice that would make you sit up and take notice.

An accurate description of Vinny Lynch would have been "really mean and full of himself." He had recently been charged with false imprisonment, armed robbery, aggravated battery, carrying a concealed weapon and receiving stolen property, in connection with his exploits for Capotorto. Dooher and I first met him at a car lot in Fort Lauderdale.

We entered a dark, dingy sales office and introduced ourselves to the sales manager by show of credentials. Through the corner of my eye, I noticed an individual sitting on a leather chair, about twenty feet away, wearing a black leather jacket over a white T-shirt, Levis, and dark sunglasses. He sat quietly on a brown leather upholstered chair during our introduction, saying nothing, but staring intently at us.

Dooher displayed his credentials to the manager, and asked, "Special Agent Michael P. Dooher, FBI. We're looking for Mr. Vincent Lynch. Is he around?"

The man in charge pointed to Lynch, the man seated on the leather chair. Dooher and I walked over to the man with the sunglasses and ominous expression on his face. Dooher flashed his credentials again, this time in Lynch's face, as a very official "This is the FBI. Don't mess with us" gesture.

I immediately sensed that was a mistake. The atmosphere suddenly became oppressive—even foreboding. It felt as if we had just stepped within the proximity of a coiled rattlesnake.

Lynch momentarily glanced at Dooher, studying his face, and while glaring directly into Dooher's eyes from over the rim of his sunglasses, revealed the kind of contempt that convinced both of us he was not impressed.

Suddenly, Lynch snatched Dooher's credentials, and began fanning himself with them. Dooher's authoritative countenance began to melt away.

Lynch then initiated a monologue, slowly and methodically, as he began reading the inscription on Dooher's credentials, with both fabricated solemnity and condescension.

"Well, well. Special Agent Michael P. Dooher. Federal Bureau of Investigation. My, my. Isn't that something?" Lynch was overwhelmingly sarcastic, as he continued fanning himself with Dooher's credentials, while staring at him, obviously challenging Dooher to try to retrieve them.

At that point, I committed myself to putting this jerk in prison, if it were the last thing I ever accomplished. He was making a joke out of the FBI and challenging Dooher and me to stop him.

Dooher had enough. He quickly reached out, snapped his credentials out of Lynch's grasp, and pocketed them.

Both Dooher and I were convinced that the possibility of gleaning any information about Capotorto's operation from Vincent Lynch was next to none, so we did not waste our time. As we left the sales office, Lynch knew that would not be his last contact with the FBI. He knew he had lit a fire within us, and it would be a long time before it would burn out.

Gene Flynn and I took a low profile approach in our later interviews with Lynch. We covered a lot of ground, discussing a variety of different subjects, ranging from the drug culture in Fort Lauderdale to the mission of the FBI, including the use of SWAT teams and rappelling techniques for descending rapidly on ropes down the sides of buildings and out of helicopters.

All these avenues of conversation were exhausted in our efforts to flip Lynch to get him to talk about Big Jimmy. Nothing worked.

The depth of meanness in Lynch's violent character surfaced vividly in the last interview we had with him, just prior to arresting him. We were discussing how rappelling was useful in evacuation techniques and rescue efforts. Suddenly, Lynch stunned me with the following comment:

"You know, McPheters, some day you and I are going to rappel out of a helicopter into the ocean, and you aren't going to come back up."

I was caught off guard at first, but then regained some composure and mentally reaffirmed my commitment to put this guy away.

I responded, "Time will tell, Vinny. Time will tell."

★ ★ ★ ★ ★

From the time Big Jimmy finished serving a seven year term in the Atlanta, Georgia, federal penitentiary for his 1974 role in a conspiracy to transport a quarter million dollars worth of cocaine from South Florida to New York, he had everyone intimidated. He had lifted weights constantly while in prison, and obviously, had not cut back on his eating. He came out of prison a hulk and immediately put his voluminous mass to work, pushing people around. Weighing well over two hundred and fifty pounds and built powerfully, few people were willing to step in his way. It was, "Sure, Jimmy" this and "Sure, Jimmy" that.

While in Pompano Beach, Florida, I contacted an employee in the Palomino Lounge who had a "run in" with Big Jimmy a couple weeks before. This fellow was a big man himself, over six feet tall and weighing well over two hundred pounds. He explained how Big Jimmy became unglued with him over some past dealings, grabbed him by his shirt collar and heisted him several inches off the floor, pressing him up against the wall of the bar. It was clear the man was still traumatized over the incident.

Big Jimmy's other associates in his racketeering activities were individuals who had been operating on the fringe of mob activities for years. They were lucky not to have already been incarcerated.

In addition to Vinny Lynch, other members of his gang, including Danny "Blue Eyes" Malatesta, Angelo Bertolotti, Victor Dodaro, and Jacqueline Champion, among others, were always on hand for Big Jimmy when they were needed and were usually on the receiving end of his generosity. All of them were suspected by the authorities of having organized crime connections.

Most of the criminal activity generated by the Capotorto gang occurred from December 1974 through February 1976. Their favorite haunts were the Paddock International Club in Pompano Beach and Chi-Chi's Italian Restaurant in Fort Lauderdale.

Finding the most appropriate and effective way of prosecuting the Capotorto bunch was extremely important, since opportunities to neutralize conspiracies like these involved in organized crime activity were very limited. We were fortunate that the recent RICO legislation had been passed, which provided extended penalties for criminal acts performed as part of an ongoing criminal enterprise, and that we were now able to direct its strength toward Big Jimmy's gang.

Assistant United States Attorney John Evans had just been assigned to a new strike force, organized by the U.S. Attorney's Office in Miami and was delegated to assist us in going after Capotorto. He was a perfect pick. Innovative, hard-charging, willing to take risks, Evans was a delight to work with. In his early thirties, full of energy and enthusiasm, and ready to charge, this slim, red-headed warrior with a full mustache was the epitome of confidence.

As Flynn and I continued interviewing witnesses in the Caportorto case, more and more pieces fell into place. Detective John Stanton and his brother, David, were doing their part, supplying numerous affidavits, and firming up the allegations documenting the ruthlessness and illegal drug activities of Capotorto, Vinny Lynch, and the others.

AUSA Evans was devouring all the intelligence data we and the Stanton brothers were developing, and transforming it into a multiple-count federal indictment. This would be the first RICO indictment of its kind issued in the Southern District of Florida. Evans was both inexhaustible and relentless in his quest to take down Capotorto.

The day of reckoning finally arrived for Big Jimmy and his gang.

On February 19, 1976 bench warrants were issued for Capotorto, Lynch, Malatesta, Bertolotti, Dodaro, and Champion, pursuant to a two-count sealed indictment, returned by a federal grand jury convened in Miami. The federal charges described "a pattern of racketeering activity, which included extortion, kidnapping, and robbery, in an effort to unlawfully obtain money and drugs from various individuals."

We swept down on Big Jimmy's parents' residence in Pompano Beach early that morning, rousting the big guy out of bed. As Capotorto lumbered out of bed, he immediately began asking why we would come after him, when he had only been clearing the streets of drug dealers, a job the police had found impossible. We made it clear we were not there to argue the merits of his indictment and ordered him to get dressed . . . quickly.

The big fellow threw on a pair of gargantuan slacks and an ample button-down shirt. As he dressed, it was obvious that what had once been a cut-in-steel head-smashing physique had diminished to a flabbier form of obesity, most likely due to a decadent lifestyle of drug abuse and improvident living. The muscled mobster who had strolled out of prison years before with the bulging biceps now appeared more like a baby whale.

★   ★   ★   ★   ★

All of Big Jimmy's gang, except Jacqueline Champion and Victor Dodaro, were picked up by agents of the Miami Division. The latter two were arrested by agents in Cleveland, Ohio.

Months later when the case went to trial, Vinny Lynch managed to escape from the custody of the U.S. Marshalls, who had been holding the defendants without bail.

The trial went on, but Lynch's absence put the government at a disadvantage. That was because Lynch's mere presence, especially the cynical aura of hostility he exuded, would lead the jurors to certain conclusions as to his culpability.

After Lynch had absented himself for two days, Flynn came through for us in the most uncanny fashion that one would expect only from Special Agent Eugene Flynn.

A lot can be said about the "sixth sense" of the trained investigator, what it is, and how it comes into play. No one has ever been able to explain it, yet no one can effectively deny that it works. Some call it mental telepathy or just plain old "horse sense." Whatever it is, Flynn was really plugged into it.

We were in the booking area of the Dade County Jail, where Lynch had been held just prior to his escape. We were inquiring with some deputies regarding the details of the escape. These deputies had transported Lynch back and forth from jail to the courthouse. No one had any answers for how he got away, nor any other details of his escape.

After wrapping up a few inquiries, I noticed Flynn, shuffling back and forth in front of one particular wall of the booking area that was covered with graffiti, copying some of it down onto a notepad. He suddenly appeared extremely focused, as he copied yet more scribbling that turned out to be a specific address in the Bronx area of New York City.

"What do you have there, Gino?" I asked.

"Vinny said he had a girlfriend in New York City, remember?" he reminded me.

"Yeah, I remember him saying that, but New York's a big place, and that's just one of a lot of addresses on that wall, man!"

Flynn insisted that there was something special about that specific address that he had copied from the sea of graffiti. He advised he would send a teletype to the New York office to locate and apprehend Lynch at that address.

This was making my head spin. I just looked at Flynn with incredulity, saying nothing, thinking, *Is he serious? Is there something he knows that he's not telling me? Is he nuts? No, can't be. If he was, he wouldn't have the reputation he has.*

There were probably a hundred addresses on that wall, along with several hundred more names and phone numbers. These were from places all over the country, written by jailbirds, their family members, and their girlfriends to signal the inmates as to where they could be contacted upon their release.

And Flynn has somehow reduced all this to a formula for locating and apprehending Vinny Lynch? I mused.

How Flynn could be so certain Lynch could be located at that address remains an unsolved mystery to me to this day, but he sent that teletype, and because he did, Lynch was apprehended at his girlfriend's address by New York City agents that very night. Needless to say, I will never doubt Flynn had a "gift" that went far beyond mere human perception.

Lynch was back before the judge the next day and was subsequently convicted for his felonious extortionate activities while conspiring with Capotorto. He was sent to prison to serve several years and never got out. His propensity for violence and picking fights made him a lot of enemies behind bars, and finally one of them stabbed him to death.

Big Jimmy met a similar fate.

In April 1976, just before the trial of Big Jimmy's gang of extortionists, I flew to Salt Lake City for the annual General Conference of The Church of Jesus Christ of Latter-day Saints. My goal was to receive training and inspiration from the many general authorities of the Church that would benefit me as bishop of my Miami Third Ward congregation.

The second day of the conference, Judy called me.

"Have you heard about what happened to Capotorto?" she asked.

"Something happened to him?" I responded.

"Yeah. He'd been picking on someone's wife. The guy shot him. He's dead!"

I was not surprised. I thought of the saying, "What goes around comes around." Big Jimmy had pushed so many people around for so many years, it was amazing he lived as long as he did.

I learned that Capotorto had been threatening the wife of one of his associates and had become way too physical with her.

The husband responded by taping two handguns under a coffee table and then inviting Big Jimmy over to talk. Capotorto sat down across from him and was filled with bullet holes, while the enraged husband kept pulling both triggers, not stopping until the cylinders were empty.

Thus ended the saga of James Michael Capotorto. The rest of Big Jimmy's gang were convicted and sent to prison on racketeering charges. On February 19, 1997, an article in the Broward County edition of the *Miami Herald* announced that the Capotorto drug ring had been broken.

Strike Force Prosecutor John Evans was superb in presenting the evidence we compiled. Unlike many prosecutors, who only authorize prosecution of cases they see as ready-made convictions, Evans had been willing to take risks on a case that had great potential but no past precedents. He was a perfect match for the FBI.

★ ★ ★ ★ ★

Many years had gone by since we left the four seasons of the mountains west and our families. We were concerned about our children seeing their grandparents more often, since their health was failing and time was taking its toll on them.

On May 20, 1976, the Bureau was sympathetic, and transferred us to the Portland, Oregon office. I was subsequently released from my first bishop calling with a wonderful letter written by the Presiding Bishopric, expressing their appreciation, and dated exactly eight years to the day from the date I entered the FBI. The raise in pay we received shortly after the transfer to $23,000 a year came in handy for the move.

On July 5, 1976, we were on our way to Oregon.

19

★ ★ ★ ★ ★

BUSTING TIMBER THIEVES, MORE BISHOPING, AND BEARS

1976–1982

Upon arriving in the Portland area, we found a nice home in a country setting in West Linn on two and a half acres. It was only twenty-five minutes from the office.

At this time, Church President Spencer Kimball was strongly advocating that we become self-sufficient. We planted three gardens for fruits and vegetables, raised beef, had chickens and collected their eggs, planted fifty fruit trees, and started a beehive project to collect honey. Judy and I were given various Church assignments in the Oregon City, Oregon Stake.

I was totally surprised with my new FBI assignment. I would be spending the next few years out in the mountains, chasing timber thieves. Who had ever heard of this? I wasn't aware that Oregon's economy was so centered in the timber industry, and so adversely affected by these thieves who would knock down old growth cedar groves, three to four hundred years old, and with their heavy equipment, completely destroy the ecology that surrounded them. Nor was I aware that a large percentage of these timber thieves had criminal convictions for violent crimes, including murder. I was amazed that such dangerous individuals were being confronted in the woods, miles away from another person, by unarmed forest rangers.

My first partner was Bob Mitchell, an energetic, but serious-minded fellow in his late thirties, shorter but robust in appearance, who prior to my arrival was the only agent assigned to the forests. Our territory included the one hour jaunt out past Estacada, southeast of Portland and on up the Clackamas River, into the Mount Hood National Forest, which contained a million acres of prime old growth and second growth timber. This was all United States Forest Service (USFS) land. The national forest was bordered by the Warm Springs Indian Reservation on the east and Mount Hood on the north. Salem and the little towns around it were spread out on the west. Mount Hood, itself, commanded the full view of the Willamette Valley. Its challenging peak could be seen from everywhere and lent the impression of a living giant that could swallow up anything at any time.

I soon discovered that timber thefts from rich timberlands like Oregon were a racket yielding several million dollars annually, at the forest's expense. Beautiful, ancient cedar trees were being felled along the river and stream banks in the lowlands, where the mammoth, shallow-rooted trees thrived on the abundance of water. Douglas and hemlock trees used for construction and other significant projects were being stolen off decks piled up by lumbermen with legitimate permits. Individuals entitled to no more than a few cords of wood a year by permit, and for personal use only, were ravishing the forests with their chain saws, greedily selling all they could cut for profit. The thefts were facilitated by the newer model self-loading trucks that could pull into the loading areas for decks of logs—which had been freshly harvested, limbed, and ready to be delivered to the timber mills—and then drive away with them. At the core of the problem were many people who had adapted the mentality of the pioneers who cut what they wanted when they wanted and never thought of it as theft. They had lost sight of the fact that times had changed, and that they could no longer regard the forests as their personal property . . . their private land. The national forests belonged to everyone and needed to be protected.

I began calculating the value of one load of logs chained on a flat bed truck, heading down the highway, and taking stock of the value there that most people would not be aware of. I figured out that in 1976, a truck carrying a load of Douglas fir or hemlock would be worth several thousand dollars on the market. With cedar valued at one hundred and eighty dollars a cord, a couple of thieves could earn fifteen hundred dollars for just a night's work out in the mountains, while being virtually unobserved by the authorities.

As I became involved in working cedar thefts, I discovered why the thieves, known as "shake rats" or "cedar barons," were hauling cedar out of the woods on their backs, in two foot lengths called "bolts," prior to dumping it into their pickups. They did that because those same pieces would be cut into either shakes or shingles for covering roofs of houses, and were very expensive to procure on the market. While cutting down the trees, the thieves gave no consideration at all to the lush environment in which they had developed. We found only jagged tree stumps and muddy ruts and gashes remaining in the land left by the trucks and heavy equipment used to remove the plunder. In short, they had butchered the cedar groves and knocked down the older trees that were reseeding the forests for future generations.

The thieves would even employ helicopters to airlift loads of illegally cut cedar and old growth logs to the mills. Since many of the thefts occurred in remote areas that were inaccessible and potentially would not be discovered for years to come, no one really knew the full amount of damage and loss being sustained to the government.

When I arrived in Oregon in 1976, the hordes of timber thieves were increasing, due to the rising value of wood throughout the country. Much of it was even being transported abroad, in violation of conspiracy laws that made transportation of timber into a foreign country from a national forest a federal violation. The bureau had just entered the investigative arena of timber theft, and Bob Mitchell and I were pioneers in that arena. We were joined by special agent John McCormick from the U.S. Forest Service, who was a tremendous resource to Mitchell and me, since he was trained specifically to work timber theft cases. Mitchell and I would often have to address other cases arising in Portland, including a continuing rash of drug-related bank robberies, which would temporarily pull us off our timber cases, and McCormick would take up the slack until we returned. The U.S. Forest Service and the Bureau of Land Management (BLM) were adopting new measures to address the timber thieves, who were becoming increasingly more brazen, as they continued to raid the forests with impunity.

Mitchell became my instructor in the ways of timber thieves. He had not worked the timber very long himself, but had just been involved in a case involving six magnificent cedar trees that were illegally hewn down in the Bull Run watershed, located approximately twenty-five miles southeast of Portland. This case fired public concern regarding what was happening in the forests, since Bull Run was a gorgeous area, a popular spot for the general public and very protected. It was also part of Portland's water supply. Being an original old growth area, some called the thefts "a crime against nature."

"So how are you going to prove this Bull Run case, Bob?" I asked, sincerely curious as to his response.

He replied, "Trees produce the same telling clues that other crimes do, including annual growth rings that are as peculiar to them as fingerprints are to human beings. When we discovered those logs in the bad guys' possession, we were able to cut a circle off the bottom, take it back to the stump and match it up, ring for ring, or in other words, year for year. It's not that hard."

This was intriguing. "What else? I see you've kept the axes and wood mauls you recovered out there. Where do they fit in?" I asked.

"Those stumps from the stolen trees have axe and wood maul marks on them." He took me over to a table in an area where he had carefully stowed, tagged, and labeled the Bull Run evidence.

"Look," he waved toward the tools and wood rounds. "We have the axes and wood mauls. It's actually pretty easy. The laboratory guys come out here as expert witnesses and just match up the marks and impressions. Same way they can trace bullets they pull out of bodies to the guns that fired them. They just match the marks and creases on the bullet rounds to those same marks, called lands and grooves, in the barrel of the gun, or by matching the indentation that the firing pin makes on the cartridge to the firing pin itself. They do the same type of matching with timber theft tools and the wood itself. It's all pretty cut-and-dry science for the laboratory guys, Mike." Mitchell was smiling a little at my surprised expression, as I considered in awe this new area in forensics that I had no idea existed.

"Bob, this blows me away! How long has the Bureau been into this technology? It's all Greek to me." Mitchell knew he had my full attention.

"We're the first," he said. "We're plowing some new ground here." That was it! I knew there was something special going on in this part of the country in a new phase of law enforcement, and I was glad to be part of it.

Mitchell continued. "In this case, not only have we got what I've mentioned already, but the thieves left tire tracks that we can match to their rigs, boot prints that we can match to their boots and fingerprints on their empty beer cans that we can match to them." Mitchell had a "slam dunk" case. The Bull Run thieves were convicted.

With the technology to address this huge economic problem in Oregon, the Bureau became anxious to go after it, but only on a limited basis. There were manpower constraints, due to the other two hundred and sixty violations we were tasked with. The impact of the Bull Run case changed that, at least for a few years. The Bureau assigned a handful of agents to work the timber, as we deliberately let the word out that we were now in the woods. It was a great deterrent. Word came back through our informants that the perpetrators were shaken up, and preferred not to become involved with the FBI. The U.S. Forest Service also jumped in with both feet. While in 1976 they only had three investigators assigned in Oregon and Washington, by 1980 they had eighteen investigators in those two states and sixty more throughout the rest of the United States.

Special Agent John Heidtke developed the Bureau's Crime Resistance Program to determine the magnitude of the timber theft dilemma, the kinds of thefts involved, and the modus operandi or manner of theft utilized by the culprits. He also presented programs to forestry employees, law-enforcement groups, representatives from the logging industry, and anyone else who would listen and who might cooperate in resolving the problem. Heidtke had a background in forestry and was successful in teaching some of the investigative techniques and crime scene solutions that Mitchell and I were using in the woods on almost a daily basis.

Eventually, loggers began reporting some of their employer's illegal activities, and inside observers became informants. More cases were reported and more anonymous tips began coming in. The thieves were slowed up, but didn't give up. That was because the price for timber was still on the rise for construction projects and the cost of cedar shakes was escalating. Wood burning, as a cheaper alternative to the high cost of heating fuel, was becoming more popular. The temptation for men with sharp chain saws and a pickup with a tank full of gas was overwhelming . . . men like Allen Lamont James.

★　★　★　★　★

The highway up the Clackamas River was a daily run for James, who had to keep up with the ads he had placed in the *Oregonian* newspaper for firewood sales. Only ten cords of firewood were allowed per person per year with purchase of a permit, but that wood was for home use and was not to be sold. James had made over one hundred thousand dollars in a few short months by responding to all the requests left on his answering service with firewood obtained illegally. James had filled over twenty-seven hundred firewood orders at forty-nine dollars for every cord of wood delivered, most of which was old growth Douglas fir. He was cutting two truckloads of wood a day in areas where he had no permit. I had discovered the ads and had James under surveillance for just over two months, making sure that he exceeded his permit limit several times over, before I finally arrested him. On several prior occasions, U.S. Forest Service personnel had spotted James trucking down the highway towards town, loaded down with firewood.

I took several photos of James selling firewood as he delivered it to

Mike investigates a timber theft incident.

customers who paid only in cash. I actually hid behind a snowman once to get the photos up close. On another occasion, as James was pulling out of his cutting area at dusk, he almost drove over me because I was snapping photos up close while lying in the mud near the cutting site.

On the last day of surveillance, armed with a warrant for the theft of government property, I and several forest service officers followed James all the way from the vicinity of the Ripplebrook Ranger Station up the Clackamas River, all the way to Estacada, many miles down the highway. He had a huge load of illegal firewood and all the cutting equipment, which could be used as evidence in court and which we seized, including chain saws, wood mauls, and so on, to compliment the surveillance photographs that we took.

In the latter part of September 1977, James was found guilty of one count of a federal indictment, charging theft of government property, and was sentenced to thirty days incarceration and two hundred hours of community service. James was just one of about fifty commercial wood thieves operating in the area, selling everything they could get their hands on. Firewood thefts increased substantially in 1978. Some weekends McCormick and I would observe hundreds of trucks along the Clackamas River, loaded with firewood, a lot more trucks than there were permits.

The following month, Rollin Lee Spencer and Wayne Frank Doyle, two of my cedar thief subjects, didn't get off so easily. They had been stealing cedar bolts high in the mountains where there was heavy snow and where they thought no one would ever go to investigate. Investigator McCormick and I had received a tip they were cutting down old growth cedar and piling it up in the back of their pickup over poached deer. We knew they were cutting at night and muzzling the sound of their chain saws by running the exhaust end through a hose down into a bucket of water, so they couldn't be heard.

The one thing Spencer and Doyle didn't count on was McCormick and I driving our 4x4 rigs through the snow, bumper high, late at night. Nor were they thinking real clearly when they lit a bonfire high up on a ridge to stay warm. They were shocked, seeing us slowly drive up, as McCormick's suburban labored in four-wheel drive through two feet of new snow.

"Mr. Spencer. Mr. Doyle. I'm Special Agent Mike McPheters, FBI. This is Investigator John McCormick, U.S. Forest Service. We're out here looking for some folks that we hear are taking down illegal cedar. Could we see what kind of permits you folks have?"

Both men's expressions, formerly just curious, now turned ashen, as they stumbled over themselves, trying to say something that made sense, while gazing down at the holstered revolvers both McCormick and I wore.

"We're picking this up for some friends that told us they cut it on their permits and just needed some help hauling it in." Spencer knew he hadn't convinced anyone.

"Okay, Mr. Spencer. Then surely they gave you a copy of their permit. You know, so you wouldn't get into trouble, while you were hauling it out? May we see that?" I asked.

"They forgot to give it to us," was the reply.

McCormick weighed in. "No problem, Mr. Spencer. Give me their names, and we'll radio our office to have them contacted." Chagrined expressions ensued from both men.

"Do you mind if I take a look at that load of wood?" I asked, motioning to the pickup.

Doyle chimed in. "Go ahead. It's just wood."

I sorted through the cedar rounds that had not been cut into bolts, or quarter-rounds yet. The hoof of a buck mule deer sprang up about eight inches above the pile, as I removed an extra big round near the pickup gate.

"You fellows obviously like fresh venison, but hunting season has been over for more than a month." When I said that, I was pretty sure Doyle was wetting his pants.

On November 1, 1977, Spencer and Doyle were convicted for the theft of U.S. Forest Service cedar from the Mount Hood National Forest.

In another operation, McCormick and I shut down an operation along the Clackamas River, near the end of a logging spur, or a small dirt road built for hauling out logs. Twenty-three trees, including cedar, hemlock, and Douglas fir were hewn down by a private contractor who had only been authorized to fall some fire-damaged trees that had been carefully marked with yellow paint. We marked the stumps of the twenty-three illegally cut trees with red paint, numbering them one through twenty-three. We sliced cross-sections off the stumps, which were up to four and a half feet in diameter, with our chain saws. The cross-sections were numbered in red to correspond with the red numbers on the stumps they were removed from. Many of those cross-sections matched logs stacked in a pile nearby, next to the road we came in on. We then marked the logs matching up with the cross-sections with the same numbers as the stumps they had come from. We collected two pickups full of numbered cross-sections from the twenty-three stumps. The evidence weighed nearly a ton, and would have to be exhibited before a jury, unless there was a guilty plea. All we had to do now was contact the contractor who had the logs in the pile he hadn't been authorized to take. He didn't have an explanation that worked and had to plead guilty.

In another FBI investigation in Oregon, an individual moved his family into a trailer way back in the mountains into a totally secluded area, and logged off nearly six acres illegally. He built roads with heavy equipment, inserted a sophisticated system for draining off water, and eventually brought out over thirty-two thousand board-feet of lumber at night over obscure roads. He ended out serving a year in federal prison. The stiffest penalty imposed up to 1980 was a three year prison sentence. The biggest fine imposed was the maximum: ten thousand dollars.

My timber theft investigations took me all over the state of Oregon, working a case in Coos Bay where logs were being illegally exported out of the country, and another case in Klamath Falls, where logs were being stolen from piles or decks right off the timber sales areas by thieves driving self-loading trucks. The brazen nature of these thieves was without precedent.

★ ★ ★ ★ ★

In July 1978, I was advised my road trip up the Clackamas River was being terminated. The Bureau was once again de-emphasizing timber thefts. I was transferred to Squad Five to work white-collar crime under supervisor Jim Riddle. I took my unresolved timber theft cases with me, and continued actively pursuing my target case: the Hank Westbrook matter, where huge amounts of timber were being exported from the Oregon coast to the Pacific Rim countries, in violation of federal law.

★ ★ ★ ★ ★

The first couple years working timber thefts in the Mount Hood National Forest were truly enjoyable. I loved the leisurely drives up the Clackamas River and the contact with the U.S. Forest Service people, who were mostly all outdoors enthusiasts like me, and who loved hunting and fishing. I'd be home by a reasonable hour in the evenings for family time and working on our projects for becoming self-reliant. Our hens were furnishing all the healthy brown eggs we wanted, and we were eating our "friar-cross" chickens, which were a combination of White Rock and Cornish birds. We were harvesting corn, tomatoes, peas, beans, several kinds of squash, potatoes, pumpkins, strawberries, and cucumbers. We were picking huckleberries and blueberries. Judy had her hands full with canning, and we'd continue to raise a couple beef each year. Our grass got so high one year, we had it bailed into grass hay. It yielded three and a half tons, thirty bails to a ton. Many of the meals we were eating were completely produced from food we had grown and raised.

Life had been good, with a balance of energy going into the timber theft investigations, time with the family and the "gentleman farm" duties. I even had time to climb Mount Rainier with some fellow agents. Then one night the phone rang! It was President James Bean, our stake president.

On July 26, 1978, I was called to serve as bishop of the newly-created West Linn Ward. President Bean was waiting for me at our home, where two other couples were also there waiting for Judy and me to accompany them to a Relief Society luau. President Bean signaled for Judy and I to follow him over to where my bureau Suburban was parked and showed me a letter signed by the First Presidency, indicating their approval to have me succeed Bishop Douglas Westenhaver as bishop of the West Linn Ward. When I was set apart, I was promised I would be delivered from "harm, evil, or accident" if I fulfilled my calling. I was told if I did this, my work would be satisfactory to my employer and that I would be happy and fulfilled. I was grateful for that assurance and for another opportunity to serve. Judy told me this time I had to "get it right."

There were a lot of problems members were having in the ward. There were some huge obstacles I had to help them confront and overcome. Jumping right in and helping them address those issues converted those previous leisurely days, driving up the Clackamas River, into a "full court press" again; but from the Miami experience as bishop, I knew what that was all about. An event soon occurred that taught me that any obstacles people were confronted with in life could be overcome, even if they came in the form of a seven-foot tall bear.

It was July 27, 1981, at the Multnomah County fair. An animal trainer was displaying Sampson, a huge black bear, in the cinnamon brown phase, while controlling him with a hand-held chain, looped around the bear's neck. Sampson was de-fanged and de-clawed. Three times a day, he would take on four wrestlers, one at a time. My kids liked the idea of seeing what their dad could do with this animal. The fact that he was almost seven feet tall and weighed over six hundred pounds didn't faze them. After all, what were dads for, if not to furnish some classy entertainment for their kids once in a while? Besides, they decided it would be the perfect family home evening opportunity.

I caught Sampson at his 7:00 PM appearance. I was the first of four dummies to climb up onto the stage and confront him. As I watched the bear lumber through the crowd and up the stairs, he didn't appear over-whelmingly large. That didn't happen until he stood up on his hind legs, the position he was in as I ascended the staircase. Suddenly, I had a lump in my throat. Agent Phil Miller was there to take photographs . . . photographs that would be displayed to the entire Portland office staff. Now wasn't the time for me to turn into a weenie.

As I waded into Sampson, I immediately realized that all that loose weight hanging down from a bear that appears jelly-like to the casual observer, feels like steel-belted tires when you latch onto it. The other thing I immediately became aware of was that bears have really bad breath!

As we waltzed around the stage, both of us on two feet, or in Sampson's case, paws, it really did appear that we were dancing with one another. He was leaning on me, and I had my head tucked into his front shoulder cavity. Within a few seconds, I was tiring under the weight.

I knew it was now or never, as I took a wide stance, rotated my upper body around with all the strength that I had and threw Sampson across my hip. He went down on his back, with all four paws up in the air. Had it not been for the photos Miller gave me later, I would never have believed that I executed that move so well.

Once Sampson was down, I positioned myself over his shoulders and neck, and kept him pinned down for a few gleeful moments, when I had him

Wrestling Sampson
Mike later wrote a poem about his experience

totally off balance. The crowd was going wild, seeing the underdog human winning out.

Then Sampson rolled over on me. During the three or four minutes Sampson was on top of me, flattening me like a pancake and pummeling me in all the wrong places, I learned a little about overcoming your problems and endurance. I learned something about meeting overwhelming odds in life, as we often do. I learned just how overpowering some of the bears in our lives can be, but of even more importance . . . I learned that a bear, even a big bear, could be thrown. That is the lesson I had to learn as a bishop, to pass onto my people, and as an FBI agent to resolve some complicated cases.

Wrestling Sampson caused me to wax poetic:

> It was at the Portland Fair when I wrestled that bear, that I
>   first gained the conviction, I think
> After pinning that bear that was out of its lair
> That a bear's breath really does stink!!!
> The bear was a black one, in the cinnamon brown phase
> Weighed six hundred pounds and was seven feet tall
> When it stood up and faced me, I was truly amazed!
> I thought my heart surely would stall!
> The bear took on four challengers straight in a row
> I was first. What a dumb thing to do!
> We locked in real tight . . . I was plumb full of fright, and
>   knew that my Doomesday was due.
> He gnawed on my shoulders. He thumped with his snout,

and leaned on my smaller physique

Now I had to do something . . . before I gave out

And oh! How this bear's breath did reek!

I said "This is it. It's now or never!"

And threw him over my hip

I pinned him all right . . . and thought I was bad. Had him
    down thirty seconds or more

But "No sir! No more." I then hit the floor

And then came the gore. He started to roar! Wouldn't take
    any more

His snout hit me more . . . and some more . . . and some
    more. Hey, where is the door?

I don't want anymore. I'm too beat up and sore!

It lasted for three or four minutes, I'd say

The beating he gave me that day

But a lesson I've learned about bears, methinks

When you get near them, their breath really stinks!

20

★★★★★

FINDING D. B. COOPER'S MONEY

Every Saturday following Thanksgiving, the small town of Ariel, Washington, located near Mt. Saint Helens, comes alive to celebrate the only unsolved hijacking in the nation—the one perpetrated by D. B. Cooper. The "Ariel Store," 288 Merwyn Village Road, is the scene for a look-alike contest and other festivities celebrating Cooper's bold act. Other similar celebrations, along with various songs, movies, television spotlights, and various forms of literature, have all made Cooper famous, and scores of businesses throughout the Pacific Northwest continue to sell souvenirs depicting his daring jump.

Although many feel that what Cooper did was extremely stupid, there is little doubt that it was without precedent.

★　★　★　★　★

On November 24, 1971, I was working hijackings in Miami, Florida, most of which involved individuals demanding ransom and then wanting to go to Cuba. That day I heard that a man using the name Dan Cooper, subsequently referred to by the news media as D. B. Cooper, had hijacked a Boeing 727-100 aircraft flying for Northwest Orient Airlines, now known as Northwest Airlines, from Portland, Oregon to Seattle, Washington.

Cooper was described as a white male in his mid-forties, approximately five feet ten inches to six feet tall, with dark sunglasses, and nicotine stains on his fingers.

After the plane took off from Portland, Cooper handed the female flight attendant a note and advised her he was in possession of a bomb. He further advised her he was hijacking the aircraft. In his note, he demanded that two hundred thousand dollars in cash and two sets of parachutes be delivered to the plane, upon landing at the Seattle-Tacoma International Airport. Cooper further demanded his instructions were to be followed, or he would blow up the plane.

William Scott, the pilot, received the demand and relayed it to the FBI, who, in turn, advised the president of Northwest Airlines of its contents. Scott was instructed to cooperate with Cooper, who had just shown the flight attendant enough bomb components, including red cylinders, wires, and a battery, to convince the crew the threat was real. While the parachutes and money were being collected, the aircraft maintained a holding pattern over Seattle. The FBI had all ten thousand of the twenty dollar bills photographed sufficiently well that all the serial numbers were recorded.

At 5:30 PM, when the plane landed and Cooper's parachutes and money were delivered, he directed that everyone be released except the pilot, one flight attendant, the first officer, and the flight engineer.

At 7:40 PM, Cooper ordered the plane be flown to Mexico City at a speed of only two hundred miles per hour and at an altitude of less than ten thousand feet, with the landing gear down. Up to this point, no one had ever tried to parachute under these circumstances.

Cooper then changed the destination to Reno, Nevada and ordered the flight attendant who had been seated next to him to go to the cockpit. Next, he walked to the aft stairs and at 8:13 PM, jumped into the darkness and into a furious rainstorm.

Since that moment, there has been no proven report of Cooper ever having been seen again. Several facts make the likeliness of Cooper having made a successful landing very improbable. The area in southwest Washington over which he jumped was very remote and mountainous. He was dressed in a dark suit, black raincoat, white-collared shirt, necktie, black sunglasses, and loafers. The impact upon landing in loafers, rather than appropriate foot wear, could alone, be enough to write off the jump.

★ ★ ★ ★ ★

FEBRUARY 1980

From the time eight-year-old Brian Ingram found $5,880 of Cooper's money on the banks of the Columbia River, five miles northwest of Vancouver, Washington, our entire FBI office had been scouring over the area where Brian had made the exciting discovery. The 294 deteriorated twenty dollar bills were still bundled and bound by rubber bands. The outside edges were frayed and diminished, giving them the appearance of mini-bills. The serial numbers, however, were still intact and matched those that had been delivered to Cooper. The money was discovered adjacent to the river and only a couple inches underneath the surface of the sandy beach.

It was assumed that the money, found nine years after the hijacking, may have been dredged up or washed down from one of the tributaries of the Columbia, possibly the Washougal River in southwest Washington. The Bureau believed the discovery of this money reinforced the theory Cooper never survived, since he would not have left the money behind that he jeopardized his life for.

While sifting through a parcel of the beach assigned to me, I turned up portions of soil containing pieces of paper currency approximately two inches wide, but still containing serial numbers that matched Cooper's demand money. I preserved each piece as evidence by storing them in plastic bags, tagging them with my initials and the date and case number. I kept digging. By late that night, and with the help of a good rake, I had found numerous pieces of the money, all of which matched up. I documented my discovery as one of the most interesting reports I had ever written.

Finding the money produced a euphoric surge of tingling satisfaction, knowing I had in my hands the same money Cooper had in his, when he leaped from the airplane nine years earlier.

Later on, while still in the Portland Division, I joined in additional searches for the remains of D. B. Cooper throughout the wilderness of southwest Washington. I and another agent discovered some interesting looking bones near a river. We bagged them and took them to a state crime lab technician, who indicated they were from wild animals, and not from Cooper.

In a subsequent assignment in Pendleton, Oregon, I developed a suspect whose description matched Cooper's and who was gone from his residence in Pendleton at the time of the hijacking. He returned with a limp, had nicotine-stained fingers, wore the same kind of sunglasses Cooper had worn during the hijacking, and had a good deal of money. This was in the late 1980s. Although my suspect was good, we had to wash him out when it was discovered that he was checked into a hospital the day of the hijacking.

★   ★   ★   ★   ★

In October 2007, the Bureau advised it had produced a partial DNA profile of Cooper from a necktie he left behind before he jumped.

On December 31, 2007, the FBI published new composite sketches of Cooper never-before-seen and fact sheets online for the public to view, hoping that would revive memories that would help to identify the famous hijacker. The Bureau concluded that Cooper probably did not survive the jump, but were then, and still are today, very interested in identifying him.

The FBI has withdrawn its theory that Cooper was either an experienced sky diver or a paratrooper, since they learned from their contacts with paratroopers and skydivers that these people would never jump without a light source during a rainstorm.

The mystery of D. B. Cooper lives on.

21

★★★★★

PORTLAND SWAT

SEPTEMBER 1980

The next few years in Portland were punctuated with a host of different assignments, ranging from working white-collar crime cases to interstate prostitution to interstate pornography. I was also assigned to work on supervisor Ken Lovin's bank robbery squad my last years in Portland. Lovin and I had been roommates during our initial training at the FBI academy. Since Lovin was the SWAT team coordinator for the division, and I was one of the more experienced members of our team, he and I made a lot of fugitive arrests and drug raids together.

Either Lovin or I were often the first ones through the door. We loved it. I would be way too excited to be afraid. We would hit the bad guys early in the mornings, while they were in bed. Five or six in the morning was a great time to hit the residence with a warrant, knock the door down with a heavy, metal cylinder object we called "the key," and if we were lucky, take the whole door frame with it. Just before rushing in, we'd often throw in smoke grenades we called "flash bangs." The affect on our bad guy was overwhelming. He never had quite enough time both to recover from the shock and get his hand on his guns. Before he knew it, he would be handcuffed on the floor face down, and we'd be hauling away his drug stashes and tagging them as evidence.

Our SWAT team continued regular training in cross-country skiing, white-water river navigation techniques, building clearing, firearms, mountain drills, and various other techniques. I trained local, county, and state SWAT units all over the state of Oregon and also taught firearms at the

Oregon State Police Academy at Monmouth.

The day came when I was called as the SWAT team leader. On September 8, 1980, I headed up our team's response to three barricaded subjects in the Ringside Restaurant in Portland, who were holding twelve hostages. We were in position from 2:30 AM until 4:30 AM, when the subjects finally came out in the center of a human circle with their hostages handcuffed around them, so we wouldn't shoot.

Another SWAT response was to terminate the activity of some individuals being sought for drug peddling and bank robberies. The gang was run by Larry Burhoe and Gary Scott Anderson. Our episodes with these guys were action-packed. Burhoe had shot at one police officer, stabbed another, and had subdued two other officers and handcuffed them to a tree. He was extremely hardened, and definitely a "professional" criminal. We anticipated a shoot-out with Burhoe. Supervisor Lovin and I assisted the assigned case agent and other agents in interceping him, Anderson, and a woman by the name of Lynette Spaise at a store in Salem, Oregon. I jumped out of the passenger side of a Bureau car that Lovin was driving with an M-P 5 fully-automatic rifle trained on Burhoe, while Lovin got the drop on the other two subjects. Burhoe resisted my order to get down on the ground, forcing me to do it for him. Within seconds, eight to ten officers from other police agencies confronted all three subjects with drawn guns.

The most interesting assignment for our SWAT team did not come from the garden variety criminals from the state of Oregon, but from a religious commune which had been expelled from India and subsequently took root in Central Oregon . . . the Rajneeshes, or the followers of the Indian spiritual leader . . . Bhagwan Shree Rajneesh.

22

★★★★★

THE RAJNEESH EXPERIMENT

1981

Rajneeshpuram was a commune of followers of "Rajneesh" Chandra Mohan Jain from India, a fifty year-old enigmatic and controversial Indian mystic and spiritual leader, more commonly known as Bhagwan Shree Rajneesh. Rajneesh arrived in Oregon with a few of his followers on August 29, 1981. The commune residents, called sannyasins but known locally as Rajneeshes, lived on sixty-four thousand acres of property previously known as the "Big Muddy Ranch," located in Wasco County in the remote reaches of Central Oregon and nestled between the John Day and Deschutes rivers. The commune was carved from empty desert hills into a city of seven thousand people, and eventually had all the trappings of an urban city, including police and fire departments, malls, an immense convention center, restaurants and townhouses, and a 4,200 foot airstrip. It was briefly incorporated as a city in 1981, but under extremely tumultuous circumstances. Eventually, because of controversies and ensuing criminal actions, the stage was set in Rajneeshpuram for a historic showdown with the federal government.

While assigned to the Portland, Oregon office from 1976 to 1982, I covered the Columbia Gorge road trip for a short time, which included the Oregon communities east of Portland, perched along the southern banks of the Columbia River, including Hood River and The Dalles. Rajneeshpuram was located on the eastern edge of my territory and about sixty-five miles south of the Columbia River.

When allegations of prostitution, drug trafficking, and involuntary servitude were brought against the Bhagwan's commune in the spring of

1982, I was sent out to investigate. I was advised that the point of contact at Rajneeshpuram was Ma Anand Sheela, the spokesperson for the burgeoning enterprise in the middle of nowhere. Rajneesh, the Bhagwan, had taken a self-imposed vow of silence, and therefore, was unavailable. Ma Anand Sheela was his personal secretary and representative. I arranged to meet her in Madras, Oregon, not far from Rajneeshpuram. There we sat down in a café for an interview over lunch.

Ma Anand Sheela was an attractive lady, thirty-two years old, who was born Ambalal Patel Sheela in Baroda, India. She had been introduced to Rajneesh by her parents just before she left to study at Montclair State College in New Jersey at the age of eighteen. She returned to India four years later and began her career working with the Bhagwan, assisting him in his teaching enterprises. She then returned to the United States where she married Jay Silverman, a resident of New Jersey, thus becoming known also as Sheela Silverman. It was Ma Anand Sheela that represented the Bhagwan in purchasing the ranch near the village of Antelope, and naming it Rancho Rajneesh.

When I met Ma Anand Sheela, she was dressed in casual clothes, rather than the bright red and orange attire worn by most Rajneeshes. She was about five feet four inches tall, medium build, and dark-complected with black hair cut short. She had an oval-shaped face with a fairly prominent nose and a captivating smile. Although she claimed to be a vegetarian, she seemed to relish her cheeseburger with fries, topped off with a chocolate shake.

From the outset of our conversation, Ma Anand Sheela seemed anxious, a little too anxious, to convince me that everything happening at the commune was in good tastes and in harmony with all federal and state laws. She seemed a little indignant when I questioned her regarding allegations of involuntary servitude, responding that every member of the Rajneesh community had invested a great deal of money just to live there, as much as thirty thousand dollars apiece, and that most of the residents had come from outside of the United States, including from the Middle East, Japan, Australia, and India. She adamantly emphasized that the residents were highly educated, many having master's and doctorate's degrees. She characterized them as strong-minded individuals who could never be forced or held against their will.

As I questioned Ma Anand Sheela specifically regarding the rumors of prostitution, she broke out in laughter.

"What's so funny?" I asked.

"They don't need to pay for anything! People there are free to do what they want regarding sex," she said, smirking.

Ma Anand Sheela's statement was consistent with what I would eventually determine: that free love was a vital ingredient in popularizing the social structure of Rajneeshpuram and was strongly supported by the Bhagwan's teachings. The residents were mostly single adults or couples with no children whose sex lives were unrestricted by any social parameters. It became strikingly obvious that the environment of the Rajneeshes really didn't lend itself to prostitution.

Regarding the third allegation of illegal drug use and drug trafficking, Ma Anand Sheela categorically denied that activity was permitted in the community.

My curiosity about these people, clad in red and coming from all parts of the world to follow a spiritual leader who had become an outcast in India for his inflammatory philosophy, was overwhelming. Now that I had reviewed all the pending allegations against the Rajneeshes with Ma Anand Sheela, I wanted to know much more, and she seemed more than willing to enlighten me about her people and their turbulent history.

"Tell me more about what brought you here," I asked.

"It was better here for Rajneesh, our leader." She spoke the Bhagwan's name with a clear reverence.

"Can you tell me more about him?" I asked. "There seems to be a lot of unanswered questions regarding your leader, especially among the local residents throughout Central Oregon. People are becoming a little unsettled about all these new foreigners moving in."

It was common knowledge that when the Rajneeshes first arrived to take over the ranch, the Bhagwan informed the local authorities that he only intended to have a small farm and a religious following of about fifty worker disciples. However within one month, zoning permits were requested to move thirty-six trailer homes onto the ranch which were shortly thereafter occupied by one hundred and seventy people. The Bhagwan had quickly become a subject of intense curiosity and random conjecture. I was not going to press Ma Anand Sheela for explanations regarding these inconsistencies at this stage of the investigation. These were matters that would eventually be resolved by local authorities. I had already gleaned some background on the Rajneesh, before talking to Ma Anand Sheela.

Rajneesh characterized himself as "the rich man's guru." Unlike many religious teachers, he advocated that lack of material possessions wasn't a genuine virtue in the spiritual sense. He, at times, wore very expensive watches, expensive clothes, and had seventy-four Rolls Royce automobiles. His followers' goal was to obtain 365 of these vehicles, so that each day of the year their leader could drive a different one down the road winding through his many throngs of admirers. It is felt by many that he did this partly to assert his support for the inherent value of personal wealth and partly to offend the sensibilities of the local populace outside of Rajneeshpuram, much like he had the people in his home country of India years before. Rajneesh became known as the "sex guru" in India and the "Rolls Royce guru" in the United States.

Ma Anand Sheela was intent on erasing any doubts I had about the Bhagwan.

"Rajneesh is a great leader and a good man who was never really understood in our own country. In India he was a philosophy professor whose real name was Mohan Chandra. Rajneesh was a nickname he acquired in his childhood. He began lecturing in 1957 at colleges and universities. In 1971, he changed his name to Bhagwan Shree Rajneesh," she explained.

I eventually discovered that although Rajneesh had what was called a "golden tongue" in Hindi, and was considered a very intelligent man by his peers, he was asked to transfer from his teaching post at Raipur Sanskrit College in India because the Vice Chancellor there thought he was jeopardizing his students' morality and religion.

"What does his name mean?" I asked.

"The word *Bhagwan* means 'the blessed one,' 'lord or god.' *Shree* means 'master.' In India he taught what he called 'human potential psychotherapy' in a setting we call an ashram, which is a community Rajneesh formed to uplift and enlighten his people." Ma Anand Sheela paused momentarily, to make sure I understood. Then she went on.

"All of us that follow him are really 'sannyasins', although they call us Rajneeshes, because we follow the master. To be a sannysin in the real sense is to renounce the worldly life style as one knows it outside of the commune. It is a more advanced step of Hinduism. Here in Oregon our commune is actually called the Rajneesh Foundation International," Ma Anand Sheela continued.

"When Rajneesh's ashram in India became so popular, everyone wanted in, but there was no room. The government in our country prevented him from expanding because of its regulation of the land. They were unfair to Rajneesh and cancelled his tax-exempt status. Then they billed him for millions in back taxes. I came to Oregon and found this place. Here we can keep to ourselves, it has a good climate, and we can find room here for many followers." She smiled as she contemplated a bright future for Rajneeshpuram.

"I understand there were controversies surrounding the Rajneesh's teachings in India and subsequently in New Jersey, before he settled out here." I was anxious for an explanation.

"In the 1960s Rajneesh spoke a lot against socialism, as he traveled through our country. He also spoke against Mahatma Gandhi and institutional religion. The people resented him for that, but he felt he had to be loyal to what was in his heart, and taught his conscience. His teachings regarding sexuality were not accepted. They called him the 'sex guru'. As I mentioned, the local people became wary of him and rejected him, but he drew many Westerners to him. He offered special therapies from what he described as the 'Human Potential Movement'. He was just too permissive for the Indian people, and by the late 1970s, he had apparently exhausted the patience of our government. We first relocated in New Jersey for a short time, but that didn't work out, so then we came here." Ma Anand Sheela seemed pleased that I was listening intently and appeared sympathetic to their plight.

I couldn't help but compare the hostilities towards Rajneesh and his followers to the persecutions and expulsions of my own Mormon predecessors who were forced out of upstate New York, Ohio, Missouri, and Illinois by vicious mobs and conspiring state officials, including governors. I thought of the fragile hopes those pioneers had of surviving, having to abandon their homes in the middle of winter, to flee into the frigid wastes of the plains, while making their way to Utah, with hundreds dying along the way. However, the contrasts in motivation for the two groups were stark. The Mormons were forced, under mob rule, to abandon what was theirs, and then were forced to abandon the comfort of their homes in the dead of winter. The Rajneeshes left India and New Jersey voluntarily, free to choose their own time of departure. The Mormons were seeking a destination where they could strive to live a higher law that called for avoiding moral excesses. The Rajneeshes seemed to be seeking a refuge where they could shake off their moral compass and give vent to their lust. For the Mormons, family life was the core of their culture, with God-fearing children the crowning achievement of their existence. Few of the Rajneeshes even had children, or if they did, declined to bring them into the commune. The Mormons were accountable to their Heavenly Father. Rajneesh was the god to his people and taught them that the "New Man" shouldn't be trapped into the institutions of family, marriage, or institutional religion.

I asked, curiously, "Was Rajneesh's permissiveness toward sexuality his central theme?"

"No, of course not!" Ma Anand Sheela answered defensively. "He taught all about the benefits of meditation, the importance of celebrating important facets of our lives, the meaning and essence of love, the importance of being creative and the magic of humor. These are all things that are so important, yet the people in my country couldn't understand that."

Ma Anand Sheela did not mention that Rajneesh had falsely applied for a medical visa, claiming he needed medical treatment for cancer that could only be obtained in the United States. Nor did she mention that the Bhagwan had little regard for Central Oregon's land use laws. His followers would continue to construct various kinds of edifices in defiance of local laws. He would also establish his own city council, which would grant the commune its building permits. He would soon be reprimanded for not advising government agencies about what he was doing. Within a year the Rajneeshes would be involved in legal battles with the local populace regarding these land use issues. Nor did Ma Anand Sheela mention that the Bhagwan was arranging sham marriages for foreigners coming into the commune, enabling them to remain illegally in the United States. This would all be discovered later.

Ma Anand Sheela invited me to follow her back to the commune, where I could see for myself and draw my own conclusions.

Prior to driving into Rajneeshpuram, we skirted the small ghost town of Shaniko, with its old restored hotel, and passed through the little town of Antelope, located eighteen miles from the ranch with its population of fifty inhabitants and its post office, which became a major focal point for disseminating Rajneesh's voluminous supply of writing. The post office became the conduit for millions of dollars coming into the commune from external adherents and sympathizers bent on promoting the Rajneesh experiment.

The first sight that captured my attention was a huge, earth-filled dam the Rajneeshes had built, upon which they had painted an enormous dove flying out of a huge circle. The bird was red with a rose-colored hue outlining it. This was the Rajneesh symbol. I was impressed with the sight of hundreds of people walking around dressed in orange and red clothing, each one wearing a locket around their neck with the Bhagwan's picture on it. Most of the residents appeared to be in their twenties through forties, and obviously from many different corners of the world.

Next we drove by a huge convention center under construction near the center of the town. Ma Anand Sheela advised this was where the Bhagwan would occasionally come to lecture and to motivate his disciples. She spoke little about the Bhagwan, leaving the impression that any reference to him was off-limits, not to be trodden on by outsiders, and that to take me into confidence regarding their revered leader might amount to "casting pearls before the swine."

Ma Anand Sheela showed me truck farming areas where fruit and vegetables of multiple varieties were being cultivated for the many thousands of residents and future visitors. We passed by poultry farms where eggs were produced and some chickens slaughtered, although Ma Anand Sheela was quick to remind me that most of her people were vegetarians like her, therefore reluctant to eat meat. She also pointed out that one section of the poultry farm was designated for hens past their laying years that had served their purpose, producing the eggs necessary for the menu. Those old birds were now being given their well-earned retirement, along with the older roosters that had been for breeding. She reminded me how much more humane this was then sentencing the poor creatures to the chopping block.

Next stop was the cavernous dining hall and kitchen areas that were state-of-the-art in every way imaginable. They were huge utilitarian areas that would normally be found in large government or military complexes. The décor was in excellent taste, with the ever-present circular bird symbol dominating the common view. I was introduced to an elderly Greek lady who Ma Anand Sheela advised held three post-graduate college degrees but had found her life's fulfillment in cooking sumptuous meals for important visitors.

"They [Rajneesh residents] just come here to be under the Bhagwan's influence" she exclaimed. "They have voluntarily dropped out of ordinary society and have surrendered themselves to something much better and more meaningful."

I asked, "What do they all do here?"

She responded, "Most of the residents, like that cook, are pleased to work ten hour days, seven days a week, just for the fulfillment of doing what they have always wanted. But it's always work with their hands that they relish, always in common endeavors: farming, ranching, cultivating the land, providing fish and game, cooking, cleaning, and building. Doing all those more simple things they have always yearned to be doing while they were sitting at their desks in big offices, being micro-managed by people less intelligent."

Suddenly I got it!

These people were dropouts from society . . . people who really didn't care to be encumbered with normal societal stewardships, like raising children. They were attempting to escape the status quo parameters of society. With their own resident god, they could receive the go-ahead for giving vent to all the fleeting pleasures in life . . . with no one to report to on Monday morning, or any morning, except the Bhagwan. The way they viewed life, they were "good to go."

"If they work the ten hours required every day, where do they find the time for taking care of the house, cooking, and personal business?' I asked.

"Not a problem." Ma Anand Sheela retorted. "All their domestic work is done by others, including making their beds, washing their laundry, and cleaning their homes. Their food is even cooked for them and meals are all taken together. They have nothing else to do, outside of the work they are assigned to. Everything is done for them by others, who, like them, work seven days a week."

"Even with everything being done for you, it still seems to me that the '24-7' schedule thing would get old pretty fast." I wondered if she would be at least, a little realistic.

"If they didn't like it, they would leave," she insisted. "They don't leave. And more are coming all the time. The relatively small number we have now is being augmented rapidly. In the summers, during the special festivities, there will be thousands more, coming from all over the world. Many will stay."

I then followed Ma Anand Sheela to her home, a fairly generic, modular dwelling, much like all the others. It was obviously hastily constructed, but well done with furnishings that were well-appointed and rich in appearance. She and her husband, Jay Silverman, known in the commune as Jay Anand, were obviously considered people of distinction.

Jay Anand greeted me with a firm handshake. He appeared as a typical American in dress and bearing. He was light-complected, tall, and lanky. He communicated with joviality and seemed very good-natured. It was apparent, however, that Jay Anand, although the man of the house, had accepted his role as Ma Anand Sheela's number one supporter, and had voluntarily relegated himself to his superior wife, the second-in-command of Rajneeshpuram. He had personally witnessed that role evolve from a student he had met and fallen in love with from India in his native New Jersey to what she had become. He seemed to find satisfaction in the prestige of being the husband of Ma Anand Sheela, even to the extent of adding her middle name to his own.

Following the short chat with Jay and Ma Anand Sheela, and after having again been absolutely assured there was nothing amiss in their community or with their leaders, I excused myself, returned to Portland and submitted my report that at least, on the surface, no federal laws were being violated. That all changed quite abruptly in the ensuing months.

Both Jay and Ma Anand Sheela contacted me by telephone a couple of times over the next few months, just to say "Hello" and to invite me back whenever I wished to return. I have often wondered if they were calling just to provide friendly cover for all that was going on.

The little city of Antelope, next door to Rajneeshpuram became a center of conflict between the Rajneeshes and the local populace. More land use conflicts arose, due to the Rajneesh's misrepresentations regarding their plans to expand their population. A public-interest group called "1000 Friends of Oregon" challenged the Rajneesh's right to expand, resulting in Antelope denying them a business permit for their mail-order operation, the major source of the commune's income. The legal pressures from both federal and state government, as well as from the media, increased against the newcomers.

In April 1982 Ma Anand Sheela ordered a sufficient number of Rajneeshes to move to Antelope that would enable them to gain control of the city council prior to the November elections. After that she began a "Share a Home" project to recruit homeless people who could vote from various parts of the United States to be bused to Rajneeshpuram to help her people win two seats on the Wasco County Commission. After that effort failed, the same street people were no longer needed and subsequently bused just to the outskirts of the commune and dumped.

Adding tremendous concerns to the local Oregonians was the fact they had developed information, proved to be accurate, that the Rajneeshes had begun stockpiling arms and had supplied their security guards, which they called the "Peace Force," with semi-automatic rifles and other state-of-the-art weaponry.

Almost all the media attention was negative regarding the Rajneesh's activities. In 1983 Ma Anand Sheela, in a jealous frenzy, announced to the commune's residents that the Bhagwan would speak only to her and to her alone. She was suspicious of someone usurping her authority and position and was asking herself, "Who else has been communicating with the Master?" thinking only she had that privilege. She had heard rumors that others in the commune were infringing on her stewardship as the Bhagwan's sole mouthpiece and confidante. *Who are they?* she kept asking herself. *I've got to know!* She subsequently ordered the medical area and the operating room next to Rajneesh's bedroom bugged.

Another area in the commune, called "Jesus Grove," was found to contain a clandestine laboratory and additional eavesdropping equipment. In fact, over three thousand tapes with sixty to seventy thousand phone calls were discovered, in addition to an eavesdropping monitor discovered in the Bhagwan's living room, just underneath a panic button. Additional bugging devices were located in fountain pens, ash trays, and clothes hooks. Ma Anand Sheela's quest to electronically eavesdrop on the Bhagwan's quarters and learn the identities of her competitors for Bhagwan Shree Rajneesh's confidence launched the beginning of the most grandiose wire-tapping case in the history of the United States and was the eventual reason for twenty-three federal indictments being returned against the perpetrators.

Many of the Rajneeshes began doubting whether Ma Anand Sheela was really representing Rajneesh's interests. Many commune members tired of her authoritative leadership style and left the commune.

In March 1984 Rajneesh predicted that AIDS would destroy two-thirds of humanity and emphasized again the importance of creating the New Man, in order to prevent annihilation of the human race. The Bhagwan's continued commentaries and warnings about global catastrophe were considered extreme overreaction and infuriated the people of Central Oregon even more. The Rajneeshes adapted a bunker mentality. I recall seeing Ma Anand Sheela in a television interview wearing a holstered revolver and appearing extremely defiant. I asked myself, *Could this be the same person that I had interviewed just a few years before in Madras?*

As time passed, tensions increased between the Rajneeshes and the locals in Antelope, Shaniko, Madras, The Dalles and the other outlying communities. Rajneeshpuram had become a powerful entity, both economically and politically. Its population had risen to seven thousand. Local citizens were intimidated by the presence of so many thousands of foreigners dressed in red and orange, many whose languages they couldn't understand and whose culture was yet an enigma to them. They felt the Rajneeshes had failed to explain themselves. They were leery of a culture with its roots now deep in their county, but whose leader, mute with his self-imposed vow of silence, had yet to impart one word to them. Ma Anand Sheela and Rajneesh's other avid supporters did little to quell the fears and concerns of the Oregonians, as they continued on the defensive, isolating themselves even more. The Rajneesh security forces began maintaining surveillance of all incoming traffic from their three guard stations. Visitors were now being photographed and their license tags recorded and forwarded ahead to commune headquarters.

More and more of the news media began taking notice of what was happening in Central Oregon and exploited its potential for juicy coverage. Ma Anand Sheela favored the media, especially the television appearances, where she would continue appearing armed, signaling to the country that the Rajneeshes were becoming a power to reckon with and should not be taken lightly. These actions, seemingly designed to provoke people, were driving the local populace into frenzy, as they took note of Ma Anand Sheela, thumbing her nose in their faces.

In September 1985, prior to the Wasco County elections, Ma Anand Sheela went way out-of-bounds, ordering commune members to integrate salmonella poisoning, which had been processed in Rajneesh laboratories, into the salad bars of ten restaurants in The Dalles, Oregon. Over seven hundred and fifty people became ill and several were hospitalized. The idea was a drill to determine whether this measure, designed to keep Oregonians from voting in the forthcoming November elections, could succeed, allowing the Rajneeshes to take over two of the county commission seats. This action was the first instance of a chemical or biological terrorism attack in the United States. The scheme failed miserably.

During that same time period, Ma Anand Sheela assembled a hit squad to assassinate United States Attorney Charles Turner from Portland, Oregon, who was appointed to investigate illegal activities in Rajneeshpuram, including the salmonella bioterrorism attack in The Dalles, as well as charges of illegal wiretapping, immigration fraud, and sham marriages. The conspirators purchased false identification and handguns and began stalking Turner, but were unsuccessful after an investigation by the FBI into the salmonella attack was instrumental in discovering the plot. The perpetrators were all subsequently identified and sentenced to up to five years in federal prison.

As if all these efforts of the Rajneeshes to wreck havoc were not enough, there was also a failed conspiracy in 1985 to murder the Bhagwan's personal physician.

On September 13, 1985, Ma Anand Sheela saw the handwriting on the wall and fled the commune with some other followers for Europe, ending up in Germany.

On September 15, 1985, Rajneesh broke his vow of silence and reported in a press conference that Ma Anand Sheela and several others had left the country, allegedly to look for another location for their commune. He accused Ma Anand Sheela of planning the salmonella attack and poisoning The Dalles water system. He claimed she had tried to murder his doctor, his dentist, his girlfriend, and the district attorney. He, basically, blamed everything that had gone wrong on Ma Anand Sheela.

On October 28, 1985, Ma Anand Sheela and two of her accomplices were arrested in West Germany when authorities found a wiretapping facility and salmonella poisoning facilities in her house. She was hastily extradited back to Oregon, before she could flee to Switzerland, where she was a citizen.

As more and more recruits continued streaming into Rajneeshpuram, with its promise of free love and unbridled free agency, the Bhagwan had continued to allow the foreign newcomers to bypass immigration laws upon expiration of their visas and to make their residence permanent. He began arranging illegal marriages of those new on board with the permanent residents of the commune, marriages that were that in name only, all in violation of U.S. immigration laws. This illegal activity, combined with the salmonella food poisoning, the attempt on the life of United States Attorney Charles Turner, an attempt to murder the Bhagwan's physician and Ma Anand Sheela's wiretapping of the Bhagwan's residence to satisfy her concerns, was the fuse for another bomb that was ready to go off.

On October 23, 1985, a thirty-five count indictment was issued by a federal grand jury convened in Portland, charging Rajneesh and his followers with conspiracy to evade immigration laws and illegal wiretapping activities. This required an FBI response. I was called in from Pendleton, Oregon as part of the Portland SWAT team to respond to Rajneeshpuram to provide armed support for the agents who were to execute search warrants on the commune. We were joined by SWAT team contingents from neighboring divisions in Washington and Utah.

As we drove into the center of Rajneeshpuram in our SWAT transport vehicles, I jammed a fully-loaded clip of .223 caliber rounds into my M-16 automatic rifle, leaving the port open to where I could activate it by merely hitting the thumb release. With that awesome weapon cradled in my arms and my sidearm fully loaded and dangling from my belt, and feeling the extra protection of the Kevlar vest against my chest, I paused to consider the very real predicament we could be advancing into. I gazed at my fellow team members, all a little apprehensive, as they, like I, were visually combing the hillsides adjacent to the road underneath us, checking for any sign of the red clad uniforms of the Rajneesh security guards, who might be training their guns on us. We all attempted joviality, but none of us were kidding ourselves. This was life-threatening. We had been advised that if search warrants were executed on the Bhagwan's residence, we would be greeted with automatic machine gun fire from the Peace Force, who we knew were heavily-armed. We had advance intelligence they were set up on the hillsides above us and around us. In our position on the lower road, and from their vantage points in the surrounding hills, we could be prime targets. We had also been warned that there was a plan to create a human barricade of Rajneesh women and children surrounding the Rajneesh's residence that would have to be addressed if we attempted to arrest him. We had been advised that the Bhagwan's security people had more weapons than all of Oregon's police departments. The tension was palpable. This was not going to be just another arrest we would be involved in. This would be a battle . . . maybe a battle to the finish.

At the last minute, and to everyone's relief, negotiations took place that negated the need for hitting the Bhagwan's place, and SWAT was called back. The party was over . . . at least for the moment.

On October 27, 1985, the same day Ma Anand Sheela was arrested in Germany, Rajneesh and several followers were also arrested in North Carolina aboard a Learjet. They had fifty-eight thousand dollars in cash, plus a million dollars worth of watches and jewelry. They were escorted back to Portland, Oregon, where the Bhagwan entered an "Alford Plea"—wherein he didn't admit guilt concerning the immigration violations, but admitted there was enough evidence to convict him. The charges were concealing his intent to remain in the United States and another count of arranging sham marriages. He was sentenced to ten years, which sentenced was suspended. He was then placed on five years' probation. He was also fined four hundred thousand dollars and agreed to leave the United States that November, not to return for at least five years. Rajneesh traveled to several countries to try to restart his commune, but was refused residence in Nepal, Crete, Switzerland, Sweden, England, Canada, Ireland, Uruguay, Spain, Brazil, and Jamaica. He was finally able to return to India in July 1986. The red and orange dress code for his followers was abandoned in 1987.

Rajneesh's health began deteriorating in 1987. He claimed he was poisoned by U.S. Authorities, charges that were never substantiated. In December 1988, he took upon himself the name Osho Rajneesh, indicating he no longer wanted to be called Bhagwan Shree Rajneesh. He died on

January 19, 1990 of heart failure at the age of fifty-eight.

Ma Anand Sheela was sentenced to ten years in a federal prison in Pleasanton, California, on charges of assault, attempted murder, arson, wiretapping, and the salmonella attack. She was released in 1988 on good behavior after serving just two and a half years and went to Switzerland. The assassination conspiracy against the United States attorney was discovered after she had left the United States for Switzerland. Switzerland subsequently refused to extradite her and tried her in a Swiss court, sentencing her to "time served."

According to a later report in the newspaper, *The Oregonian,* Ma Anand Sheela was running two private nursing homes near Basel, Switzerland where she is known as Sheela Birnstiel.

The Oregon Supreme Court ended all litigation against Rajneeshpuram in 1987. By then the commune was both empty and bankrupt. Even the seventy-four Rolls Royces used for the Bhagwan's daily rides were sold to a Texas used car dealer at a public auction. Connecticut General Life Insurance Company owned the mortgage on the property and bought it back, after satisfying the back taxes.

The Big Muddy Ranch was again sold and was later being used by a Christian youth camp, called "Wildhorse Canyon," and operated by "Young Life."

I've been back twice since the commune died out. Rajneeshpuram is no longer shown on state maps, and the little town of Antelope has reverted to its old name.

Bhagwan Shree Rajneesh's Oregon commune is now windswept and barren.

23

★ ★ ★ ★ ★

ON TO PENDLETON:
THE "LET 'ER BUCK" COUNTRY

SUMMER 1982

The Bureau established a new transfer policy, designed to assure that all special agents hired after October 1, 1969, that had not yet served in one of the larger twelve FBI divisions (New York, Los Angeles, Chicago, and so on), and were not yet in their third office, be available to fill the vacancies in those offices caused by retirement and other attrition.

Although that policy caused a lot of anxiety and consternation for many agents, it opened up a vacancy in Pendleton, Oregon, the largest one-man office in the lower forty-eight states and the home of the world's third largest rodeo: the "Pendleton Roundup."

The Pendleton Resident Agency covered eight counties in Eastern Oregon, and was bound by Washington to the north, Idaho to the east and Nevada to the south. It included twenty-seven thousand square miles tucked in among the Blue Mountains, the Umatilla Indian Reservation, the Wallowa-Whitman National Forest and the Jordan Valley. It was beautiful, breath-taking land. Any agent assigned there was over two hundred miles from headquarters in Portland and was the Bureau's representative for one-third of the state of Oregon.

I applied for the Pendleton opening and received the appointment on August 24, 1982.

Those orders also necessitated my release as bishop of the West Linn Ward.

As an FBI agent, tasked with dealing with the dregs of society day after day, I had so appreciated a ray of light, some positives, to filter out

156

the darkness that could so easily ebb into my daily itinerary. Interviewing the vibrant, positive youth of the West Linn Ward often provided me that refreshing uplift. I was there for them to give them strength, encouragement, and direction; yet it was me that would come away uplifted and refreshed by my contact and activity with them.

Knowing I had touched a young life here and there, and helped launch their energy in the right direction, brought me huge satisfaction. No matter how sordid and distasteful my day may have gone in dealing with hardened thugs on the street who had no regard for the law or for the rights of others, and who continuously lied to me, visiting with the youth about their feelings, aspirations, and challenges, and knowing deep down they were listening to me, and that I was making a difference in their lives, was an awesome, invigorating feeling that eclipsed the negatives.

I will never forget their appreciation, voiced both verbally and in writing:

> *"Thank you for asking me as I walked out the door of your office if I wanted to hear from 'our missionaries'—that question changed my life."*
> *-Rhonda*
> *(Joined the church and served a mission)*

> *"Bishop, you have been the best inspiration in my life. Without your example and your love and concern for me, I'd probably never have made it to the temple."*
> *-Laurie*

> *"I feel such a strong love for you. You made me want my mission bad!"*
> *-Doug*

Little remembrances like that provided the antidote for whatever the negatives were out on the street. I would miss that . . . .for a while.

24

★ ★ ★ ★ ★

THE SHOOT-OUT

In his recent book, *My FBI,* former FBI Director Louis Freeh made the statement that as FBI agents, we must be willing to lay down our lives at any time. Never was this total commitment made manifest more clearly to me than in a mountain ranch house in Oregon, where death and I came very close to meeting one another.

The Book of Mormon gives a fascinating account of a young Jew who was ordered by his father to obtain some brass plates from an evil man named Laban. The young man, Nephi, offered Laban a fortune in gold, silver, and other precious items for the plates. Laban immediately seized all that was offered and refused to give anything in return. He even tried to kill Nephi. Eventually Nephi gained an advantage over Laban, killed him, and acquired the brass plates, which contained the record of his people, a record his family would need for inspiration and enlightenment as they embarked upon a perilous journey across the ocean to Central America.

It wasn't until a year after I had been assigned to the Pendleton, Oregon, resident agency of the FBI that I heard of another man by the name of Laban, who in a very real sense, would make me realize the truth of Director Freeh's statement.

★ ★ ★ ★ ★

AUGUST 12, 1983
The dry, mountain heat permeated throughout the wheat lands of northeastern Oregon, a mile and a half from a small community, referred

to by many as "the jewel of the Blue Mountains," but more commonly called Elgin.

It would have been like any other Friday were it not for the green Datsun pickup, bearing a Florida license tag, that pulled into the driveway of Robert McClure's yellow, ranch-style farmhouse, located on the north side of Highway 82.

Paul Garrett and William Kinsey emerged from the vehicle, obviously exhausted from days on the road.

Garrett, a Floridian, age fifty-three, weighed over two hundred and twenty pounds and stood six feet two inches tall. He was a take-charge personality, with a deep southern drawl and a commanding voice.

Garrett's accomplice, William Ray Kinsey, from Georgia, was in his late forties, slightly built, and substantially more withdrawn. Kinsey had begun authoring a book about living and dying with honor.

Both men were involved in the deep sea salvage business off the coast of Florida. They were smart enough to have invented and patented a mini-submarine used for retrieving marine treasure but reckless enough to drive all the way across the United States to extort drug money.

Working outside on some farming details was forty-five-year-old Robert James McClure, totally oblivious to the arrival of the two men, who were approaching with guns drawn. As Garrett and Kinsey cast their shadow over the area where McClure was working, Garrett's voice boomed out.

"We've come for the money, Bob. You give it to us now, and we won't harm your wife and kids. You don't, and we will!"

McClure gasped as he gazed up into the barrels of two drawn revolvers. Somehow he'd truly believed that the passage of the past few years and his relocation to such a remote part of the country would have prevented this day from ever arriving

McClure's mind began rambling. *Surely Garrett couldn't have got out of prison that soon! And how could he have found me so easily?*

McClure's memory focused on that day in April 1981 at Port Mayaca, a tiny village in Florida's everglades on the east side of Lake Okeechobee, when the Martin County Sheriff's office arrested Garrett and some other crew members after detecting residue from what had been a huge load of marijuana.

McClure and Garrett had orchestrated a major marijuana smuggling operation together, transporting fifty-five thousand pounds of marijuana in a shrimp trawler captained by Garrett, from Colombia to South Florida.

When McClure, an expert in radios and electronics, realized the U.S. Coast Guard had caught wind of the operation due to Garrett's failure to clear customs, he alerted Garrett to the impending apprehension of their pay load. Garrett's crew quickly dumped most of the marijuana shipment overboard.

The trawler was able to elude the Coast Guard authorities by turning into some of Florida's inland waterways in Martin County, but subsequently ran aground on a sand bar.

McClure, who had directed the operation from Florida, boarded the ship and salvaged thirty-two hundred pounds of the marijuana, promising to get back with Garrett to split the profits. He escaped before the boat was seized, but Garrett and his crew were all arrested when marijuana residue was discovered.

McClure never delivered Garrett his cut. It seemed apparent that McClure had used the drug proceeds from the Colombian deal to buy his large wheat farm.

Garrett served several years in prison for his part in importing the marijuana, but he never forgot McClure's empty promise. He was well aware of the value of what McClure had gotten away with and was still eager for his share.

It was soon after his release that Garrett teamed up with Kinsey and drove from Florida all the way to Oregon, where suddenly he became McClure's worst nightmare.

The FBI and the U.S. Probation Department in Portland knew nothing regarding McClure's involvement in the Colombian marijuana deal. We had been made aware, however, that he had previously been involved in an illegal drug operation out of the Bahamas and had struck a deal with the U.S. Drug Enforcement Agency (DEA) to cooperate in future drug cases, in order to avoid prison.

★　★　★　★　★

McClure had frozen at the sight of Garrett and Kinsey. The thought, *He's back and he'll kill us!* seized his consciousness, as he faced the two men and conjured up a gimpy smile.

"Well, Bob, you look like you've seen a ghost. Never thought this day would come, did you?" Garrett blurted out from behind his drawn .38

caliber revolver, trained on McClure's head.

"Hello, Paul. I can't believe it's you! I was wondering when we'd be able to get together . . . and take care of things. You know?" Beads of sweat were already appearing on McClure's forehead.

Garrett motioned for McClure to open the garage door a short distance away, as he and Kinsey followed McClure inside.

"All right, Bob. Let's cut to the chase! You owe me one hundred and fifty thousand dollars, for my half of that stash. Where is it?" Garrett was steaming, as his eyes quickly surveyed the garage's interior for anything of value.

McClure stammered, "I had every intention of getting back with you, Paul. I didn't know where they sent you up or how to get it to you. You left no instructions."

"Not good enough, Bob. Where's the dough?" Garrett was delighting in the discomfort he was causing. He inwardly enjoyed seeing McClure stammer all over himself.

"I got four thousand stashed over there." McClure motioned toward a coffee can on a shelf, by a jar full of roofing nails.

Garrett snapped up the cash in twenty-dollar and fifty-dollar bills, pocketed it and grabbed McClure by the right arm.

"Today's Friday, Bob. You've got until Monday morning at ten o'clock to get me the rest. Ten o'clock, Bob, or your wife and kids are dead. Got it, Bob?" McClure knew Garrett meant what he was saying.

McClure's mind was racing as his pulse quickened. *These guys have come all the way from Florida in that truck. They know where I live. They have seen my family. How do I come up with that kind of money? Even if I sold the farm, I couldn't get it that quickly.*

McClure thought of how easy it had been to purchase the farm with the drug proceeds. Selling it that fast would be next to impossible.

"All right, Paul. All right. Be here at 10:00 AM Monday morning. I'll find a way to have your money here. Just don't hurt my wife and kids. Please!"

Garrett let go of McClure's arm, playfully ruffled his hair, and quipped, "Sure, Bob. 10:00 AM. Sure. We'll be here."

McClure swallowed hard as he caught a glimpse of the revolver protruding from Garrett's waistband as he walked away.

★ ★ ★ ★ ★

The one-man resident agency I covered out of Pendleton, Oregon, was one of several outposts of the Portland Division of the FBI. It was the largest one-man resident agency in the lower forty-eight states.

During my eight and a half years in Pendleton, I worked homicides on Indian reservations, aggravated assaults, sexual assaults, and a host of other felonies. I also investigated numerous drug operations and many of the other 250 FBI violations that occurred anywhere in my territory.

It was not uncommon to receive a phone call from Portland headquarters like the one on August 12, 1983, advising me Robert McClure had been extorted for $150,000, with an implication that his family would be killed if he didn't deliver. I had worked far too many cases of violence, mayhem, and death to view this complaint as anything unusual.

However, this case did have an interesting twist.

McClure, who was skilled in electronics and had worked for a firm in Beaverton, Oregon, had moved from Beaverton, Oregon, to Florida, where he was again employed in the electronics industry.

What I didn't know anything about was McClure's past involvement with Garrett in the Colombian drug deal, when he was supposed to be cooperating with the DEA, in return for them cutting him slack for his involvement in a prior Bahamas drug smuggling case.

On August 15, 1983, when McClure's attorney in Florida contacted McClure's U.S. probation officer in Portland, Oregon, who was supervising him on his probation stemming from his involvement on the Bahamas drug-smuggling case, McClure had only given federal authorities half the story, completely distancing himself from any prior illegal involvements with Paul Garrett. McClure had only disclosed that Garrett and Kinsey had visited him, extorted four thousand dollars from him, and demanded an additional one hundred and forty-six thousand by the following Monday. If the extortionist's demands were not met, his wife and children would be killed. McClure's U.S. probation officer in Portland had been notified of all this by his attorney in Miami, who advised McClure had called in a frenzy, fearing for his life and that of his family.

It was Friday. I knew I had to respond to this threat by the following Monday, the day Garrett had warned McClure to turn over the money.

Once I terminated the call from McClure's probation officer with the details of McClure's confrontation with Garrett, I was immediately on the phone with Ken Lovin, my supervisor in Portland.

Lovin and I had been roommates during part of our rookie training at the FBI academy, and I was confident I would get all the help I needed. Before my transfer to Pendleton, I had been the SWAT team leader for a short time in Portland. I was counting on the team rolling out and supporting me in the ensuing confrontation on Monday. After all, I was alone and 207 miles away from another agent.

Such was not to be the case.

Once I filled Lovin in on all the details, he asked, "Mike, what is the possibility of you putting together a team of local officers to help you out there? We have been hammered with bank robberies the last few days, and need every man we've got, including the SWAT guys."

While tapping my pencil against the old hardwood desk, I ran some fast calculations through my head regarding the logistics of pulling an extortion response scenario off with an ad hoc response team that would be organized "spur of the moment."

I responded, "That shouldn't be a problem. We've got some good local guys out here in all three branches: the state police, the county, and the local police in Elgin. John Zea, the chief there, is dynamite to work with. I'll handle it."

Lovin and I had teamed up on a lot of SWAT operations, including narcotics raids, fugitive arrests and dynamic entries, where we kicked in doors, cleared rooms, and grabbed the bad guys. He knew what I could do, and I had put him at ease.

"I'll let you know how it goes, Ken." I hung up, and got on the phone with Elgin Police Chief John Zea to set up a planning meeting with the Oregon State Police and Union County Sheriff's office.

★   ★   ★   ★   ★

When Monday rolled around, I was tasked with setting up the game plan. In a meeting with officers from all the involved agencies at the Elgin Police Department, Chief Zea turned the meeting over to me.

I asked the state police to block off Highway 82, both east and west, once Garrett and Kinsey arrived on the scene. I further requested state police snipers to position themselves in the wheat fields adjacent to the McClure farmhouse, where they would be backed up by other local officers, who would not be visible, but in a position to respond immediately. All officers would be shuttled into their locations, and no vehicles would be left visible.

Garrett and Kinsey would be allowed to enter the house, but if either of them produced weapons, officers outside the house would apprehend them before they could gain entry. McClure would invite them to sit down at the kitchen table, where there would be a large bowl of grapes. McClure was to involve them in the kind of conversation that would elicit statements regarding their complicity in the extortion.

Senior Trooper Patrick Montgomery and I would be positioned inside the house, where we could overhear, and later testify to any incriminating statements in court.

If either Garrett or Kinsey displayed a weapon, or became physical with McClure, he would utter the word "grapes," or would offer them grapes from the table. That signal would prompt Montgomery and me to quickly respond, arrest the subjects, and separate them from McClure. The outside officers would then storm in and assist us.

Once we finished formulating our plan, Montgomery and I jumped into the back of a pickup and lay in prone position, so as to remain invisible until we bailed out near the farmhouse.

Local and state officers took their positions in the surrounding wheat fields. Montgomery hid in the master bedroom of the single story residence, and I hid in the bathroom, adjacent to the garage where McClure had given up the four thousand dollars to Garrett three days before.

McClure's wife and three children had been evacuated and secured at a safe location. McClure, who remained in the house with us, picked up the phone and dialed Garrett's cell phone number that he had been given the prior Friday, which we had been unable to trace. I listened carefully as McClure commenced his dialogue with Garrett and set up a meeting with him. He committed to having the balance of the money together that Garrett was pushing for. He told Garrett he had some now and that he would have to raise the rest in Florida at a future time. Garrett agreed to leave McClure's family alone if he turned over a substantial sum of cash, but no set amount was agreed upon.

In McClure's subsequent debriefing, he advised he didn't know where Garrett and Kinsey were when he called them, but since they indicated they were coming out very shortly, he assumed they were close. He further indicated Garrett knew he didn't have all the money but seemed excited to get his hands on whatever was available.

Because of McClure's duplicity, we never had the chance to fully execute our plan. There was no way McClure was going to allow Garrett to sit down, and then engage him in conversation, knowing full well that if he did, the entire history of his involvement in helping Garrett master-mind the Colombian drug deal would be revealed.

McClure knew that the quickest way out of this mess for him was to remain as silent as possible, then wave to Garrett and Kinsey, as they were being escorted to the county jail in handcuffs.

Within minutes, through a window and from behind a curtain, I noticed both Garrett and Kinsey driving slowly by McClure's farmhouse, looking the house over for any sign of a trap.

Montgomery, who had a vantage point from which to observe the highway, broadcast to all officers: "Be advised, they drove by towards the left."

McClure, who had his nose glued to another window, stated in a voice obviously betraying his anxiety, "They went by. They didn't stop. They're watching."

I softly spoke into my radio, again reminding McClure: "Remember. Grapes. Guns. You see guns, say 'grapes.'"

McClure was becoming more nervous by the minute. He asked, "Is that what I say?" as if that instruction hadn't already been drilled into him numerous times.

I repeated the instructions, "If you see guns, say 'grapes.'"

Knowing he would never carry out the plan as outlined, McClure patronized me with a nod, "Okay."

I queried Senior Trooper Montgomery as to whether he had his handcuffs. I sensed how every detail pertaining to the forthcoming arrest needed to be executed with perfect precision.

My next remark was again directed at Trooper Montgomery.

"McClure's going to be watching out the window for them. If he sees that they got their guns out when they come in, he's going to say 'grapes'. And that means that he's going to head right for the bedroom and hide, and you and I will take them down as soon as they come in."

"Okay" came the response. Montgomery understood.

Then I added, "And don't hesitate to shoot. If they bring that gun up to level, don't hesitate to blow them away."

Montgomery answered: "I won't. But I'm going to wait for you to come out first with the shotgun."

Another minute went by. Garrett exited the pickup and headed slowly toward the farmhouse on foot. Kinsey continued driving a little farther down the road.

McClure abruptly interrupted our dialogue.

"There they come!" he warned.

Montgomery asked, "Are they coming in?"

McClure advised, "He's going to walk in. He's walking in. The other guy's leaving. Now you want to take him [Garrett] down in here probably, don't you?" McClure needed constant assurance we would stop Garrett before Garrett could get to him.

Montgomery, seeing Kinsey driving away, asked, "Do you want me to have their cars [officer vehicles] stop that pick-up?"

"Yeah," I responded, but there was no need.

Kinsey drove only a few more feet, then exited the pickup and lay down in the wheat field, adjacent to the farmhouse, approximately seventy-five feet away on the west side. From there he could partially observe his partner with his binoculars. He had a thirty-eight revolver tucked in his waistband. He was totally oblivious to the fact he was covered by snipers from the moment he sat down.

Twenty more seconds passed. "Does he have a gun, Bob?" I asked.

"No, but he's probably got it in his pocket." McClure responded.

I continued preparing McClure.

"Bob, now we might let you talk to him. If he doesn't have his gun out, we're going to let you talk to him. Get him to make some juicy threats."

Appearing to be in complete compliance with the plan, McClure said "Okay." He continued, "He's probably got his gun in his front pocket. I can see it in his pants."

Montgomery then queried, "He's going to come to the front door, isn't he?"

McClure answered, "I don't know. I can tell when he turns, okay? He's probably coming in the back door, I believe. Yeah, he's coming in the back door. This is where I'll let him in when he comes behind."

Again, I repeated, "Remember, Bob: 'Grapes,' okay?"

"Okay."

Twenty more seconds passed before McClure opened the door, and Garrett walked in.

McClure initiated the contact, facing Garrett hesitatingly. "There you are."

Garrett was a stout man in his mid-fifties, with an obvious paunch, plenty of grey in his hair and a wrinkled brow. He was wearing denim trousers and a short-sleeved, plaid shirt. His face was stern and serious. Although his voice resonated as deep and authoritative, at the same time it seemed somewhat wavering and apprehensive.

Garrett started first, immediately taking charge of the conversation: "Whew, I want it to be quick!"

McClure responded, "Look, I've got a little money for you. Will you leave my family alone and . . ."

Garrett cut in, "Look, Bob. Let me tell you something."

McClure continued, "You threatened my family!"

Garrett quickly broke in, "Wait a minute! Hold on. Listen to what I'm saying. Right now!"

Then, with pointed emphasis, Garrett got right in McClure's face, and with overpowering authority while elevating the tone of his voice to match that authority, warned, "Believe me, I don't want your stash. I don't want nothin' that I don't believe belongs to me. I don't want to hurt you. I don't want to hurt your family. You've known me for a good many years. That's always the way it's been."

Then with an added bit of cold steel that left no doubt in the ear of the observer of just how far Garrett would go to back up his words, he added, "Unless you would make me. Understand that? Understand that? Okay. You can put that as a general agreement. All right. Play it cool."

By this time, McClure had uttered a succession of "okays" in hasty agreement, punctuating every sentence that Garrett blurted out. It was obvious that by then the appearance of Garrett's revolver bulging out from his hip pocket had taken its toll on McClure's nerves. He was ready to do whatever Garrett wanted.

Garrett continued, "This is very difficult for me, and I think you know, I thought you knew better. I mean, than to mention my name on the phone, but that's spilt milk."

McClure, just wanting to find a way to get this over, continued bending over backward to agree with Garrett on every sentence, each time with an acquiescing "Okay" or a "Yeah."

Finally, McClure couldn't wait any longer to escape from Garrett once and forever.

Unfortunately, McClure's idea of resolving his extreme discomfort had nothing to do with the game plan. He knew that if he sat down at the kitchen table with Garrett to induce him into making those statements that we needed to convict him of extortion, the probability of Garrett saying something that would implicate McClure in the Colombian drug deal was way too high.

McClure decided to drive the case in another direction, and instead of sitting down with Garrett in the kitchen, he headed straight for the garage.

Garrett was becoming suspicious of a set-up, and began to stammer. "But, uh . . . I . . . I . . . I . . . The bottom line is, I feel uncomfortable!"

"Do you want me to get this package or not?" McClure asked, referring to the money.

Garrett's response: "Let's . . . Let's talk." He then walked several steps in my direction, following McClure toward the door to the garage.

They would have to pass directly in front of me.

Garrett continued, "This . . . this is a hell of a strain on me and you, sir. I don't want to get set up!"

McClure responded, "And I don't want to set you up. I'll go back there and get it." This made sense to Garrett, who recalled grabbing the four thousand dollars from a shelf on the garage wall just three days before.

At this point, I could sense the mounting tension and apprehension in the room, as both men walked toward the garage where they would pass directly in front of me, and from where I would have to make a decision that could have devastating consequences, unless I did everything right.

It was obvious that McClure had jettisoned the game plan to avoid detection. He had a lot of questions to answer before the day was done, and even more to answer two years later, when I would track him down in Alaska, and make him pay for his deceit.

The words that were spoken from that moment on, by me, by Paul Garrett, and by other officers present were etched into my memory forever, as I came as close to dying as any agent in the history of the FBI.

Garrett and McClure continued moving in my direction, approximately ten feet away.

As I cradled a 12 gauge shotgun in my arms, waiting to apprehend Garrett when he passed by me, I was confident. After all, this was my weapon of choice. The magnum buckshot loads were the equivalent of firing off nine .31 caliber pellets each time I pulled the trigger. For me, this spelled maximum firepower and maximum protection.

But as Garrett approached, something didn't feel right. I sensed I was holding the wrong weapon, although it was what I was trained to use in a situation like this.

I felt a keen prompting, a still small voice, telling me to put down the shotgun and draw the .38 caliber snub-nosed revolver I packed on my hip.

I listened to that quiet prompting and put down the shotgun. I grasped my revolver, bringing it up to waist level.

I began to vacillate again.

This is crazy! I can't give up my fire power, especially if his gun is out. All those years of FBI training and teaching police departments correct fire-arms procedures can't go out the window. In life-threatening situations like this, I need maximum firepower.

Natural instincts were at war with spiritual promptings, as I gave in to my reasoning, holstered the revolver, and again picked up the shot-gun.

Garrett was now just a few feet away, with McClure just ahead of him. I had the distinct impression everything was happening in slow motion.

The promptings came again, clear and crisp, like the wind rolling off the branches of pine in the nearby forests. They were not unfamiliar. I had heard them before as a young missionary in Uruguay, seeking spiritual help, as a new bishop, struggling to help the people in my congregation, and as a father, praying to guide my children in truth. I knew I must follow them.

This time I paid more attention. I began to realize I was on the brink of a decision that would determine whether I lived or died.

It was clearly being manifested to me that Almighty God was trying His best to communicate with me.

I knew I needed to listen.

For the second time, I drew my revolver and put down the shotgun. It was a decision that saved my life.

Garrett was feeling something amiss . . . something definitely wrong, but he was unable to sense what it was, as he muttered to McClure, "You know right where to get it, don't ya? Yeah."

As Garrett came within five feet of me, he became even more apprehensive, and continued stammering, "You know, that's . . . that's like . . . like walking into a lion's den, man. You . . . you . . . you wouldn't . . . you wouldn't do that . . ."

McClure passed in front of me first, with Garrett four feet behind him. I knew it was now or never, if I were to save McClure from what would surely be a fatal encounter with Garrett. Extortionists kill their victims rather than leave a living witness who could later identify them.

I quickly stepped out into the corridor with my revolver drawn, between Garrett and his victim and yelled, "FBI, freeze!"

I had never looked down the barrel of a gun before. I have been told that when you're on the other end, that barrel looks more like a cannon barrel. I didn't see anything like that. All I saw was Garrett's .38 caliber revolver coming up to chest level, pointed right at me.

Instinctively, I fired and shot Garrett through the heart.

My bullet lodged in his spine, causing him to collapse onto his back. From there, he continued firing, even as he lay dying .

I immediately ducked back into the bathroom, crouched down, and peered around the door. Garrett fired three more bullets at me. His second and fourth rounds were .38 cartridges, loaded with pellets that penetrated into the door that I had been standing in front of. His third round, a regular bullet, also penetrated that door, which took on the appearance of Swiss cheese.

I fired again at Garrett from crouched position, near the bathroom entrance. That shot missed Garrett's head by an inch, struck the edge of the kitchen/dining area cabinet, and ricocheted back, rolling up to my feet.

With his last breath, Garrett continued shooting at me from where he lay on the floor. One pellet struck my trigger finger. Although I felt a definite sting, the round never penetrated my hand.

By now, Garrett was in his death throes, but still firing haphazardly in my direction.

★ ★ ★ ★ ★

Trooper Montgomery walked calmly out from the dining room area, and from four feet away, fired three rounds into his head.

In less than six seconds, nine shots had been fired.

The Oregon State Police crime lab personnel recreated the dynamics of everything that happened during the shooting incident. Their report indicated that Garrett was three to four feet away from me when he fired his first shot, and that I returned fire at the same distance.

When I yelled at Garrett, I threw him off guard sufficiently enough to cause him to raise up on his first shot at me. His bullet passed one quarter of an inch over my left shoulder, and embedded in the door that lead into the utility area, just before the garage. According to the lab report, and lucky for me, that bullet was a defective load that "key holed" into the door behind me

Had I not listened to those promptings, and used the shotgun instead of my snub-nose revolver, the extra second or two it would have taken me to bring the shotgun up to level would have allowed Garrett a second shot, before I got mine off. The distance would have been less than two feet . . . a sure hit.

Providence was on my side that day. I listened to those promptings, and by so doing, my life was preserved

Outside in the adjacent wheat field, William Kinsey had been watching the farmhouse nervously, as he heard the nine shots. The officers observing from outside had been studying him continuously throughout the entire incident. Upon hearing the shooting inside the house, and seeing officers enter, Kinsey panicked. He knew the end was near.

An Oregon State Police sniper yelled at him, "Put your weapon down and freeze!"

Kinsey, slowly and deliberately, put his revolver up to his head, cocked it, and pulled the trigger.

It was over.

I walked over to Garrett, who had drawn his last breath, kicked his revolver away, and told Trooper Montgomery, "Okay, if that's the way it's got to be, that's the way it's got to be. You call who you have to call, and I'll call who I have to call. Don't let this bother you. Just remember one thing. He tried to get us first."

Once the shooting was over, and it became clear everything was under control, I silently thanked the Good Lord for helping me come through unscathed.

That night on my way home, while reliving the events of the day, I felt no remorse. I knew even though I'd taken the life of another human being, it was either him or me, and he fired the first shot.

I again reflected back on the story of Laban in the Book of Mormon, how he had tried to kill Nephi and his brothers, and how instead, Nephi was able to kill him when he found him in a drunken state, and how this facilitated Nephi and his people in securing the brass plates with their genealogical records (1 Nephi 3–4).

The scripture reads:

> And it came to pass that I was constrained by the Spirit that I should kill Laban; but I said in my heart: Never at any time have I shed the blood of man. And I shrunk and would that I might not slay him.
> . . . I also knew that he had sought to take away mine own life; yea, and he would not hearken unto the commandments of the Lord; and he also had taken away our property. . . .
> Behold, the Lord slayeth the wicked to bring forth his righteous purposes. (1 Nephi 4:10–11, 13)

That night I contacted my bishop, Richard Lemmon, not because I felt guilt but because, like Nephi, I had never taken a life before and needed assurance. Bishop Lemmon understood.

It was the next day, while searching through Garrett's pickup, that I received that assurance. The interior of the vehicle was cluttered with evidence of other crimes, including illegal weapons, pedophilia, stolen property and cash, indicating Garrett and Kinsey were most likely involved in thefts, assaults, and possibly homicides in a crime spree between Florida and Elgin, Oregon.

Of major significance was the content of Garrett's wallet, especially his driver's license. The document, which was worn, frayed and bent on the corners, bore the pertinent Florida state inscriptions. The picture on it was of a man appearing much younger and somewhat thinner than the man I had last seen stretched out on the floor.

The name on it will be etched on my memory forever. It was Paul Laban Garrett!

★ ★ ★ ★ ★

During the next two years, the events leading up to the Elgin shootout were unraveled by Special Agent Mike McBride, assigned to the Bureau's Fort Pierce, Florida resident agency. His investigation led to both Robert McClure and Arnaldo Mellado being indicted by a Florida federal grand jury for narcotics violations, based on their complicity with Paul Garrett.

The indictment charged that during his 1980–1981 residence in Lantana, Florida, McClure helped formulate and direct Garrett's smuggling operation from off the Florida coast, and that he subsequently boarded the shrimp trawler and off-loaded thirty-two hundred pounds of marijuana. Mellado was also charged as an accomplice in setting up the drug deal in Colombia.

How Mellado's involvement came to light was an amazing story.

Several weeks after the shoot-out, Agent McBride called me, seeking information on a suspect he developed by the name of Arnaldo Mellano, who he believed may have been involved with Garrett and McClure.

"Hey, McBride, remember that first big car ring case that Jim Hufford, the White Knight, and I investigated in 1969, where we indicted all those car thieves and ended out being in trial for six weeks?" I asked.

"Yeah," McBride responded, "you and Hufford both put on about twenty-five pounds, eating all that Cuban food at that little dive by the courthouse."

"Okay, go to the Miami files and pull the file on the 'Pillo Gang.' Look for a picture of Arnaldo Mellado, one of the guys we put away. I think that may be the same guy as your Arnaldo Mellano. Show that photo to your witnesses. Good chance that's your guy," I assured McBride.

Shortly thereafter McBride called back and said, "Bingo! Same guy."

At the time of his arrest, Mellado was running the same gas station and towing service he had operated when I had arrested him over a decade before, as a subject in the "Pillo Gang" car ring conspiracy. In that case, he had used his business as a base of operations for processing fraudulent registrations for vehicles stolen in New York and New Jersey and transported for sale to Miami's Cuban community.

★　★　★　★　★

Subsequent to Robert McClure being indicted in the latter part of June, 1985, in West Palm Beach, Florida and the arrest warrant being issued, I flew from Seattle to Ketchikan, Alaska, where I was met by Lieutenant Ron Leighton and other officers from the Ketchikan Police Department, who accompanied me to McClure's residence, a run-down wooden house in Ketchikan's fishing section on Tongass street.

Warrant in hand, I paused for a moment on the front steps of McClure's house. A strange combination of triumph and closure prevailed over my feelings.

I knocked on the weather-stained door, and a tired McClure appeared, with a flowing beard, reflecting astonishment and appearing as though he had aged twenty years rather than just two.

A slow, startled look of recognition crossed his face, as he remembered the day, two years before, when I had saved his life. The circumstances were so different now, as I placed him in handcuffs.

On the afternoon of July 25, 1985, the following article came out in a national UPI release:

An Elgin, Oregon rancher, who was the target of a two year-long FBI undercover investigation, has been arrested in Alaska, and charged with smuggling fifty-five thousand pounds of marijuana from Colombia to Florida four years ago, agents said Thursday. Robert James McClure, forty-seven, was arrested in Ketchikan, Alaska, late Tuesday night on a federal indictment issued by a Florida grand jury, and charged with four counts of federal narcotics violations. Arnaldo Mellado was picked up in Miami on the same violations.

25

★ ★ ★ ★ ★

CALLED AS BISHOP
IN PENDLETON

APRIL 20, 1984

I was called into Portland, Oregon, for an all-agents conference and presented a special in-grade promotion for superior performance for my past year's work for the Bureau in Pendleton. The SAC announced that I had contributed significantly to the division's statistical accomplishments. I was feeling fine . . . maybe even a little haughty. After all, I was taking down a lot of bad guys out in the far reaches of Oregon and beginning to gain a lot of confidence.

Some of that confidence began to ebb when on May 20, 1984, I was called as bishop for the third time to preside over the new Pendleton Third Ward of the Walla Walla, Washington Stake. I found myself beginning the balancing act again, running the FBI operations in eight counties constituting the eastern third of the state and coordinating the activity of several hundred members of my congregation. When David Hafen, the stake president, extended me that sacred calling again, Judy looked at me and smiled that familiar "Here we go again!" smile. Then she looked at President Hafen and exclaimed, "Well, President, this is the third time. I hope he gets it right this time!"

It had been only two years since I had been released as bishop of the West Linn Ward, and although I had always held another calling when I wasn't serving as bishop, I had lulled myself into a false sense of security, thinking I had escaped the "full court press" duties of being the bishop, at least for many years to come.

Judy just looked at me, took my hand, and said, "Well, I guess our breather is over!"

McPheters family in Pendleton

On June 24, President Hafen set me apart and gave me some very significant assurances, promises, and direction:

> I was told the Lord loved me and it was He who had called me.
> I was promised I would lose no member of my ward, if I would labor with the youth.
> I was advised to spend sufficient time with my family and to make them a priority.
> I was blessed with the ability to talk to people successfully.
> I was assured my family would be blessed in giving me their support.
> I was promised I would be protected in my profession, so that I could serve for several years.

As time elapsed, and as I devoted myself as a bishop in Pendleton, I was blessed to excel as an FBI agent. The proof was there. By the end of 1984, the year I was called, President Hafen announced at a stake conference that our ward was leading the stake in activity and accomplishment. During that same time period, I obtained one-tenth of the Portland Division's criminal convictions.

The Lord had revealed the formula to me for success in my work with the Bureau: devote yourself to Him and you'll be blessed in your profession. It really did work! I had learned that principle previously, but the eternal truth of it would manifest itself even more clearly each time I was called to serve. The more I put into my church calling, the more interesting and rewarding my FBI assignments were. In fact, the most productive parts of my career with the Bureau were when I served as bishop. For me, knowing I was acceptable enough to the Lord to serve Him in the capacity of a bishop gave me the confidence to excel out on the street.

26

★★★★★

THE MOUNTAIN METH LAB

DECEMBER 30, 1984

The whirring sounds of a snowmobile were familiar to the country people in the small town of Elgin, Oregon. They used them all the time, not only for recreation, but for hunting elk and deer, gathering firewood, and for checking on livestock. But this one was coming right down the center of Main Street! With smoke belching and deafening rumble emitting from the machine, while holding the town's ears hostage, it was obvious that the snow machine was far removed from its element. The most perturbing part wasn't the fact the rider was in violation of local city ordinances, since snowmobiles were not permitted within city limits, but it was the total disregard the rider was displaying for the sensibilities of those around him.

Far removed from more appropriate venues, like woods and snowfields, the rider, a Caucasian male, age thirty-five, slightly balding with brown hair down to the bottom of his neck, seemed to care less about the fact he was violating the law. His lanky frame, at six feet six inches tall and two hundred pounds, was punctuated by a brown skullcap, a heavy parka, and Levis. Actually, he would have looked like anyone else in town were it not for the holster on his hip, with a .44 magnum Blackhawk revolver in it.

The rider, later identified as Robert Charles Mayer, had recently purchased a beautiful, expensive log home up in the woods just a few miles out of town. He figured no one in "a little hick town" like Elgin would care about the gun or where he rode his snowmobile. After all, he thought, probably everyone out here has a gun on them. This is the real west. Besides, after just getting out of the state penitentiary in California for dealing methamphetamine, Mayer was concerned about whom he might run into.

Jerry Weir, an Elgin Police Department officer, was one of the first people to take notice of Mayer's raucous entry into town.

"Hey, fella, can I have a word with you?" Officer Weir asked, as he cautiously approached the rider.

"Sure, man! What's up?" came the response.

"We have a city ordinance here against riding your machine in the downtown area. And what's up with that hog leg on your hip that you're toting?"

"Well, sir, thanks for cluing me in about your snow machine laws. Being from California, I never would have thought that would be a problem out here." Mayer was anxious to deflect any further curiosity or confrontation with the law.

Officer Weir continued. "All right. I'll just issue you a warning today, but I don't want any repeats, okay?"

The officer's sixth sense was kicking in, as his curiosity about the new fellow in town was mounting. "Now, what about my second question? I've got a real problem with that gun you're carrying. Although, it's not a violation of the law to have it, I need to tell you, you're the first guy I've seen in town packing a handgun in full view, especially a .44 magnum! It's disrupting, and you're liable to upset some of the local folks."

"No problem, sir. You won't see me in town with it anymore. I promise." Mayer seemed sincere.

Officer Weir took the serial number off the gun, as well as the identifying data from Mayer's California driver's license, determined his current address, and then let him go.

★ ★ ★ ★ ★

Shortly after Mayer had been contacted, my phone rang in the Pendleton office.

"Hey, Mike. Chief John Zea here. I've got something out here I think you'll be interested in. You may want to check it out." Zea reviewed the details of his officer's contact with Mayer. Chief Zea advised he suspected the Mayer confrontation would evolve into something big in the drug arena and was concerned his department didn't have the manpower and sufficient resources to take on the case.

"So what you're telling me, John, is this guy just shows up out of nowhere on a snowmobile, packing heat?" Zea had pressed some of my hot buttons.

"There's more to it than that. I just ran him through the National Crime Information Center (NCIC). He has two prior drug convictions. The most recent one was an arrest in California where he had developed a methamphetamine laboratory. He served hard time in prison there and was released just a few months ago."

My interest intensified. "So we got an ex-con in possession of a firearm now with a propensity for making meth. Interesting, John. Very interesting! That's one federal strike for sure, plus a lab in embryo."

"That's still only part of the story, Mike. I talked to the local realtor in town that sold him his place up on a mountain near here with well over a hundred acres, for two hundred and fifty thousand. The guy has no job and drives a new Dodge Ramcharger. Part of the home sale included several hunting rifles. He gave me all the serial numbers. There's five or six more federal charges!" Now I could tell John was frothing at the mouth.

Waves of excitement were cascading into the conversation now, bouncing back and forth between us.

Bingo! I thought. *Chief Zea has outdone himself on this one.* We had a two-time convicted felon for narcotics trafficking, in possession of multiple firearms, living in a remote ranch with one hundred acres, several miles outside of town on a mountain overlooking a valley that he paid a quarter of a million dollars for in cash. Plus the guy's driving a new vehicle, and no visible means of support.

You bet I'd let John turn this one over to the FBI. We were ready to strike gold here.

"John, this is awesome information. You know I'll take this case. Anything else?" I asked.

"Yeah. The realtor says Mayer has two or three truckloads of stuff coming in with some movers, but the loads will be intermittent. He's already moved in more than enough furniture to set up housekeeping for him, his wife, and a ten year-old son. He told me Mayer expects these other special shipments will take two more months."

John was through talking. Now, he was testing my response, curious as to how I would proceed, now that he had handed me the baton.

Zea and I had both put two and two together. "John, are you thinking what I'm thinking?"

"You know I am," came the reply.

I proceeded. "I say we watch him for two or three months and wait . . . then hit him! He's undoubtedly setting up a secret meth lab out there in no-man's-land. He thinks he's way under the radar, otherwise he never would have showed up in town driving a machine down Main Street with that Blackhawk on his hip. Let's not push him. We'll give him a couple of months to start cooking. I'll alert the Union County Sheriff Office, since Mayer lives on their turf."

"Okay. The realtor knows Mayer pretty well. He's positioned himself to know when things are going down out there." I could tell John was relishing the prospect of joining the Bureau and Union County in taking down a major drug operation in his own backyard.

I went on. "John, you're the key player here, even though it's on the county's turf. When your man, the realtor, tells us Mayer's receiving his goodies, I'll get a warrant for him and a search warrant for his residence and surrounding outbuildings, based on the guns. That will get us in the door. If we're lucky, Mayer will be cooking meth. If we see he's got sufficient product and precursors to meet federal guidelines for prosecution, we'll get an additional search warrant to search for all the drugs and accompanying ingredients, and any cash, vehicles, and other assets appearing as ill-gotten gain. We'll seize everything he has that appears could have been purchased with drug money, especially since he has no visible income. Let's see if we can get lucky!"

"I'm in!" Zea was jazzed. "Let's wait him out."

★ ★ ★ ★ ★

Two and a half months passed. Mayer had been seen in town off and on with his wife and son, driving his Ramcharger. The realtor had stayed in touch with him, but reported nothing of interest during that period.

Then the call came.

"Hey, Mike. John here. Our boy's up to something! A couple U-Hauls arrived at his place yesterday with a lot of boxed-up goods." Zea was bouncing off the roof and ready to roll.

"Let's give him a few more days, John. If it's the precursors for the dope and the glassware, he should be cooking by then. That'll give him plenty of time to unpack and set up. Let's hit him in four days." I was sure the timing would be good.

"Okay. I'll advise the county. How about 6:00 AM?" Zea asked.

"Right on, John. Nothing like an early morning drug raid to start the day. These types like to sleep in." I was loving this case already.

On February 27 I obtained warrants for Mayer's arrest and to search his house, but Zea and I still decided to wait a few more days to execute them.

On March 5, at 6:15 AM, Zea and I, along with four FBI agents from Portland, and a couple Elgin PD officers met up with several Union County Sheriff deputies at a road spur off the main highway that lead into Mayer's residence, a fairly modern, two-story brick house.

It was mid-winter and cold but beautiful. The pine groves leading up to the fringe of the log home were accented with a blanket of snow almost three feet deep. Deer trails were visible ascending and descending the snow banks, thirty to forty feet apart along the road leading into Mayer's driveway. Wisps of smoke were climbing up from the chimney, signaling that people were already stirring in the house, and that we were probably arriving too late to preserve the element of surprise.

Chief Zea then called Mayer and asked him to come to the police department to answer a few questions about his parole agreement.

We left one FBI car and one county vehicle at the place the spur intersected the main highway to prevent Mayer's escape. The rest of us drove slowly up to the house. We were just slowing up in our five vehicles, ready to park, when the garage door sprang open and Mayer charged out in his Ramcharger, obviously with his gas pedal floored. He had seen us driving up and decided to make a break for it.

We radioed the two units back at the intersection and alerted them to Mayer's escape attempt, instructing them to block the road. As we pursued our drugger, who was by himself, vehicles were skidding all over the ice, wheels grasping for a little traction. As we began to close the distance, Mayer surged forward from us with his head start. A county unit passed him and positioned itself in front of the Ramcharger, while Zea and I closed in on his side. The marked car in front of Mayer slowed to a halt, forcing him to stop. Mayer was hemmed in with nowhere to go. Within seconds, he was gazing down the barrels of drawn revolvers and shouldered shotguns.

"Turn off your engine, Mayer, and toss your keys out the window!" I ordered.

Mayer complied, voluntarily placing his hands behind his head with his fingers interlocked. He knew the drill.

I continued. "Now get out, with your hands in the air and walk backwards towards us!"

Mayer complied in total silence, as sheriff's deputies threw him down on the ground and handcuffed him, while I flashed my credentials and identified myself.

"Mayer, we have a federal warrant for your arrest for being a convicted felon in possession of a firearm, namely, a Blackhawk .44 magnum revolver. Where is it?" I awaited a response that never came. I continued with the Miranda warning.

"Okay, Mayer. You have the right to remain silent. Anything you say could be used against you in a court of law. If you decide to answer questions now, you may stop at any time. You have the right to an attorney. If you cannot afford an attorney, one will be appointed for you. Do you understand these rights?"

"Yeah," came the indifferent response. Mayer had seen the handwriting on the wall and knew he was going back to prison, but this time to do federal time.

I continued. "We have a search warrant for your house and any adjacent outbuildings to look for some rifles you bought recently and the Blackhawk. You still have those guns?"

"I ain't sayin' nothin,' man. You guys can talk to my attorney," Mayer muttered.

Chief Zea weighed in. "Have it your way, Robert. But we do need to know who all might be in that house. Can you at least give us that much information?" Zea was definitely a people person.

"Only ones there are my woman, a woman friend of hers, and my kid. That's all!" came an angry response. "But I'm sure you guys know that already." Mayer's complexion was reddening. There was still plenty of fight in him.

We decided not to take Mayer's word for who all was in the house. Sheriff's deputies maintained custody of Mayer, while the rest of us approached the house. For our safety, and to preserve whatever evidence was inside the house that could be destroyed, I kicked in the door. The frame went down with it. Adrenaline was pumping.

Mayer's wife, Genee, came to the door entry area, with her eyes looking down at the door and frame, then back at us, obviously frightened and apprehensive. As we advised her of the circumstances of her husband's arrest and the fact he was currently in custody, she showed no sign of surprise. She maintained a resigned and forlorn expression, as I advised her we held a search warrant to look for rifles we knew were recently purchased by her husband, who was a convicted felon. She told us where the rifles were.

★　★　★　★　★

Upon entering the residence, I had detected the pungent odor of methamphetamine, and the odor of its sickening poison was settling into my nostrils. The smell was emanating from the basement. Upon descending the staircase, the smell was becoming overwhelming, signaling that either the dope was cooking, or had recently been finished. Then was the time to take maximum precautions, in light of the many meth labs that had blown up in hidden kitchens and dingy cellars in the past. Lives had been lost and people maimed in such incidents, because of meth makers that really didn't know what they were doing.

As we secured the basement, we were not surprised to find a room full of vials, flasks, and other kinds of glassware and paraphernalia, being used to add to the supply of finished product that we discovered, ready to be distributed to Mayer's dealers, who were anxious to get their hands on it for distribution at top price out on the street.

Another adjacent room was discovered that was full of chemicals and precursors used to produce the methamphetamine, including muriatic acid, alcohol, iodine, anhydrous ammonia, dry ice, lye, and other items. There were also rubber gloves, rubber tubing, strainers, coffee filters, hot plates, thermometers, in addition to all kinds of glassware, all of which were used in the production of meth. The amount of finished product we found far exceeded the quantities necessary under the federal guidelines for prosecution of controlled substances. Mayer was using one room just to store the precursors for the meth and another room to store all the glassware and paraphernalia to cook it.

Now we clearly had a two-prong case against Mayer for the federal courts: one for several counts of firearms in possession of a convicted felon and another for the illegal production and distribution of a federally-controlled substance.

Zea and I had timed it just right. It couldn't have been better. Once we had concluded the search, we had seized ten rifles, eight handguns (including the Blackhawk .44 magnum revolver), thousands of rounds of ammunition, two boxes of dynamite, seven thousand dollars in cash, several diamonds and other precious stones, some valuable coins, some gold and silver products, over thirty-five thousand dollars worth of chemistry hardware which we later donated to Portland State University, and enough finished product and precursors to produce almost six million dollars worth of methamphetamine in street value.

Scott Lawrence, Drug Enforcement Agency (DEA), in Portland, advised that although he calculated Mayer was producing two or three pounds of methamphetamine a week, he estimated the lab was capable of producing ten pounds of meth or "speed" a week, with a wholesale value of one hundred and forty thousand dollars and a retail value of three hundred and eighty thousand dollars. Other agents from the DEA described the drug bust as possibly the biggest to date in Oregon and one of the biggest in the history of the Northwest.

Joe Powers, a DEA chemist from the San Francisco DEA laboratory, advised that from his analysis of drug heists from the eleven western states their lab covered in the prior ten years, Mayer's operation was the second largest he had seen. He further indicated the finished product Mayer had produced was eighty percent pure, making it some of the purest meth he had ever seen produced.

In addition to what we found in the house, we also seized ten vehicles, including the Dodge Ramcharger and other passenger cars, some pickups, snowmobiles, and a few other vehicles. We also seized Mayer's house, under the federal forfeiture statutes. Under those forfeiture laws, there were "adoption" provisions, allowing us to transfer ownership of all these assets over to the Union County officials, whose very limited operating budget was instantly and royally enhanced.

Once the search was completed and the items seized were loaded into a U-Haul truck for delivery to the Portland FBI office, I jumped onto one of the snowmobiles and searched Mayer's acreage for any additional "fruits of the crime." I found nothing additional, but truly enjoyed the outdoor search in the woods surrounding the Mayer residence, while privately relishing the success and blessing of our endeavor.

Meanwhile, Chief John Zea was celebrating in the privacy of his small office, back in the city that Mayer had so haughtily termed "the little hick town of Elgin."

Several months later, on May 13, 1985, Robert Charles Mayer pled guilty to the drug charges, in exchange to dropping the weapons charges, and was sentenced to twelve years in the custody of the U.S. Attorney General.

The guilty plea paved the way for the local Union County authorities to keep many of the items we seized at Mayer's residence, including four vehicles, a backhoe, and a boat.

It was subsequently rumored that the Union County Prosecutor was driving around in a new Dodge Ramcharger.

27

★ ★ ★ ★ ★

OTHER PENDLETON HAPPENINGS

1985

While in Pendleton, I continued to be called upon to assist the Portland Division SWAT team. During the first quarter of 1985, we joined in a nation-wide raid on the "Bandidos Motorcycle Gang" at Bellingham, Washington, near the Canadian border. We arrested several of them for drug trafficking.

★ ★ ★ ★ ★

During that same time period, we conducted operations against the "Neo-Nazis" on the Oregon-California border. This was a militant group that violently manifested their hatred for African-Americans and Jews.

★ ★ ★ ★ ★

We put a drug operation out of business at "Ten Mile Lake," near Coos Bay, Oregon, after quietly crossing the lake in the middle of the night on small boats and making a stealth attack on the drugger's cabin at 4:00 AM.

My assignment was to take the point and "neutralize" the subject's pit bull with a well-placed head shot, if it began barking and giving away our position. I didn't like the idea and neither did Stan Renning, a veteran agent who happened to love dogs and was one of the best football players ever to come out of the state of Montana. Stan could get pretty hard-nosed when it came to killing dogs. It was finally agreed that I would either mace the animal or try to knock it unconscious, or just scare it off any way I could, but no shot would be fired.

Handling the dog turned out to be a moot point. When we ascended the second floor of the cabin onto an adjacent deck, the dog was waiting. When the pit bull realized he had camouflaged visitors arriving in the pitch black of night, and stared into our blackened faces, he began backing up rapidly, whining, in low, guttural staccato, and finally tumbled off the edge of the deck. We observed him quickly pick himself up and lumber off into the woods without a sound.

With the dog out of the picture, we hit the door and arrested the drug trafficker, whose only request was that one of us would "adopt" his dog. The man's other associates in drug trafficking were also arrested in other locations that day. A huge stash of methamphetamine and other chemical precursors were recovered.

The same day an FBI agent brought home a dog.

★ ★ ★ ★ ★

Summer 1986

It had been a boring, quiet day in downtown Pendleton. I was pulling out onto a street, just around the corner from the Pendleton Police Department, when I observed a Native American man and woman in their mid-thirties staggering out of a tavern and screaming out profanities, as they worked their way down the opposite side of the street that I was parked on. Several women and children who were shopping in the area were being forced to take in their rudeness and profanity.

I pulled up just across the street from them and rolled down my window on the driver's side.

"Hey, you two need to cut back on the profanity! Look at the people around you here. I'm a law enforcement officer. I'm ordering you to not be so disorderly."

Upon hearing me from across the street, the man, barrel-chested, shorter than average, but very stout, looked around, confused, trying to hone in on my voice. When he finally observed me through his drunken stupor, his face flushed with anger, and he started across the street for me.

I rolled up the window and called the police department for a back up, knowing that what was about to transpire, me being assaulted, would constitute a local violation that would have to be tried in the Umatilla County Courthouse.

I anticipated correctly. Just as I finished rolling up the window, a fist made contact with it, knuckles first, and blood splattered all over the glass next to my head. As the assailant pulled back his fist, he stared at me through reddened, inebriated eyes, and then walked away with the woman following him. Neither of them could think ahead enough to realize the police department was only a block and a half away, and they were walking right towards it.

I rounded the corner and parked about a hundred feet from the police department, as I watched Officer Ted Burrows walk out and confront the couple. Knowing he was the one that would now need a back up, I exited my car and walked towards him and the couple I had radioed him about.

"Hi, Ted! Here's what happened with these two." Just as I said that, the man turned around, and noticing I was next to him, tried to deliver a round-house punch. I grabbed his arm, took him down into the dirt, and was going to handcuff him, when I felt the pain of something hard banging into my ribs. The woman had come up behind me before Officer Burrows could stop her and was kicking me as hard as she could.

While keeping the man's head wedged into my chest with my left arm, I grabbed the woman's arm, pulled her down to the ground and pinned her with my right arm. I'd never had to subdue a woman before, but under the circumstances, it didn't bother me a bit. Burrows and a couple other officers from the police department had both subjects into custody within seconds.

As I pulled myself up off the ground, covered with dirt, bloody scratches on my neck, and my shirt untucked, I noticed my son, Shad, was standing a half a block away, having taken in the whole scene. He had a story to tell in school the next day.

Both the man and woman were convicted under county law for assaulting me.

★ ★ ★ ★ ★

Being a bishop and an FBI agent simultaneously, I tried to be as nice and as charitable as possible with people I had to arrest. A lady in Halfway, Oregon, who I caught embezzling thirty thousand dollars from a bank confessed her crime to me and later wrote me a "Thank you" card for being a "nice guy".

There were other times, however, when I had to temper my quest for being humane with realty and my need for self-preservation. One such instance occurred when I had to transport an individual I had arrested from Vale, Oregon, to Ontario, Oregon. I was unable to find a local officer to accompany me in transporting the subject, a twenty-nine-year-old Hispanic male, six feet five inches tall and 270 pounds, and very muscular. I was forty-six-years-old and weighed only 200 pounds. I could barely get the handcuffs to go around his wrists. After I had placed a belly chain around the subject, then looped it through the handcuffs and seat-belted him in the passenger seat, where I could keep an eye on him, the conversation between us went something like this:

I spoke first. "Terry, guys as big as you have been known to break out of these handcuffs and restraints before, and since I don't have anyone with me to watch you while I drive, and since it's a fifteen-minute trip from here to Ontario, we need to get one thing straight."

"And what's that?" he replied, looking inquisitive, yet apprehensive.

I continued. "You behave and we'll have a friendly visit on the way to Ontario. But if you don't, I'll have to shoot you."

Terry understood and said jokingly, "I'm too young to die." We had a nice chat on the way to Ontario, where he was booked in on a "material witness" warrant without incident.

★　★　★　★　★

New cases, with new investigative challenges, were always popping up in Eastern Oregon. It was as if a huge Pandora's box was suddenly opening, with all kinds of new looks.

On August 6, 1987, George Raymond Cree was charged with sexually abusing his own three-year-old son on the Umatilla Indian Reservation and then fleeing to Portland to avoid prosecution. Special Agent Jim Russell, a top investigator out of Portland, met me at the airport and accompanied me to "Flossie's," a gay bar downtown, where we found Cree, arrested him, and made arrangements to have his son cared for.

★　★　★　★　★

On April 1, 1987, Richard Lee Vieyra, a major supplier of cocaine to Baker and Union counties, was sentenced to prison, following a three month investigation where I was able to convince a couple to cooperate and testify. They both had been addicted to cocaine through attending parties where small amounts of the drug in powder form, called "lines," were doled out. They were so hooked that they would go days at a time without eating, while inhaling powder up their noses. When their marriage was on the brink of dissolution, and they knew they would face criminal charges for illegal possession of a controlled substance, they chose to cooperate with me and the local authorities and bring down Vieyra and his gang of conspirators.

★　★　★　★　★

On July 21, 1988, I made an appointment with Michael Farley, who had robbed several banks in Portland and Seattle, representing myself as Jim Wilson, a Pendleton realtor. I told Farley I had some land I wanted to show him east of Pendleton, near Meacham, Oregon. I had heard from an informant, who gave me Farley's phone number, that he was looking for land there and that he had enough bank robbery loot to buy it. I had checked out the land the day before, so I could talk intelligently about it. Farley agreed to meet me at a Denny's restaurant in Pendleton the following day. The local police had been alerted and were standing by.

When I pulled in at Denny's at the appointed time, Farley was sitting out in the parking lot in his car with the window rolled down on the driver's side.

I approached him. "Hello there, Mr. Farley. I'm Mike McPheters, with the FBI."

He flashed a smile and began laughing. "Sure you are! I know who you are. You're Jim Wilson, the realtor. FBI! Right. That's funny. So, shall we go in and visit for awhile about that property?" He motioned toward the restaurant.

"Hey, Farley, I really am with the FBI. I'm not kidding, and you are under arrest for bank robbery. I am not Jim Wilson. I am Special Agent Mike McPheters, FBI."

Farley was now out of his car, standing in front of me, but beginning to turn toward Denny's restaurant. "I'm sorry, man, but if you're not Jim Wilson, I don't know who you are. But Jim Wilson, the guy I'm supposed to meet must be in that restaurant, waiting for me, and that's where I'm going!"

I flashed my credentials and again identified myself as an FBI agent. I then pocketed the credentials, drew my revolver, pulled out my handcuffs, and snapped them on Farley's wrists. He was speechless and wet his pants.

I accompanied Farley back to my office, where he admitted to six bank robberies: three in San Diego, two in Portland, and one in Yakima, Washington.

28

★ ★ ★ ★ ★

KIDNAPPED

JULY 9, 1985

For five-year-old Amanda Sargent and her two sisters, the day was just another warm, sunny adventure, to be enjoyed frolicking with their friends in the public swimming pool at Yantis Park in Milton-Freewater, Oregon. This is where the three girls spent at least half of their long, carefree days during summer vacation. It was about 3:00 PM. Their mother, Phyllis, left Amanda in the care of her sisters at the pool for a few hours, while she was at work.

Milton-Freewater was a sleepy laid-back community of about six thousand residents, just south of the border with Washington in northeast Oregon. The city enjoyed a very low crime rate, in spite of its diversified demographics, divided between North American and Hispanic elements.

As Amanda and her sisters were splashing one another and cavorting about, the last impression to ever enter their minds was that they were being watched.

Patrick Thomas Redmond was a white male, age fifty-seven, approximately six feet three inches tall, with a lithe, slim build, grayish-blonde hair, full mustache, reddish complexion, with chiseled facial features, and a hardened appearance acquired through outlandish living and a protracted prison stint. He, deceivingly enough, bore a genuinely kind, grandfatherly appearance. He had been released from prison on October 5, 1984, with an insatiable appetite for little girls still intact. Redmond had been sought on parole violation charges by local authorities since February.

Small towns like Milton-Freewater, with unsuspecting populaces, were prime targets for recidivist offenders like Redmond. He drove slowly around the block that encompassed the public pool area, with his eyes narrowing, honing in on Amanda. He was tantalized, almost to distraction, by her little pre-pubescent body, clothed in a bright blue swimsuit under a green blouse and pink shorts. He had parked and re-parked his car repeatedly to facilitate his focus on Amanda, to the exclusion of all the rest of the children in the pool area. He had allowed his inner excitements to run away with complete disregard for the possible repercussions of the action he was intent upon carrying out.

Redmond was a loner, a deprived pedophile who cared little about anything other than indulging his sick cravings that only little girls could satisfy.

Little Amanda, with her cherubic grin reflecting her gleeful excitement, laughed as she plunged repeatedly into the shallower end of the pool, her favorite spot. She was of average height and weight for her age. Her brown hair was highlighted by short bangs tumbling down over her tiny face with pretty petite features.

After having studied Amanda's childish form and countenance and having listened to her innocent, high-pitched laughter for over two hours, Redmond knew that he had to have her and that he would go to any lengths to separate her from her sisters . . . those other girls who she always seemed to gravitate towards.

Redmond made every effort to park as close to the water fountain as possible, where he observed the sisters to separate occasionally to quench their thirst. His pulse quickened as he anticipated they would separate again at some point. He resolved to force himself to be patient as he formed his plan to entice Amanda away. He waited apprehensively as he sat parked in the driver's seat of a cluttered older model, a 1969 pale green Chrysler Newport bearing Washington license tags.

Since Redmond had been released from prison, he had been living with his wife in a mobile trailer park near Ogden, Utah. He would be heading in that direction again, once he had Amanda to keep him company. He would be careful and take care not to draw attention to himself in the pool area. Besides, the longer he was parked there, the more he would walk about and would begin to blend in with the environment of Yantis Park. In his own sick mind, he would reflect a grandfatherly image, consistent with his age and appearance. Perhaps Amanda would even think he was just an employee there.

As Redmond pursued his fixation upon Amanda, he thought, I can wait. It will be worth it. She'll come for a drink soon. He was right. At approximately 3:00 PM, Amanda walked in the direction of Redmond's vehicle, close to the water fountain and somewhat distant from her sisters and the pool personnel. As she walked slowly toward the water fountain, it became obvious to Redmond that Amanda had taken note of him, seated in the driver's seat. He lowered the passenger window and slid over from the driver's side, calling out to her.

"Hi there! I've really been enjoying the day here at the park. I bet you have too. Would you like to go for an ice cream? Tell me, what's your favorite flavor?"

"Chocolate," responded Amanda.

"Well, hop on in, and I'll take you back to the ice cream shop. I'll have another one and get you a chocolate double-scoop. Then I'll bring you back to your friends."

"Okay," responded Amanda excitedly, as she began to savor the thought and flavor of her favorite ice cream.

After two or three steps, however, she had second thoughts, stopped and stared at Redmond, who had become a little more emboldened as he opened his passenger door, got out, stood up, and invited her in.

"What's your name?" Redmond asked.

"Amanda," she responded warily, as she gazed at Redmond with his graying hair and friendly countenance. She perceived he was a kind man, much like her own grandfather. He was just trying to be nice. She took a step closer to the car. She hadn't eaten for several hours, and now the concept of chocolate ice cream was overpowering. Since Redmond wasn't coming across as a threat, she took a few more steps toward the green Chrysler, as Redmond reiterated his former statement that he'd have her back within just a few minutes.

When Amanda was within Redmond's reach, she suddenly felt a grimy lock on her right wrist, as she was pulled off-balance and whisked into the Chrysler. As Redmond slid across the passenger seat with Amanda in tow, he reached over her with his left hand and locked the passenger door. He then raised the window to mute Amanda's futile cries for help.

With his left hand on the steering wheel and right foot on the gas, Redmond drove slowly out of the Yantis Park area, inconspicuously, with his right hand over Amanda's mouth, pushing her downwards onto the floor and out of sight. He continued driving until he reached a quiet, dirt road, just out of the city limits, where he slowed to a stop, removed Amanda's clothing, and unleashed the first installment of his pedophiliac frenzy, an act that would be repeated continuously over a two day period.

★ ★ ★ ★ ★

Milton-Freewater was thirty-five miles from my office in Pendleton. The phone rang at 3:30 PM, with a call from the Milton-Freewater police, advising me regarding Amanda's abduction. The local police had an all points bulletin out for Redmond's vehicle, with his description, after a clerk at a Milton-Freewater motel where Redmond had taken Amanda had suspected something was wrong and furnished the license number on Redmond's Chrysler. They had described him to the police. The Chrysler was registered to Redmond at an address in Walla Walla, Washington. The police had checked out that address and the motel in Milton-Freewater with negative results.

Subsequent to the all points bulletin being issued by the Milton-Freewater Police Department, intense efforts were made by the Walla Walla, Washington Police Department, the Oregon State Police, the Umatilla County Sheriff's Office, and myself to assist the Milton-Freewater authorities.

Within an hour of being notified of Amanda's abduction, I was in Milton-Freewater, checking the area around Yantis Park, where Amanda had disappeared. I touched base with the local police department and obtained all the descriptive data they had available regarding Redmond's identity from his vehicle registration. I also contacted Amanda's parents, Harvey and Phyllis Sargent. The Sargents had no suspect in mind, but passed on the information to me regarding Redmond that they had gleaned from talking to Amanda's sisters.

I felt frustrated and inept, as the image of my own three daughters flashed into my mind and considered how innocent and precious they were. I couldn't begin to imagine how I would feel if what was surely happening to Amanda would ever happen to them. I knew about men like Redmond, who eke out the lives and souls of their victims and rob them of their childhood . . . men who live forever in crazed perversion, bent only on satisfying their sick lust. I knew that in most instances men like this were usually careful not to leave living witnesses of their depravity. It infuriated me that Redmond had a healthy head start and ample time to have his way with this innocent little person. I knew that we would arrest Redmond eventually, since we had him identified, but thought, *What would Amanda suffer in the meantime?*

Once I was assured the police had entered all the descriptive data regarding Redmond and his vehicle into the National Crime Information Center (NCIC), so that he would be identified and arrested if stopped by any questioning officer, I began patrolling the city on my own, thinking maybe Redmond was still around.

I also spent hours that day searching all of the areas adjacent to Milton-Freewater: nine miles north to the Washington border near College Place and eleven miles south to Athena and Weston, Oregon. This was all to no avail. Redmond had taken Amanda thirty-four miles south to Pendleton and headed east on I-84 towards his home in Ogden, Utah.

Two days later, I received a phone call from the Salt Lake City FBI Office that to this day qualifies as one of the happiest moments of my FBI career. Amanda had approached a truck driver in Liberty Park in downtown Salt Lake City. She was confused, frightened, and hungry, but alive! Amanda had approached the truck driver and told him she had been kidnapped from another park in the state of Washington. She told local authorities that Redmond had dropped her off at the park around noon the day after he had abducted her and told her to play at the playground while he went to get some hamburgers, but he had never come back. I was overwhelmed with joy, as I anticipated being able to communicate that news to Amanda's parents.

Harvey and Phyllis Sargent were reunited with Amanda at the Metropolitan Hall of Justice in Salt Lake City the morning after she was found in Liberty Park. Phyllis indicated that Amanda seemed to be unaffected by what she had gone through, saying, "She still has that sparkle in her eye!" Harvey said it had been very tense for them, while they waited for word of Amanda's appearance, but indicated they never lost faith she would be found. "You have to have hope," he stated.

I was given another great bit of news the next morning when I was notified by the Ogden Police that Redmond had been apprehended by them and the FBI early Thursday morning at his Ogden home, where he was found asleep in the same car he had abducted Amanda in. The officers indicated they had located "strong physical evidence" that Amanda had been in the vehicle. The arrest had taken place between 1:00 and 2:00 AM.

I filed a federal complaint against Redmond for kidnapping. The prosecutor, Eileen Bowman, was a lady gifted with skill in dealing with child witnesses. She was determined to take Redmond down with a life sentence. Aggravated Kidnapping was one of the few federal charges that would bring a life sentence. Redmond was a prime candidate.

Ms. Bowman was meticulous in her preparation for trial. We spent days acquainting Amanda with the U.S. Court system. We accompanied her and her mother into the U.S. District Court room in Portland, Oregon, where the case would be tried. We visited with her for hours, as casually as possible, about Redmond and what he had done to her, continuously emphasizing that she was not at fault for anything that had happened to her but that she was the victim of a depraved human being, who was evil to the core. We educated Amanda in the courtroom procedures, familiarized her with the witness chair, and described the judges, the court reporters, and indicated where her antagonist would be seated, as well as his legal counsel, and assured her that from where the prosecutor and I, as well as her parents, would be seated, we would never be more than a few short seconds away from her.

After several interviews with me and the prosecutor, and always with her mother present, Amanda began to respond. It was then that we discovered how amazingly adroit this little girl was, as she described how she was abused. Weeks later, at Redmond's trial, little Amanda, who had then turned six, had her chance to tell what happened to a jury.

Ms. Bowman had reviewed the questions with Amanda in such a way that she wouldn't be surprised or embarrassed by any of them. However, in spite of all our preparation, we had feared it would be a daunting challenge for a six-year-old girl to accomplish what lay ahead of her. Would Amanda freeze once Redmond entered the courtroom? Would she be re-traumatized when she was asked to recall to a jury of people she didn't know the terrible things that had happened to her? Would Redmond's attorney badger her to the point that she would misspeak or stumble?

None of that happened. When Amanda took the stand, she did it with poise and self-control, rarely found in a six-year-old speaking to strangers in a child-friendly home setting, let alone before a judge in a black robe, twelve adult jurors who she didn't know and who were staring at her, and a room full of attorneys and legal staff, as well as a courtroom full of reporters and onlookers.

Ms. Bowman, the federal prosecutor, asked Amanda to explain and expand upon her two-day nightmare. She did so artfully, displaying a childish innocence and overpowering credibility. She explained the crimes Redmond perpetrated upon her in the same vile terminology he used while forcing himself upon her. She conveyed the details of her captivity and abuse to an irate jury, who observed Redmond with pent-up contempt.

The government offered expert forensic testimony, including presentation of fiber hair transfer, fingerprints, and direct testimony from several key witnesses, including Amanda, FBI agents that arrested Redmond, and others.

As the jury cast angry glimpses toward Redmond during the trial, he became gravely aware that he would soon spend the remainder of his life incarcerated among inmates who, in spite of their own crimes, would despise him for what he had done to a little five-year-old girl. He panicked inwardly as he heard his attorney raise argument after argument in his defense, all of which he knew appeared totally fabricated and transparent to the jury.

During the trial, it was clear that the jury was angered by Redmond's attorney's efforts to confuse and intimidate a six-year-old witness, and as his attorney did this, Redmond further realized how quickly his stock was soaring south with the jury.

On December 23, 1985, when all the evidence was in, Redmond's defense was deflated. The jury was only out forty minutes, and returned a verdict of guilty, convicting Redmond of kidnapping. He was subsequently ordered by the Court to serve a life sentence at a high-security prison in Marion, Illinois.

For me, the satisfaction of Redmond's life sentence was eclipsed only by the joy of that telephone call I had made to Amanda's parents, advising them she was found safe in Salt Lake City. The case was a supreme triumph for the FBI, made possible by the courage and mental strength of a five-year-old girl who suffered depravity and inhumane abuse that no child should ever have to endure.

Amanda's parents, family, and friends worked diligently to help her retrieve her childhood and overcome the memories of her abduction.

29

$\star\star\star\star\star$

THE DEMISE OF KENDALL ARTHUR

DECEMBER 1986

Indian Reservation work has always been some of the more dangerous work the FBI has been tasked with. Never has that been proven more poignantly than on June 26, 1975, when Special Agents Ron Williams and Jack Coler were attacked by members of the American Indian Movement (AIM) in the Jumping Bull compound on the Pine Ridge Indian Reservation at Oglala, South Dakota, and were shot to death by tribal members there.

Leonard Peltier, accused of executing one of the agents who was wounded at point blank range, and other AIM members were subsequently held responsible for the killings and were prosecuted and incarcerated. For a fifteen year period, from 1982 through 1997, I investigated crimes committed by Native Americans on the Umatilla Reservation in Eastern Oregon and the Northern Ute-Ouray Reservation in Northeastern Utah, which was located thirty miles from the Vernal Utah FBI office. I worked among the Umatillas, Paiutes, Nez Perce, Warm Springs, and Northern Ute tribes.

The FBI shares concurrent jurisdiction with the Bureau of Indian Affairs (BIA) for investigating felonies (crimes punishable by one year or more in prison or at least a $1,000 fine) that occur on Indian Reservations. The Bureau shares the same jurisdiction on other government reservations, including military bases and national parks.

While assigned to the reservations, I was called upon to assist BIA investigators and tribal police officers in felony investigations and was often asked to assume a lead role in investigating homicides, assaults resulting in serious injury, and child abuse cases. When a tribal member was found deceased, I determined whether the death was natural, a suicide, or a homicide. That decision was based upon gunpowder burns, proximity of weapons near the crime scene, angle of bullet entry, witness testimony, or the absence of any of these. Alcohol was found to be a common denominator or the causal factor in the majority of the deaths.

Some of the homicides were almost predictable. When certain tribal personalities were out of prison and on the same reservation at the same time, the fireworks were almost sure to go off . . . like the ongoing feud between Kendall Arthur and a man by the name of Big Sammy. These two men who both resided on the Umatilla Indian Reservation near Pendleton, Oregon, hated each other with a passion. When they were both out of prison at the same time, the local police would be notified and the entire community put on alert for drive-by shootings and drunken assaults. No one seemed to know the exact source of animosity between these two men, because it was always something different. During my eight and a half years investigating crimes committed by these two men, I sent them both away to prison repeatedly. Kendall Arthur had a slight edge on Big Sammy for recidivism (repeat offenses). I had arrested him previously for being a convicted felon in possession of a firearm, sex offenses, and property crimes. His last offense, however, had the most devastating ramifications.

I had just finished my weekly youth interviews on a Wednesday evening, trying my best to convince some teenagers it was in their best interest to avoid R-rated movies and alcoholic beverages when the phone rang in my church office.

"Hello. This is Bishop McPheters."

The voice on the other end was urgent. It was the dispatcher from the Umatilla Tribal Police Department. "Agent McPheters, the Chief asked me to notify you that Kendall Arthur is at it again. This time he's hit Johnny Tall Bear over the head with a wood maul."

A wood maul? I thought. *You've got to be kidding! No one's going to survive that.*

"Did Tall Bear die?" I asked.

The dispatcher replied, "No. He's in intensive care at the hospital in Pendleton. They say he'll survive."

"How many witnesses are there, and where's Kendall Arthur?" I asked.

"Arthur's girlfriend, Martina Irene Reed, was supposed to have been at the crime scene when the crime occurred. We think she may have hidden Arthur's gun. Tall Bear's in no condition to be interviewed. There were a couple of other witnesses who still haven't been identified. As far as we know, Arthur's gone, but no one knows where."

I recoiled instantly, when I heard the word "gun." The thirty-six-year-old Arthur was a convicted felon several times over. I knew we may never be able to convict him for the wood maul assault, but if he had a gun on his person when he did it, under federal law, that would be a surefire "slam dunk" conviction for "Felon In Possession of a Firearm," an offense that would keep Arthur off the streets for another five years.

"Did you say gun?" I asked anxiously.

"Yeah. Martina had it," was the response.

It was already about 8:30 PM. I knew Arthur was "out-of-pocket" and Martina may be drinking. The other witnesses were probably tribal members that would not be going anywhere. Besides, I needed to talk to everyone when they were sober.

"Tell the chief I'll be out first thing in the morning, and I'll need an officer there to assist me with the interviews, if you could arrange that," I asked.

The dispatcher assured me an officer would be available.

I was up bright and early and headed out for the Reservation, seven miles out of Pendleton. The tribal officer assigned to help me drove ahead on the road that led out to the house where Kendall Arthur had bashed in Tall Bear's head with the wood maul. Although several witnesses had been present at the crime scene and had surely witnessed the assault, no one wanted to go into any detail, knowing that if Arthur discovered who had ratted him out, there would be another wood maul incident or a bullet in the back of someone's head. But that wasn't the only reason. The Native American instincts were to protect their own people where someone's future was at stake, even if that person had acted maliciously or criminally. It would not be ethical in Indian culture to betray someone to the police or to expose them to outside influences which could harm them, including white men and even tribal police officers.

★　★　★　★　★

That fact of tribal culture had become clear to me previously, when I had responded to a Christmas Eve assault by tribal members, all cousins, residing in a community near Goldendale, Washington, near the Columbia River, along the southern border of the state. In a drunken rage, several family members all began arguing over ownership of some family dogs. One young woman ended up spending the night out in a snow bank with a lacerated forehead, having been scalped by her cousins. Another male cousin had his head split open with a hammer. The young woman survived and began recovering the next day, but the man ended up in a Portland hospital, where I was assigned to interview him.

As I approached the young man, who's head wrapping gave the appearance of a turban, and identified myself and stated the purpose of my interview, he handed me a piece of paper and pen, indicating that he was unable to speak.

I came right to the point. "Who did this to you?" I asked.

The victim looked at me, curiously hesitant, and then with extenuating complications, barely scratched out the names of two of his assailants, his own cousins.

I asked for more details. He again picked up the pen in his right hand, the paper pad in his left, and commenced writing. His pen never touched the paper, as he strained to see his writing surface on it. He became increasingly frustrated, realizing his writing was not there. He was void of any understanding or recognition as to why not. As his pen hand continued passing several inches over the surface of the paper without ever coming close to touching it, it was obvious the young man felt he was losing his mind. The terror in his eyes betrayed the serious damage to the portions of his brain where the hammer had repeatedly fallen, the same parts that controlled the motor skills in his hands that, under normal conditions, would have permitted him to write.

Months later, when I was subpoenaed to testify in State court for the prosecution, regarding my interview with the young man, he denied ever having contact with me and ever having furnished me any information regarding the identities of the cousins who had almost killed him. In fact, none of the family members who had seen me at the hospital that night would acknowledge that I had even been there. Because of this collective effort by the family to completely erase my presence in the victim's hospital room that night after Christmas Day, I was not even called upon to testify. I drove the one hundred and sixteen miles back to Portland, never knowing what the final outcome was, but fairly confident the two guilty cousins would go free. Apparently the young lady who was scalped and thrown into the snow bank also conveniently forgot the identities of her assailant cousins.

Based on the Goldendale investigation, I was not surprised that witnesses in Tall Bear's assault were playing games with me.

★　★　★　★　★

As each witness we contacted at the scene of the Tall Bear assault skirted the issues and insisted on remaining anonymous, one central piece of information kept emerging, and that was that Arthur's girlfriend, Martina, had hidden Arthur's gun so the police wouldn't find him with it. I knew we had to interview Martina and find that gun.

First came Martina. The interview was fruitless. She denied any knowledge of the wood maul incident and categorically denied ever seeing Arthur with a gun. That denial would become disastrous for her, just a couple months later. I searched the area adjacent to the crime scene for several hours with numerous tribal police officers assisting me, but we never recovered the gun.

Two months later, I received a call from the sister of Leah Alice Tahkeal, age twenty, another of Arthur's girlfriends, who advised me Arthur had returned to the reservation several weeks prior and had began a relationship with Leah, who moved in with him into a cabin near the community of Adams in the Thornhollow area, several miles away from reservation headquarters. The sister said that at first Leah would come home every few days, but they had not heard from her now for several months. She said that was very unusual for Leah, who had a young son who missed her very much and who she normally would have visited by now. Leah's sister stated she went to Arthur's cabin the day before, but no one answered the door. She noticed snow piled up on the roof that would normally not be there if a fire had been burning inside. She also noticed that around the cabin there were no car tracks or footprints. She had smelled something strong and noxious near the cabin and indicated she feared it was Leah's body. She supplied all the details regarding the location of the cabin.

I immediately briefed police Chief Robert Wilcox and asked him to meet me at the police department in a half hour. Soon he, I, and another tribal officer were on our way to Arthur's cabin, for which I had obtained a federal search warrant. As we walked up to the front door, the smell of death was overwhelming. We forced the door, entered, and found ourselves surrounded by four walls of a living room covered with blood splatters.

Hanging on the entrance to a bedroom was an old Spanish-style sword with blood stains all over it. We immediately could predict who we would find in the bedroom, and we were right. Lying there naked, face up on the bed, with an eagle feather between her breasts to help take her into the Spirit World, was Leah Tahkeal, the sister of the young lady who had called me earlier. The body contained several entry marks, lacerations and punctures, where the sword had been repeatedly thrust. The hands of the corpse were placed ceremoniously over the stomach. Her feet and lower body were carefully arranged with the toes pointing straight up. Her eyelids were shut, while her head was positioned so it could be looking directly to Heaven. It was obvious the girl had been dead at least a couple months.

We contacted the state medical examiner, Dr. William Brady, then cordoned off the cabin and preserved the sword as evidence. The Chief summoned other officers to assist in preserving all the crime scene evidence and in taking photographs.

We knew it would be at least a half-hour before the other officers, the state medical examiner, and lab personnel arrived. That gave us just enough time to pursue information written in the most interesting evidence Arthur had left behind, a spiral notebook located near the victim, and in the apparent handwriting of Kendall Arthur, which read as follows:

> *I am here to say my last saying. I have killed twice. Whether anyone can believe this, I never meant to. Martina is buried between two pine trees, out by the front road. Leah Alice is laying here beside me.*

It appeared that Arthur had spent some time lying with Leah, after he killed her. The note continued:

> *I truly wish I could lay beside her and follow. Although I know in due time, I soon will. I love Alice, love her so very dearly—and Martina. I have no excuse for these actions except alcohol and jealousy. I am sober now. It is morning and I see the aftermath of horror. It is so terrible. I wish I had never awakened. Alcohol has won. You people will never understand, except that I am a twisted person, but not until consumed by the booze. I do not know what I am going to do, but I hope I die soon. Prison is worse than death.*

We searched the forest grove behind the cabin and found two huge pine trees about eighteen to twenty feet apart, within forty yards of the cabin, where the earth had obviously been disturbed. We shoveled in earnest, and within minutes struck onto a foot and ankle protruding from a bundle, wrapped in canvas. Within ten minutes, I was lifting Martina's body from her shallow grave.

This was the same Martina Reed that had made it impossible for us to arrest her future murderer, just a few weeks before . . . the same Martina that had "stood by her man" by hiding his gun, to protect him from the law, allowing him to run free and eventually take her life. The irony of Martina's death haunted me. I recalled the day on May 10, 1984, when I had arrested Arthur for raping, beating, and threatening to murder another woman on the reservation. Martina was a member of the Yurok Tribe, and had come to Oregon from California and had moved onto the Umatilla Reservation two years prior to her death. She had two children living in California and one in Canada, who would never see their mother again.

Because of the advanced state of decay of the victims' bodies, Dr. Brady, the State Medical Examiner, was not able to determine the exact cause of death, so he had to pronounce that both women had died of "traumatic asphyxiation," which only means the victims stopped breathing because of a traumatic incident . . . something other than natural causes.

That afternoon, I obtained an arrest warrant from the United States Attorney in Portland, Oregon, for Arthur, based upon the murders of the two women, and entered that information, along with all his descriptive data, into the National Crime Information Center, so he would be picked up if stopped by any local law enforcement agency. The manhunt for Arthur intensified considerably over a large area, from the Reservation to Pendleton, to Portland. The Oregon State Police also searched for him through several of the rural areas of the state.

We determined through local tribal sources that Arthur had gone to Portland and was living somewhere near the "skid row" area of Burnside. There, FBI agents began patrolling with the fugitive's photo.

On December 23, 1986, Special Agent in charge of the Portland office, Theodore Gardner, had assigned a large contingent of agents to look for Arthur. U.S. Magistrate William Daley had issued warrants for him for the death of both women.

By now, BIA investigators and tribal police were searching the area near Arthur's cabin for other potential victims, believing they may have a serial killer on their hands.

Arthur was spotted on Christmas Eve by FBI agents, walking through the Burnside area, where they took him into custody. He was taken completely by surprise, thinking that since two months had passed since the murders, he was home free. He was lodged in the Multnomah County Jail, where he refused to speak to anyone. His attorney immediately filed a motion to have his notebook, with his incriminating statements, declared inadmissible as evidence.

On Monday, December 29, 1986, Arthur was arraigned in U.S. District Court in Portland and charged with Second Degree Murder for the death of Leah Tahkeal. On December 31, 1986, a federal grand jury in Portland returned two bills charging Arthur with First Degree Murders for the deaths of both women.

It had been apparent through Arthur's entries in his notebook, following the death of the two women, that he was a very disturbed individual. He had been raised by his relatives on the Umatilla Reservation, subsequent to his mother's death when he was a young child. Later, he worked as a farm laborer during the intervals when he wasn't incarcerated for assaults, property crimes, and sex crimes. He considered the reservation his home, but his mere presence made a lot of people in the Thornhollow area very nervous.

Once Arthur was captured, he sought to be elusive from the moment authorities began interviewing him. On February 21, 1987, I made the 207 mile jaunt from Pendleton to Portland to interrogate Arthur in the Multnomah County Jail. I had obtained a federal court order to take handwriting samples from him.

When Arthur was brought out from his cell, he was defiant.

"I have nothing to tell you guys!" were his first words, even before we advised him of his Miranda Rights. Once he was advised of his rights, I came right to the point.

"We know you killed Leah and Martina, Kendall. You want to tell us about it?" I asked.

"You got nothing. I'm not talking about this, because I don't need to," was the response, both curt and authoritative.

"What about this, Kendall?" I pulled out a time bomb in the form of a spiral notebook written by a crazed man, living in a remote cabin up the Umatilla River with two of his girlfriends—a note confessing he had murdered them both.

Arthur's eyes mirrored immeasurable anxiety, as his eyebrows began twitching up and down. I knew he had forgotten about the notebook, and that he must have written it while in a drunken stupor, or a drug-induced high, then had inadvertently left it behind and had forgotten about it. Arthur stiffened, as if he'd been hit hard by a brick, coming out of nowhere, a brick not even remotely anticipated. He calmed down a little and sat quietly for about twenty seconds, gazing remorsefully at the notebook. Finally, with great pain, he forced his eyes away from it.

He finally spoke, "I'm out of here!"

"I don't think so, Kendall" came my reply, as I pulled out the court order, signed by a federal judge, ordering handwriting samples. "You can either give me your handwriting or have the judge order the county deputies to take it from you, but you have to do one or the other, and I might be a little more congenial to work with than those guys. What do you say?"

Arthur flashed a fleeting glimpse of recognition, acknowledging that he knew that I was right.

He nodded his approval, muttering, "Okay."

I was not forensic-trained nor had I ever taken handwriting samples, but two people had died needlessly. I had a court order and a captive audience, and I didn't feel the need to summon a lab technician to travel all the way across the United States from Washington D.C., to tell me something I was sure I could discover myself, in about twenty more minutes with Kendall Arthur.

I had previously identified certain letters in the spiral notebook which were written in an unmistakably unique way and consistently repeated. I extracted the words from the notebook that contained those letters and used those words in other totally unrelated sentences, so that when Arthur wrote out those sentences, he had no idea which individual letters I'd be honing in on for identification purposes. I had him write out the test sentences at various speeds and intervals, knowing he would try to mask his normal writing form. I didn't know if this procedure was standard forensic lab protocol or not, having no experience in those techniques, but it worked! The similarities between the test sentences that Arthur provided and the note left at his cabin were unmistakably and overwhelmingly incriminating. When I pointed out those similarities and consistent patterns to Arthur, he seemed crushed.

I asked, "Kendall, what really happened to Leah and Martina?"

His face reflected an ashen expression of despair, agony, and resignation.

He asked to leave and was instantly permitted to do so.

Two days later, on December 23, 1987, Arthur was scheduled to appear at a pre-trial hearing, where his attorney was going to argue against the spiral notebook being admissible as evidence. When the jailer approached Arthur's cell at 5:00 AM with his breakfast, he found him hanging from an overhead pipe with a bed sheet tied around his neck.

Once the tribe heard of Arthur's death, in accordance with tribal tradition, his cabin, now considered to be both evil and shameful, was torched and burned to the ground.

30

★ ★ ★ ★ ★

RELEASED AS BISHOP IN PENDLETON

JUNE 1987

Prior to being released as bishop in Pendleton, I spoke at the Pendleton High School baccalaureate services three times for the classes of our oldest three children. There were always three speakers from different faiths. This cross-section of the Pendleton religious community provided an ecumenical flavor of unity that was unique and binding, as we worshipped together as a town and lent spiritual support to the youth of our community, as they moved on with their education and work.

Before leaving Pendleton, I thought a lot about all that had transpired in our chapel on the north hill, overlooking the city. This was the place where I found refuge in the bishop's mantle in the evenings and Sundays, while I roamed over eastern Oregon during the work day, doing the bidding of the Bureau. I had spent a significant portion of my life in this town, trying to make a difference, while wearing two hats. That chapel and those memories inspired the following writing, entitled "The People Who Pray on the Hill":

The night's shadows are pierced by the Chapel's bright spire
From the north it commands a full view
Neither Darkness or Gloom should cast here their mire
For there's too much that we need to do
The building with beauty is an Ensign to all
It has its own mission to fill
But what of the Souls who accepted the call?
The People who pray on the hill?

Mike and Judy McPheters

When immersed in the waters by Priesthood's firm hand
We vowed to sustain and obey
As He gave us our blessings, sought He to command
Our test is to work and to pray
Now, what of Affliction and Sorrow and Grief?
Sometimes we suffer so much!
Don't testimonies dwindle without some relief?
Oft times we get out of touch
From the Spirit—the source of our strength and His love
From the teachings that help us so much
So our Chapel stands tall, but sometimes we fall
As we struggle with life as we will
But we should never forget that He loves us all. Yes,
The People who pray on the hill
On a far away mount called Golgotha by some
Three crosses went up in a day
Would the thieves at His side have known when he died
That He suffered for more than just they?
As the blood escaped through the pores of His skin
The eve before He shouldered the cross
Would the disciples have known that He saved them from Sin?

Would they sense the imminent loss?
And what about us? Far removed from the Scene
Have we fully accepted His gift?
Have we given ourselves with hands and hearts clean?
Do we believe that He crossed that Great Rift?
Are we willing to bless one another with Works?
To love those who step out of line?
To pillow a head without food or bed?
To take faith and quit seeking a sign?
Do we give of our time, of our Spirits sublime?
To add to this Church we adore?
Are we void of our pride that sets Salvation aside?
Will our Charity row us ashore?
Yes, the Chapel stands tall and beckons to all
To come forward, to listen, and mill
But the brick's only as strong as the hearts in the throng
Of the People who pray on the hill

By: Bishop Mike McPheters
(April 14, 1985)

31

★★★★★

A Dynamic Entry

April 1988

Making what the FBI SWAT teams call a "dynamic entry" is one of the most exciting aspects of law enforcement. It's where a team of officers "breach" or knock down a door quickly, in order to enter and secure a residence to obtain a tactical advantage over the occupants of the dwelling that might be unfriendly or aggressive. That advantage often insulated us from gunfire or other forms of resistance from our fugitives.

We would often either kick in the door of the target residence or use what we called a "key," which was a heavy, cylindrical piece of metal, weighing thirty to forty pounds. It had a couple of hand holds welded on it to swing it. When this much weight was swung directly into a door at full speed, the door would seldom remain upright. In fact, more often than not, the door frame would also collapse, along with the door.

On April 18, 1988, our SWAT team was ready to raid a house occupied by Mexican drug traffickers in Portland. Special Agent Gil Jarman was assigned the key. He stood six feet four inches tall, weighed close to three hundred pounds, and probably could have walked through the wall of the target house. His duty was to smash in the door. Then I was to be first through the entry to help clear the interior rooms, order everyone to "freeze" in Spanish, preserve any evidence, and help handcuff the occupants.

Our entry team consisted of five SWAT guys who would run in, once Jarman took out the door. We were ready.

"All right, Gil, on three, hit the door!" I whispered, as the excitement of the moment was coursing through my veins. My nervous system was on high alert.

Gil nodded that he was ready, as he stood to the left of the door with the key cocked back at an angle.

"OK, Gil, one . . . two . . . three!" I launched myself into the entry full throttle, as I caught a glimpse of the key flying round house toward the door.

Suddenly, I was in the midst of wood flying in every direction and a door and frame collapsing around me, as I felt a hint of pain in my left leg, totally eclipsed by the thrill of the moment.

I continued through the entry, screaming "Federales! Federales! Que no se muevan! Manos arriba!" It meant "FBI! FBI! Don't move! Put your hands up!"

In roughly three minutes, we had three subjects down on the floor and handcuffed and recovered a stash of guns and cocaine.

Once the house was secured inside and out by a small army of FBI agents, Gil sauntered up to me with a puzzled look on his face.

"I'm sorry about that, Mike," he stated sheepishly.

"About what, Gil?" I asked.

"For hitting you with the key. You went through just as I clobbered the door. That's when I smacked you in the leg. I'm surprised you're still walking!"

When he said the word "leg," I recalled the surge of pain I'd felt going through the door.

I suddenly became aware of the numbness in my left leg and had to sit down.

"Thanks, Gil, for hitting me in the leg, and not the head!"

32

★★★★★

THE BOLIVIAN CRISIS

MAY 25, 1989

I worked a huge variety of criminal cases during the eight and a half years I was assigned in the one-man resident agency in Pendleton, Oregon. However, one phone call I received on May 24, 1989 had nothing to do with anything happening in my territory. That call sent me from the mountains of Eastern Oregon to faraway Bolivia.

The call came during breakfast. I had not yet gone to the office. It was Kelly Brown, a family friend.

"Mike, I just heard on the news that two Mormon missionaries were gunned down in La Paz, Bolivia, but Shad wasn't one of them."

Judy and I breathed a sigh of relief. Our twenty-year-old son, Shad Michael, was serving a two year Church mission in the Cochabamba, Bolivia, mission, not far from where the two young men were killed.

Kelly continued, "Their names were Elder Todd Wilson and Elder Jeffrey Ball. They were killed by terrorists from a group called Zarate Willca. That's all I know for now."

"Thanks, Kelly. If you hear anything else, let me know."

The thoughts were racing through our mind: *Just how bad are things in Bolivia? What kind of danger is our son in?*

As Judy and I looked at one another, we mirrored ashen expressions of apprehension and concern.

That's when a light came on in my mind as I recalled a recent investigation the FBI had conducted in the Philippines, involving the murder of an American marine captain. Shortly thereafter, Congress had passed legislation giving the Bureau authority to investigate the deaths of U.S. citizens murdered on foreign soil.

"I've got to see if I can get on that case in Bolivia," I told Judy. "That is, if the Bureau's going to work it."

Within two minutes, I was on the phone with SAC Danny Coulson, Portland office.

"Hey, boss! My son's down in Bolivia where the two Mormon missionaries were just killed by terrorists. He's involved in the same work they were. I need to know two things: Is the Bureau going to get involved? And if so, can I go?"

"I'll check into it and let you know." Coulson hung up. He was a man of action. I knew he would call me back that day.

Two hours later, the phone rang. It was Coulson.

"Okay, McPheters. You're going to Bolivia. You'll be part of a small team working with Dwight Dennett, our legal attaché in Bogota, Colombia. Go on up to San Francisco tomorrow, get a diplomatic passport, and you're on your way."

"Thanks, boss," I hung up the phone and started helping Judy pack my suitcase.

I flew out to Portland bright and early the next morning, and from there to San Francisco, where I obtained my diplomatic passport through the American embassy.

The next day, I was headed to Bolivia.

Fourteen hours later, I exited the aircraft at the La Paz Airport at an elevation of fourteen thousand feet, situated high in the Cordillera range of the Andes. The thin air sent me reeling backwards a little, as I tried to keep my balance, while toting two suitcases, and forcing enough air into my lungs just to keep breathing. I subsequently heard all kinds of stories about people flying into La Paz, including the Catholic Pope, just a few weeks before, who was administered a drink made of coca leaves, the key ingredient for cocaine, to counteract the altitude sickness. I would pass on that.

As we descended from the airport into La Paz, a distance of about two miles, we descended nearly two thousand feet to an elevation of twelve thousand and five hundred feet, but that was still just fifteen hundred feet less than the peak of Mount Rainier, and I was feeling it!

La Paz was a different and unusual city. The people were a dark, comely kind, seemingly well-disciplined and orderly . . . especially considering the abject poverty in which they lived. They seemed to be a humble, child-like people with beautiful little children—cherubs with pixie countenances and dark, bottomless eyes. Bolivians seemed to do very well with what they had. In the early mornings, beautiful children, spotless and in white tunics, would leave for school from homes sometimes fashioned from cardboard or whatever might be available.

A million La Paz inhabitants crowded into a valley on top of some of the highest mountains in the world, with Mount Ilimaru on one end and Mount Ayena Potosi on the other. Fashionable hotels were present down in the lower part of the highland valley, but thousands of poorly built adobe brick homes clung from the sides of the mountains surrounding it.

Many other people resided in the high alto plano areas near the city, where they cultivated the food necessary to sustain themselves.

That first night in the Hotel Plaza, a nice upscale hotel in La Paz, I breathed in short gasps, forcing air into my lungs while trying to sleep. For the first time in my life, I appreciated breathing.

I felt better the next morning but didn't exactly spring out of bed. I was breathing a little easier, although still a little nauseated from spending my first night at twelve thousand feet above sea level.

I had to report at the Bolivian national police headquarters by 8:00 AM, so I showered, dressed, and sauntered down to the main floor for a Latin-American breakfast, consisting of croissants and hot chocolate, followed up by a bowl of hot oatmeal.

After eating, I returned to my room and flipped on the television. The local newscasters were ranting and raving, protesting the presence of the FBI, questioning the right of the Bureau to be investigating their people. I quickly learned the reasons they resented our presence.

Apparently, prior to the two missionaries being killed, rumors had been circulating that the United States was considering invading Bolivia in order to eradicate their cocaine crop. This was based upon a recent visit by U.S. Secretary of State George Schultz, who had emphasized the urgency for Bolivia to step up coca leaf eradication, since too much of it was coming into the states illegally.

Mr. Schultz's motorcade was firebombed and his wife almost killed, perhaps as a result of that declaration.

There was also discussion circulating that the United States planned to build a new airport in La Paz that would be used to launch the invasion.

Both these allegations put the local news media into a feeding frenzy, as they gobbled up and commented on every little tidbit of propaganda they could find.

The reason Schultz's visit and his demands caused such a stir soon became obvious.

The average farmer in Bolivia earned the equivalent of approximately four hundred American dollars a year. Where he would make one dollar for a bushel of corn, a bushel of coca leaves would bring him maybe ten dollars. Meeting the Americans' demands would, in essence, wipe out the prospect of any economical prosperity.

The result? A terrorist group, Zarate Willca, was formed to make a statement denouncing "American Imperialism." The left-wing terrorists had threatened "war to the death" against "Yankee invaders."

The terrorists proclaimed, "The violation of our sovereignty cannot go unpunished. The Yankee invaders who come to massacre our fellow farmers are warned. . . . We the poor have no other road than to rise up in arms. Our hatred is implacable and our war is to death."

Pablo Zarate Willca was a peasant farmer who led a revolt in 1890 against a law permitting the sale of communal land used by peasants. Many local people believed the Willca group was a splinter faction of the Shining Path terrorist organization in Peru.

The young North American Mormon missionaries, with their white shirts, black and white badges, and light complexions, were extremely vulnerable and were being targeted as rich imperialists who dressed well and built beautiful churches. They were victims of the first politically-motivated murders of Mormon missionaries in history.

The little-known, anti-American Armed Liberation Front of the Zarate Willca people was not specifically opposed to the Mormons or to their teachings. They were only opposed to the North American presence. They clearly perceived the United States as an aggressor, bent on eradicating their coca leaf crops, and depriving them of any hope for financial prosperity.

Elders Wilson and Ball, both twenty years old, were shot down in cold blood, as they returned to their apartment, located in a remote section of La Paz. They had resided in a neighborhood around the corner from a church that was seriously damaged by a bomb explosion the prior year.

They never had a chance. The perpetrators had been waiting in a yellow taxi, armed with semi-automatic shoulder weapons. They were subsequently identified as Johnny Justino Peralta-Espinoza, Victor Eduardo Preito-Encinas, Simon Mamani Quispe and a female, Susana Zapana Hannover, all native Bolivians in their late twenties or early thirties.

One missionary died immediately, and the other succumbed to his wounds en route to the hospital.

Those homicides were preceded and followed by other firebomb attacks on other North American church buildings, as well as Mormon chapels.

We learned that the female subject, Susana Hannover, a medical student who had tipped off the gunmen as to the location of the missionary apartments and their routine, was a recent "convert" to the church, who apparently became a member for the express purpose of collaborating with the Zarate Willca organization.

Each of our five-man team had special assignments.

Dwight Bennett, the assistant legal attaché from Bogota, Colombia, worked exclusively with the U.S. Embassy in La Paz under the jurisdiction of the Department of State.

Richard Ford, who I had first met when he was a young boy living with his parents in Uruguay, was now an FBI agent assigned to the Washington, D.C. Field Office. He was also fluent in Spanish and was assigned to work with Dwight Dennett in his liaison through the Department of State, in addition to coordinating with the Church.

Robert Murphy was from the Forensics Unit of the Bureau's laboratory in Washington D.C. All the evidence from the shooting incident was assigned to him to review.

Salvador Escobedo, an FBI polygrapher, was sent from the San Antonio Division. He worked exclusively in administering lie detector tests.

I was assigned to do exactly what I hoped to do and that was to hit the street and figure out what happened, how it happened, and who was responsible.

One of my initial assignments was to enter the elders' apartment and review their correspondence, notes, miscellaneous materials, apartment furnishings, and general living area for any clues or leads as to what may have made them vulnerable to their untimely fate. Everything was in order and appropriate. It was heart-rending and difficult to review the missionaries' letters to and from their families and loved ones. I became aware of the Herculean efforts put forth by these two young men in doing their work. I read of the love and appreciation they had for their families

I studied the imprint of the bullet holes at the gate leading into their apartment and swallowed hard as I contemplated what had happened there.

I was paired to work with a local investigator, Major Luciano Escobar, who was attached both to the U.S. Embassy and the Bolivian National

Police. Luciano, with his million dollar smile, was both very aggressive and extremely astute. We shared the same philosophy as to investigative techniques and interviewing procedures and spent most of our time working the slums and poorer areas of La Paz. We were well-matched. My level of Spanish was sufficient to keep me in the loop, as Luciano led out in the interviews.

At the end of each day, we met with the highest command level of the Bolivian National Police and reported the information we had developed. Luciano and I posted the chronology of our intelligence gathering on the wall of the debriefing room daily, with all the events described that led up to the assassinations, as well as any significant developments that occurred after the elders were gunned down

After ten days, we had eighty percent of the facts and the order of events all documented. Some of the more promising leads came to me directly through members of the Church.

The missionaries had conducted their day's business in the usual fashion: arising early, having their study period, eating breakfast, hitting the street, and visiting member families to obtain references.

There was nothing out of the ordinary in the elders' afternoon and evening activities. They had continued making member visits and had dinner with a family who had anticipated their arrival.

Following dinner, the missionaries continued making their contacts, returning home just after 10:00 PM, when they were attacked.

I thought of our own son, Shad Michael, knowing he was in that same country, facing the same danger.

Following the murders, the other Bolivian missionaries were urged to keep a low profile and to alter their routine schedules. Our son apparently did not consider the recent events with any fear or trepidation. He was a district leader in the Cochabamba Mission at the time the elders were killed in La Paz. His mission president had ordered him to round up all the missionaries he was responsible for in his district, located in the Beni area of Riveralto and Guayamarin, because of the extreme isolation and ongoing threats there, and to take them across the river to Brazil, where they would be safe, at least temporarily. To accomplish that, he and his Bolivian companion rented motorcycles and hit the dirt roads, notifying all the missionaries to head for Brazil.

Since the missionaries were restricted from working for a couple weeks, Shad was given permission to spend one week with me in La Paz. When I first saw him, I noticed his suit jacket was hanging loosely from around his shoulders. He had lost thirty-five pounds from his two hundred and twenty pound football frame. He was as brown as a chocolate chip cookie and, like most of the missionaries from outside of South and Central America, was battling the internal problems brought on by parasites. He had worn out most of his clothes in the eighteen months since I had seen him, so I gave him most of the clothing I had brought down. I also put some meat back on his bones by indulging him in good Argentine cooking and American pizza and obtained some medication from the mission home that seemed to help clear up his health issues. It was a sweet reunion, but he announced at the end of our week together that he needed to get back to work. He was ready to return to his companions, not the least bit intimidated by terrorists, and ready to spread the gospel. There was one thing I asked Shad to help me with before he left.

Agent Rick Ford had became very ill with some stomach issues and needed a special priesthood blessing. In 1964 I met his family in Rivera, Uruguay when Rick was twelve years old. His father, Archie Ford, who the Church had called on a construction mission to build chapels in South America, had such a serious case of the hiccups for so many days, he grew concerned about the affect this was having on his heart. I had the opportunity of participating in a blessing and saw him healed. Now Rick needed a blessing to regain his health and do the work the FBI needed from him. Shad and I administered the blessing, pleading with the Lord to restore his health. We saw him recover the next day, and Shad left. It was the first time in my life I had experienced the satisfaction of witnessing the recovery of two generations of the same family in different South American countries, healed by the Lord's hand.

I worked closely with the Church leaders, especially the two Bolivian mission presidents, President Fallis and President Wright, as well as the missionaries under their respective jurisdictions, interviewing those who had been in close contact with Elders Wilson and Ball prior to their death. I knelt in prayer with both these fine men as they sought out the help of the Lord in the most trying time of their three year administrations. It was obvious they were both laboring under intense strain and pressure, subsequent to the death of the missionaries.

Later in the first week I was there, I met with Elder M. Russell Ballard of the Church's Quorum of the Twelve Apostles, as well as Charles Didier and Angel Abrea from the Area Presidency, who were overseeing that part of the Church in South America. I worked out of the Church office buildings located at 20 de Octubre street, and out of the mission office in La Paz.

En route to Bolivia, I traveled with Richard Bretzing, former SAC of the Los Angeles division of the Bureau, who was then head of security for the Church and had traveled from Salt Lake City to coordinate the Church response to the deaths of the missionaries. I occasionally assisted by translating for him in some Spanish-speaking gatherings.

The news media continued denouncing the presence of the FBI in Bolivia, even though the national police continued supporting us and our mission.

We were not given permission to carry firearms until we were in Bolivia over a week. Finally, after some information was provided from an anonymous source and left at one of our chapels, we were hoping to carry out some raids that might result in the case's solution. We planned to detain a few people that we hoped could confirm what we suspected was true. The U.S. Embassy finally issued us some old .357 magnum caliber revolvers that had been around a long time. Once armed, I accompanied the Bolivian Police on some raids of several suspects we had identified.

Of the several conspirators involved in the murders of the missionaries, two were killed in police raids, several were apprehended, and all were convicted "in absentia," meaning when apprehended, the fugitives would be remanded directly into prisons without another trial, where they would spend the rest of their lives.

One meeting I covered that I will never forget was Apostle Russell Ballard's meeting with the Church's local leaders in Bolivia. After addressing the grave security problems facing American missionaries in Bolivia, I heard him tell the Bolivian leaders that he would leave the room for twenty minutes, and when he returned he wanted them to tell him how they would help ensure the missionaries working in Bolivia would be kept safe.

As he left the room, I noticed the leaders were somewhat animated and very serious, as they conversed together.

When Elder Ballard returned, he asked for their plan. An elderly stake president rose to his feet, casting a wide shadow from a very portly frame, and stated: "Elder Ballard, we have decided that we cannot allow anything to ever happen again like what has happened to our North American brethren. We will begin taking more of this missionary work into our own hands."

That commitment apparently carried on into the hearts of many Bolivian Church members, because in a short few years, a temple, representing the crowning achievement of member dedication, was constructed in Bolivia.

Mike spent some time with his son Shad
while working on the Bolivian case.

Success in Bolivia TUESDAY, APRIL 3, 1990 Photo courtesy of Mike McPheters

Pendleton FBI agent Mike McPheters, right, was able to spend a day with his missionary son, Shad, when he went to Bolivia last May to join an investigation into the killing of two Mormon missionaries. Shad is standing between two Bolivian boat makers on the shores of Lake Titicaca. Mike McPheters was honored recently by the Bolivian National Police with that country's National Medal of Honor for his part in the successful investigation. See story and photo Page 3A.

Temples are only built where local members have assumed responsibility for the well-being of the Church in their area.

Before I left Bolivia, Elder Ballard approached me and said, "Solve it, Mike!"

I was never able to return to Bolivia for the conclusion of the case, since I had sole responsibility for one-third of the state of Oregon in my resident agency in Pendleton, but I have always been grateful for being able to work with my Bolivian counterpart, Detective Eduardo Morales, in putting the case chronology together and for being able to spend one special week with my missionary son.

The people of Bolivia appreciated what we had done. General Mario Molina Herrera, Commander General of the National Police, wrote a letter dated October 19, 1989 to Robert Gelbard, United States Ambassador in Bolivia, stating that the FBI agents sent for this crisis had solved the two murders, as well as the attack against Secretary of State George Schultz, and had dismantled the Zarate Willca group.

Hanging on my office wall today is a framed, decorated ribbon, green with crossed rifles, and next to it a letter, addressed to FBI headquarters, which reads as follows:

La Paz, Bolivia
October 20, 1989
Oliver B. Revell
Associate Deputy Director
Federal Bureau of Investigation

10th & Pennsylvania Ave.
Washington, D. C. 20535
Dear Mr. Revell:

It is my pleasure to inform you that on October 19, 1989, Assistant Legal Attache Dwight Dennett was decorated by General Mario Molina Herrera, Commanding General of the Bolivian National Police, with the Orden de la Policia Nacional granting the rank of "Caballero."

The decoration was presented at a ceremony attended by all members of the Bolivian National Police staff, in recognition for his assistance to the Bolivian National Police.

Presentation of the same decoration, in absentia, was also made to the following FBI Special Agents: Samuel McPheters, Richard T. Ford, Stuart Hoyt, Agustine Rodriguez Jr., Salvador Escobedo and Robert Murphy.

The Orden de la Policia Nacional is one of the highest Bolivian National Police decorations presented to law enforcement officers, who through their actions have brought credit to and have assisted in the betterment of the police.

Enclosed for distribution, as you may deem appropriate, are the diplomas, resolutions and ribbons of the Bolivian National Police Orden de la Policia Nacional for all the individuals listed.

Sincerely,
Robert S. Gelbard
Ambassador

33
★★★★★

WORKING THE NORTHERN UTES

FALL 1991

By the fall of 1991, I had spent eight and a half years by myself, covering the eight counties in Eastern Oregon. I may have begun talking to myself a little but had not yet reached the point where I was answering.

I had fulfilled my tenure as bishop for the third time, and for several reasons, felt it was time to move on. It had been a wonderful time for our family and the last period of our lives where all five kids were at home. Marni, the Pendleton High School student body president, had gone on to a year at Brigham Young University (BYU) and then on an eighteen-month mission for the Church in San Diego. Shad, our oldest son, who had been co-captain of Pendleton's football team, had also gone to college for a year, had served a two-year mission in Bolivia, and had also gone on to BYU to study. Tylee, the second daughter, Pendleton's Homecoming Queen, had also left for her first year at BYU. That only left Shayna (age 16) and Justin (age 12) at home. Like most parents, we yearned to be closer to all our children, including the three college students in Provo, Utah.

In 1991, the Bureau published two new resident agency openings in Utah, one for a new office in Vernal that would cover the northern Ute-Ouray Indian Reservation in Fort Duchesne. The opening was contingent upon the agent having experience in Native American investigations, and I'd had a lot. I put in for Vernal and was advised I filled the bill. We were soon on our way. We had never been to Vernal, but it felt good.

My initial office space was in the Uintah County Sheriff's Office on the first floor of the new Uintah County Courthouse building. My future office, on the third floor of the same building, was still under construction, and two months away from completion. The Uintah County Sheriff invited me to share an office with one of their senior deputies, Wayne Hollebeke, a tall, slender deputy with a thick mustache and dark complexion. Hollebeke was good-natured about sharing his office with the new "fed" and made me feel right at home. He had a "stash" of jellybeans in the bottom drawer of his metal desk that made good grazing. This was the same desk he had worked out of for many years under several different sheriffs. Although he had a heart of gold and a very friendly disposition, Hollebeke could look mean enough to draw water out of a rock. He used that to his advantage in successfully obtaining confessions, all with due respect for his penchant for ethics. In philosophy, he worked somewhat apart from the rest of the county officers and was definitely his own man. Over the years to come, Hollebeke and I shared a lot of ideas.

Once I was moved into my completed office, the Special Agent in Charge of the Bureau in Salt Lake City, Gene Glenn, came out to Vernal for the ribbon-cutting ceremony. SAC Glenn and I both made a few remarks to a room full of guests, followed by a stirring rendition of "God Bless the USA" by a local Church member.

Also present that day was the new agent I was assigned to break in and train: Manuel Johnson. Manuel, who was of Hispanic/Pima Indian descent, a little shorter than average, in his early thirties, medium athletic build, dark hair, and dark complexion was no newcomer to tribal ways, since he had worked for the Pima community near Phoenix, Arizona in community leadership positions.

Manuel's wife, Marni, was pretty: tall, light-complected, and descended from eastern tribes, including Algonquin and Sac and Fox.

Manuel and I both loved to work out, so many mornings we'd either hit the health club to lift weights or we would run. One fall morning, we were running north on Vernal Avenue out of town, when it was still early enough to be pitch black. As we were more or less carried away with our visiting while running along, we nearly collided into an animal standing alongside the road, directly in front of us. It was a young buck mule deer, past the fawn stage and antler-less, obviously born just that past spring. The deer seemed to have become used to people and had probably even been fed, but hunting season had almost arrived, and the deer had become far too cozy with mankind.

We decided we had to get "Bambi" out of town, but how? At first, the little deer followed us up Vernal Avenue but would stop and look as if it wanted to head back into town. We decided to keep the deer between us and just try to coax him north up Vernal Avenue, but he kept stopping, as if poised to retreat back into the city. A light flashed in my mind. If I could rub the area between the deer's ears with sufficient force, it would generate heat. Each time the deer would stop and balk, I rubbed hard and fast, in a circular motion until the space between his ears heated up enough to make him jump out ahead. Manuel and I would sprint up behind Bambi, one of us on each side, as we continued heading north towards the pine-covered foothills. There, we planned to eventually release the little creature back into his natural habitat.

By the time we were a couple of miles out of town, it was light. As the southbound traffic passed us, as we jogged north, people slowed down to take in the sight of a buck deer trotting along between a Pima Native American and a big, tall white guy.

★ ★ ★ ★

Coming out of new agent training, Special Agent Manuel Johnson was totally gung ho. He came to work each day with a utility belt containing his revolver, handcuffs, reload packs, and collapsible baton. He always had them on. Sometimes I wondered if he slept with them.

On Manuel's first arrest, we were approaching the entrance to the Fort Duchesne Police Department to obtain some current information on the whereabouts of a fugitive he was looking for. As we were about to enter the police department, I noticed the fugitive standing fifteen feet away from the door we were entering. Manuel didn't recognize him.

"Manuel, there's your guy!" I whispered as I nudged him gently in the ribs.

"Where?" he asked excitedly.

Then, upon realizing his arrestee was only seconds away, he burst into action and sprang on him like a cat, ordering the man down on his knees with his hands crossed behind his back and his right foot over his left. He then advised the surprised man of his rights, reading from the waiver form that all new agents carry with them.

Once Manuel's arrestee was in the Bureau car, and just before we booked him, Manuel looked up at me and said, "You've got to be kidding! My first bust and I almost walked right over him!" We both laughed ourselves silly.

Another interesting event for Manuel came on an occasion when Bureau of Indian Affairs (BIA) Investigator Nate Merrick asked us to respond to a questionable death to determine the cause. It was Manuel's first time doing this. Most Indian cultures attach importance to maintaining all body parts from a deceased person intact, so that the body would be whole on its trip into the hereafter or world of spirits. It was also important occasionally to remove the hands from an unidentified individual, in order to submit them to a forensics laboratory to have the deceased identified through fingerprinting. When we had finished rough drafting our report on the examination of the body and Merrick asked us to take the decedent's hands into Salt Lake City for the crime lab examination, Manuel's eyes widened completely, as he uttered, "Hands? What hands? The dead hands? The dead guy's hands? You're kidding, right?" Both Merrick and I fought to hold back laughter, as it dawned on us this was something they hadn't covered at the training academy.

Manuel's Native American presence enhanced our relationship with the tribal council and local officials. He used his experience in tribal community work and tribal affairs to our advantage, although we were never able to win over the support of a certain tribal official who knew we were onto him for his suspected involvement with drugs. This same individual protested our presence on the reservation and stirred up community members against us.

We were frequently called upon to assist BIA Investigator Merrick, an Oglala Sioux, and the local police chief with homicides, assaults, and child abuse cases. Those accused of murder invented ways of taking a life that one would be pressed to even imagine. One male victim was strangled with his shoelace, stabbed with a Phillips' screwdriver, tied to the bumper of a car with jumper cables, drug a half mile down a country road by a car, beaten up, pushed off the road into a stream face down, and finally killed with huge boulders thrown down on top of his head.

The man who instigated the murder confessed both to me and another tribal member. The two young men that were his accomplices both pleaded guilty and went to prison. The principal subject and instigator, who actually perpetuated the scheme and enlisted the help of the other two who went to prison, was eventually tried by a jury in Vernal under state charges for murder, but he was set free. The jury felt there were two people already in prison, so they should not put a third one there. The lack of logic and the ignorance of the facts displayed by those jurors were maddening, and for me, this was one of the more discouraging moments of my career.

Before Manuel and I partnered up and began responding to the

Northern Ute-Ouray Reservation incidents, there had been no FBI presence in northeast Utah, with the exception of an occasional agent who would drive the two and a half hours from headquarters in Salt Lake City to address problems that had to be handled in person. We immediately began bolstering the division's statistical accomplishments with arrests, indictments, and convictions. There were months when we had more statistics in our single office than all the Utah resident agencies combined. The tribe knew we were serious about addressing crimes which had previously gone uncontested or were serious cases which had been processed through tribal courts that were only authorized to try misdemeanors. The result was often just a slap on the hand for a case that would have drawn time in the federal penitentiary had they been tried in federal court in Salt Lake City. We were able to change that, and obtained lengthy sentences for serious crimes.

★ ★ ★ ★ ★

When Manuel was transferred out to the Los Angeles Division, after about three years, he had more meaningful statistics under his belt as a new agent than most agents achieve in the first ten years of their career.

In January 1996, my second trainee in Vernal was young Jim Cunningham, who had spent eight years in the U.S. Marine Corps and had been a helicopter pilot in the Gulf War in Kuwait. He was from Texas, married with three children, and was in his early thirties. He was stocky, muscular, and had a low profile disposition. Agent Cunningham was great to work with and filled Manuel's role as my new running partner.

Jim and I worked a reservation homicide together where the victim's body was stashed outside in the snow, underneath a stove. While I was recording the dimensions of various objects in the vicinity of the crime scene and pacing off distances from the body to other key points, Jim was taking photographs. Suddenly a call came. It was the Fort Duchesne dispatcher, advising me that John White Thunder had locked himself into his cabin, which was close by, and was holding a female tribal member captive and threatening to stab her to death. He was in possession of a long butcher knife. Tribal officers had approached the scene but were advised they should leave him alone, or he would kill the woman and mutilate himself. Both he and his captive had been drinking heavily.

Jim and I left the remainder of the crime scene work to Andy Tom, a Navajo BIA Investigator, and responded to the White Thunder incident. We approached the dilapidated cabin and noticed the window on the kitchen side was open.

As I peered in, I saw White Thunder standing in the kitchen by the woman—a pretty Ute lady in her forties. White Thunder had a huge cut on his right shoulder, about two and a half inches wide, gaping open, deep into the flesh. He was bleeding profusely.

"White Thunder! This is Agent McPheters, FBI. What can I help you with today? It looks like you're hurting." I wanted him to think I was on his side.

He replied, "I just want those policemen to go home. Then I'll come with you."

"Okay, White Thunder, it's a deal. But first, put that knife that's in your hand down on the kitchen table." I was still shouting in from outside through the open kitchen window.

White Thunder left the woman, who immediately ran outside, where she was driven away by one of the two local police units. The other officer, Greg Littlewhiteman, moved his police car a half block away to satisfy White Thunder, yet close enough to be where he could remain available if needed.

Jim and I holstered our side arms and entered White Thunder's residence. He immediately stuck out his wrists to be handcuffed, even before we said anything.

As I handcuffed White Thunder, I took note of his physique. He was tall, lean, and muscular, with a menacing curl on his lips. He seemed detached from his surroundings, even from the unfavorable circumstances he had created for himself.

After I handcuffed White Thunder, I became aware of the blood all over my hands, draining out of his shoulder. It was at that point that Officer Littlewhiteman came forward and warned me that White Thunder was an active homosexual, currently being treated for AIDS, a fact that eventually necessitated four trips for AIDS tests for me over the next year.

Before White Thunder was transported to the closest hospital in Vernal to have his shoulder wound treated, I asked, "What happened to your shoulder, White Thunder?"

"I had to show her," he answered.

"Show her what?" I asked.

"A year ago they put a metal plate in my shoulder. I cut it open so I could see it and show it to her." A half smile appeared on his face, as he tested my reaction, staring directly into my eyes.

This was too much. I couldn't be cool. "You've got to be kidding, White Thunder. Your arm's halfway cut off."

White Thunder kept smiling, apparently taking great pleasure in my discomfort. The ambulance arrived. The attendants applied pressure pads to the open wound, wrapped it, and whisked the crazy man off to the hospital.

★ ★ ★ ★ ★

As a law enforcement officer, you never know what you'll be asked to do next. One day, at Fort Duchesne, I was reviewing some case reports with BIA Investigator Merrick. A mother came in with an infant in her arms, less than six months old, yelling, "You've got to help her! Please! She's choking!" She went on to explain that the baby had inhaled a piece of hard candy. She believed Merrick could treat her baby and thrust her into his arms, repeating with anguish to please save her baby.

Nate just stood there, perplexed, looking at me. After a couple of seconds, appearing dazed, he handed the baby to me, saying, "Can you handle this?"

My first impressions were, *It's now or never! We've got to do something.* My next immediate thought was, *If you blow this, McPheters, not only will you be sued big time by this woman's family, but the FBI will no longer be welcome here, and you'll be tortured with this baby's death for the rest of your life!*

I prayed silently, begging the Heavenly Power to be present. I had no time to administer a blessing. The baby was way too small to apply the standard Heimlich maneuver. By forcing my fist in under her rib cage, I'd probably break the infant's ribs. In a flash, it occurred to me what I should do. I turned the baby over, resting her stomach on my left palm, and cradled her in that hand, and then steadying her with my right hand, I applied light bursts of pressure upward with the flat part of my left hand. With the third burst, the piece of candy dislodged from her throat and shot out of her mouth with about a pint of vomit. She cried convulsively at first, and then gradually settled down. The bluish hue of her face changed back to a bright pinkish color, as the blood gushed back into her face.

The mother looked at me, then at Nate, thanked us both profusely, and left with her baby, as I wiped the sweat off my forehead.

I turned toward Nate, saying, "Thanks, pal!" I smiled at him with a "That's really not in my job description" look.

★ ★ ★ ★ ★

One of the most gristly murders I encountered on the Northern Ute-Ouray Reservation was that of William Poleviyaoma, known to his many friends as "Biker Bill." The killer, Valentino Colorow, was a fellow tribal member.

On August 26, 1994, I testified at Colorow's preliminary hearing in U.S. District Court in Salt Lake City and related the unprecedented brutality that led up to Poleviyaoma's death and to his body subsequently being dumped in a waste disposal site.

Colorow, accompanied by accomplices Delphine Colorow and Dominic Manning, stabbed Poleviyaoma in the neck repeatedly with a screwdriver but couldn't kill him. Then they took him to the dump near Gusher, just outside the reservation, threw him down on the ground amid the garbage, and began bashing his head in with a tire rim, hitting him ten to twelve times, pulverizing his skull and fracturing his jaw, as his life ebbed away.

On May 10, 1994, an informant led us to the site of the killing. We found Poleviyaoma's body, where it had lain for three months. Although his dentures had been bashed down into his neck, they were sufficiently intact to identify him, when they were compared with past dental work. This same information eventually also led to the identification of all three of his assailants.

In the preliminary hearing, I was examined and cross-examined for over an hour by both the prosecutor and Colorow's attorney, who sought desperately, but unsuccessfully, for any thread of evidence to keep his client out of prison. Since I had obtained confessions from the murderers, I was the only target the defense attorney could shoot at. His efforts fell short, and Poleviyaoma's murderers took up residence in a federal prison.

34

★★★★★

THE BISHOP BARBER

FEBRUARY 20, 1992

The day after we moved into our new home in Vernal, I was called as bishop of the Glines Fifth Ward. This came as a great comfort in my life, assuring me that I still had the Lord's love and trust, and inspiring me to dedicate myself to serving Him well. I was given counselors like others that I had always been blessed with: men of faith, dedicated to doing all they could to help me help the people that we were called to serve.

Shortly after being called, I gained an acute insight into just how much faith the young people have in their bishop.

Nate Eaton, at sixteen years of age, made a striking appearance. He had the sculptured facial features of a very handsome young man and was an awesome basketball player at Uintah High School. He had followed the example of his father, Valoy Eaton, an internationally known western landscape artist, who had excelled as a standout basketball player at Brigham Young University.

Because Nate was fascinated with my work as an FBI agent and we enjoyed the mutual respect of kindred spirits, we hit it off right away.

There was one thing, however. Both Valoy, who was serving in the stake presidency, and I grew concerned about Nate letting his hair grow down almost to his shoulders, a style much in mode at that time among many of the young men in Vernal, and more particularly, many of the better athletes. However, since Nate was administering the sacrament each Sunday, his appearance was presenting an obstacle to his continuing to qualify to perform that ordinance. Not only that, but Nate was preparing to serve a mission later that year.

Nate's father asked him to have his hair styled more appropriately. Nate went to the hair stylist but then changed his mind.

Nate was very popular and enjoyed hanging around with others who were accepted in the "in crowd" at school. Although he strove to faithfully maintain Church standards, like most young men his age, he also sought both the approval and acceptance of his peers. Nevertheless, when his parents counseled him regarding his hair possibly becoming a stumbling block to his worthiness to administer the sacrament and to being able to serve his mission, he listened.

★ ★ ★ ★ ★

One Sunday, after sacrament meeting, and before Sunday School, I was in my church office, having just concluded an interview. When I heard a knock on my door, I opened. It was Nate Eaton. He was standing there with a pair of scissors in his right hand, dangling down from his side.

"Bishop, I have a request." He was as serious as I had ever seen him.

"Sure, Nate! What's up?" I inquired, although I just received a pretty good hint when I observed what was in his hand.

He continued. "Would you cut my hair to where you think it should be?" I was instantly filled with admiration for this young man who had come to me, probably knowing that I had never cut anyone's hair in my life, willing to risk his appearance, in order to be obedient.

I knew I had to do this. I felt Nate's faith.

"Sure, Nate. I'll need help. Will you kneel with me in prayer? I don't want to mess you up."

Nate and I both fell to our knees, as I literally poured out my heart to the Lord, asking Him to bless me with the skill necessary to cut Nate's hair in a way that would please Him first and Nate second.

After praying, we arose. I asked Nate to sit, while I took his scissors into my hands, pulled up a waste basket, and attacked his locks. I cut confidently, but carefully, knowing I was getting help. I worked for about twenty minutes.

When I was finished, Nate thanked me and left my office. As he proceeded down the hallway, he met my wife, Judy, who said "Hey, Nate, nice haircut!"

"Thanks, your husband cut it."

Judy was taken back. "What did you say, Nate?"

"The bishop cut my hair . . . just now."

Judy responded, "Nate, I've cut the kids' hair before, but the bishop has never cut anyone's hair in his life!"

Nate responded, "You need to go talk to him. He'll tell you."

Judy found the evidence in the waste basket, looked at me in amazement, and exclaimed, "Nice job!"

35

★ ★ ★ ★ ★

TELEMARKETING TRAGEDY

1992

Eighty-two-year-old Alma Jeffries was overwhelmed with concern, as she gazed out the window of her comfortable single-story brick home in Vernal, Utah.

Should I tell my children I've lost the money? What will they think of my judgment? Will they believe I did it for their children's college education, or will they think I'm just too old, and getting to be an easy target for any scam artist that calls me on the telephone?

Alma continued to stare out her window with a sickened, forlorn expression of helplessness that was eclipsed only by the empty sentiment of betrayal that she felt . . . the same sense of betrayal felt by so many elderly people like her that Harry Harlow had taken to the cleaners with his most recent telemarketing scam.

If only Coke were still here, she thought, sadly. He would know what to do. He would have smelled a rat before the grandkids' college money was gone.

Coke Jeffries was a well-known businessman in the small community of Vernal to whom Alma had been married most of her adult life. Coke had preceded Alma in death by many years, but prior to passing on, had left her a nice home and a comfortable sum of money to carry her through the sunset of her life.

Alma was healthy for her age, energetic, and loved to involve herself in her home projects and especially with her adult children and her grandchildren. The $230,000 Harlow had fleeced from her was to be a surprise to those grandchildren that wanted to go on to college, and Alma took great pride and satisfaction in knowing it was there for them and the fact she could be the one that could make it available. However, by the time Harlow and his gang of telemarketers were finished with her, Alma had very little left to live on, above and beyond the money they stole from her.

Harlow's den of telephone thieves originated in Los Angeles; they then moved into Las Vegas in the early 1990s. They had obtained hundreds of coins from old shipwrecks that were highly salinated and were rapidly deteriorating. The coins had very little value, due to their having been so long in the salt water.

The telemarketers placed the cheap coins into beautiful velvet containers neatly tucked into small, intricately decorated wooden boxes. Each box had a phony typed certificate, certifying the coins were from the "Admiral Gardner" shipwreck. The ship was an East Indian ship that left England in 1809, bound for Bengal, India. It went down in a storm after it crashed into the Goodwin Sands sandbar. It was completely destroyed and the cargo lost. It carried a huge amount of newly-minted coins for the British East India Company. The wreck was discovered in 1985 and the money recovered in very bad condition. The coins had the East India Company coat of arms with two lions surrounding the shield, on one side, and an inscription and the Roman numeral X with the word "CASH" on the other side. All that said, the coins had very little value.

The certificates Harlow's people issued indicated the coins were worth hundreds of times their actual value.

Harlow trained several young assistants, working multiple phone lines in a small office, to contact potential victims whom he had identified that were between the ages of sixty to eighty-five and who resided throughout the United States. His most popular targets were widows and widowers who lived by themselves and nursing home patients who still had some control over their money. Like most telemarketers, Harlow had huge lists of names of prospective buyers that he had purchased from other telemarketers, containing the information about these people that he needed.

The callers were trained to modulate the pitch and tone of their voices to sound sweet and soothing and were instructed specifically to speak slowly and deliberately, so the elderly could understand them. Harlow instructed them to visit with these older people the same way they would communicate with their own grandparents, always seeking ways to convince them that they were only contacting them so the seniors would have latitude in making decisions in their best interests. That way, more people like themselves could enjoy the brighter future that they so richly deserved.

Once their victims were hooked with their first installment on the bogus coins, they were promised a visit from either Harlow or one of his representatives who would come all the way from Los Angeles or Las Vegas and arrange to take them to dinner in a Rolls Royce or a Mercedes Benz. The con artists would chat with the victims on the phone for hours at a time, winning them over, visiting about whatever interested them. In many instances, these unwary people felt they were finally receiving the personal attention they so desired and had wished for—attention that in many instances, their own families were not giving them.

Once Alma was first contacted by one of Harlow's phone bandits in 1992 and convinced to purchase the first coin shipment, she was also promised that she would be given the "privilege" to purchase additional coins in the future that would eventually comprise an entire collection, which, in its totality, would be worth much more than the total amount of her investment . . . a sum of money that could run into the millions. Alma was won over, convinced that the return on her $230,000 would be enough to put all of her grandchildren through college and would still leave her an adequate amount for her own future.

Once Alma was given the initial Harry Harlow pitch by one of Harlow's henchmen, Harlow himself came to the phone and sealed the deal, assuring Alma of their continuous friendship, the personal visit in the luxury car topped with a steak dinner, and of course, the promise of financial security. One of Harlow's promoters present the day that Alma was first contacted, advised me that Harlow was holding the telephone up where everyone in the room could take note, and then proceeded to "ham it up" for their entertainment, making fun of Alma with various gestures and funny faces, while he was fleecing her out of her money.

★ ★ ★ ★ ★

When Alma first called my office in 1992 and asked for an interview, I instantly recognized the plight she described as a fraud by wire violation where federal laws are breached when perpetrators utilize federal instruments, such as telephone lines (wires) to defraud their victims of money or other assets of value.

Alma was as fearful of having to admit to her family she had been the victim of a telemarketing fraud, since she was heartbroken over the loss of her savings. I advised her to keep her family members in the loop and to reach out to them for their support during some trying times ahead. Alma was very close to her adult children and put her grandchildren on pedestals . . . especially the young grandson preparing to serve a Church mission.

As I studied Alma's composure and obvious inner strength and her faith in our judicial system, I asked myself, *Who could possibly want to inflict this kind of suffering onto this sweet soul, especially with such impunity and indifference?* In my mind, this kind of abuse of the elderly was second only to murder and sexual abuse.

The surprising part was that as Alma described Harlow and his young pack of thieves that had contacted her, she didn't demonstrate anger or animosity towards them. What she related to me was how her "friends" had let her down and how their "promises" had been broken. She referred to each person by his or her first name, almost with an expression of endearment, the way she would describe someone in her family. She characterized Harlow's commitments to her for visits and steak dinners as promises she had valued as sweet and tender.

Alma had absolutely refused to negatively perceive her perpetrators or to pass judgment on them, even after they had betrayed her confidence and stolen her money. Even in all the subsequent years of pushing her case through the federal court system in Portland, I never once heard Alma verbally chastise one person that had fleeced her.

★ ★ ★ ★ ★

I left on a ten day junket to Los Angeles and Las Vegas and began interviewing some of the young telemarketers that were doing Harlow's bidding, both past and present. When I tossed out the probability of federal grand jury indictments and prosecution for having committed felonies for defrauding older folks, they came to attention. Two of them, principals in Harlow's scheme, rolled over on him and provided copies of transactions they and others had participated in, not only with Alma but also with hundreds of victims from all over the country.

The documents contained entries made by Harlow, as well as original evaluations of the victims by others, some recorded in demeaning language made by Harlow's "first contact" employees. The information typically included the victim's age, address, health, amount of savings and other cash deposits, stocks, certificates of deposit (CDs) bonds, and information as to close relatives in contact with the victims, if there were any. Harlow figured these were people that could mess up his scam.

Snide, demeaning comments were included, criticizing the potential victims, and making fun of them for their gullible responses, poking fun at their senility. Comments often ran like this: "She's out of it mentally . . . but easy pickings." Such statements were rampant throughout the commentaries. These records, plus Harlow's phone call records, enabled me to start interviewing victims nationwide.

I was boiling inside. My objectivity was waning. As I continued in touch with Alma and began to see her health degenerate, it was hard not to become personally involved. As the case proceeded over the next three years, I began viewing Alma as a family member, sharing with her the pictures of my own grandchildren and describing our family get-togethers. I kept her abreast of any progress in prosecuting Harlow and his gang and of the possibility of recovering some money. Alma never lost hope, but she appeared more interested in sharing her grandson's missionary experiences and her other family happenings, and hearing about my family, than she was in me bringing up the case. She always assured me, however, that when the time came, she would be ready to testify. She turned over all her Admiral Garner coins to me, which were in their cases, neatly framed in velvet, together with the fraudulent certificates of authenticity and inflated value. I preserved these items as evidence, and turned them over to the federal prosecutor in Salt Lake City.

★ ★ ★ ★ ★

On April 10, 1993, I, along with some agents from the Las Vegas office, paid Harlow a visit at his luxury home. Two very nice Mercedes-Benz vehicles were parked in his driveway. Behind the house was a large swimming pool at the base of an artificially-created mountain with a huge waterfall cascading down from it into the pool.

I had a federal warrant granting me authority to take Harlow's fingerprints and hand writing samples. As I finished doing that, Harlow asked, "What does all this mean?"

I responded, "Harry, this means we're coming back to arrest you. I've got an eighty-five-year-old widow in Vernal, Utah, who you've stolen $230,000 from, and I'm not very happy about it." Communicating that to Harlow and seeing the pale expression suddenly permeate his countenance gave us all some temporary satisfaction.

There were obstacles in moving Alma's case forward. We contacted over two hundred of Harlow's victims throughout the country who had been scammed. Some were in nursing homes, some were deceased, having died saddened and disillusioned over losing their life's savings. I either interviewed these people over the telephone and recorded their statements or set out leads to other FBI divisions nationwide to send agents out to interview the victims in person, that is, those who were still alive and able to communicate.

Harlow and his attorney knew that as time went on and the victims continued aging, Harlow could greatly benefit. As Harlow continued requesting and receiving continuances from the court, many of the victims died or became unable to communicate. His strategy was obvious, as he delayed the case with one fabricated excuse after another, prolonging any disposition of the litigation, while Alma and the others became more and more diminished in their capacity to testify.

Another obstacle was the time it took to determine the appropriate venue where the cases should be prosecuted, since fraud by wire violations could be tried at the point of origin where the calls were made, which would be Los Angeles or Las Vegas, or at the point where the calls were received, such as Utah and the many other states throughout the country. I encouraged all FBI divisions with Harlow's victims within their territories to file additional cases with their respective U.S. Attorneys. Where those divisions were unable to interest the federal prosecutors, I encouraged the Los Angeles and Las Vegas divisions to consider prosecution, since the perpetrators worked out of offices in those venues.

While I was trying to coordinate cases against all Harlow's victims on a national scale, the U.S. Attorney's office in Salt Lake City was waiting to determine how much emphasis the federal prosecutors in other offices would put on bringing Harlow down, before they decided to present Alma's case to their own grand jury.

Meanwhile, while all this was being settled, Alma's health was taking a turn for the worse. I became more intent than ever on her being able to see some justice and possibly recover a little money.

Finally, I was granted a search warrant for Harlow's house. When I advised Alma I was heading to Las Vegas with a warrant to search Harlow's residence, she asked me to deliver a letter she had prepared for him . . . a letter written without malice, but begging he return to her some of her money.

I traveled from Vernal to Nevada, met with agents from the Las Vegas office, and together, we executed the search warrant, which gave us authority to enter Harlow's home and video-tape everything at his residence that appeared to have a value over a thousand dollars. The strategy here was to create a record, proving those items existed, so they could later be seized and used to reimburse victims. The other purpose was to find items Harlow may have used to perpetuate his fraud or fruits of the crime.

That minimal thousand dollar figure applied to almost everything Harlow had, possessions undoubtedly purchased with the savings of hundreds of the elderly that he had defrauded. There were elaborate furnishings of every kind, well-appointed furniture in walnut and hickory and of the most stylish design, opulent paintings and wall hangings, multiple electronic devices and other sophisticated video and digital toys for the children, wardrobes overflowing with very expensive and stylish clothing, and about everything else anyone would want but not need.

Before I left, I handed Harlow Alma's letter. He said he would read it. I had my doubts but knew if he did read it, he would do nothing for Alma, and he didn't.

Alma continued being patient as her health disintegrated, and as her family became increasingly concerned for her, as they cooperated in the investigation every way they could. They were extremely discouraged that the case had not yet been prosecuted. I kept the phone line busy, encouraging the prosecutor assigned the case, pushing for Harlow's arrest. I kept appraising her of Alma's fragile condition and providing her whatever information she needed from the field. I did everything within my power to speed up the prosecutive effort, but learned once again how slow the wheels of justice roll forward.

Alma passed away, still positive and hopeful, but without obtaining her due justice. I was overwhelmed with sorrow, but knew in my heart that I had done everything I could for her. As I lamented her passing, the conviction was embedded in my heart that the one thing that I had done for her, sharing my family and our lives, visiting with her about my calling as a bishop, even though she wasn't of my faith, and just being a friend, was the most important thing I could have done for her.

★ ★ ★ ★ ★

After Alma's death, I continued pursuing Harlow with a vengeance. I pressed the prosecutor incessantly for an arrest warrant and soon obtained it.

Two days later, Harlow heard a loud knock on his door. When he opened it, several FBI agents surrounded him, one with handcuffs extended.

"Hello, Harry. We're back!"

36

★ ★ ★ ★ ★

SHEEP SHOWDOWN

DECEMBER 1993

During my thirty years with the FBI, including over twenty years on SWAT teams, I was never physically assaulted; that is, not until a male ram sheep decided he had my number during a morning run in Vernal.

Rulon Lind, a member of my ward, raised sheep on a stretch of land bordering the road underneath the hill our house was perched on. Rulon, an elderly gentleman in his mid-seventies, was a beekeeper who sold his honey throughout the community, marketing his mutton on the side. Most of the time, with emphasis on "most," the sheep were penned in.

However, on this one fateful morning, his band of ewes and a huge ram, weighing close to two hundred pounds, had breached the fence and wandered out onto the road, as I was approaching. Rulon was inside his house, unaware his sheep had broken out. It was very early in the morning, so there was no one to witness my "assault in embryo."

I noticed Rulon's sheep were loose but wasn't overly concerned, and decided I'd just call him at the end of my run to alert him. What I gave no thought was the fact that I was now invading the area the ram felt was his extended private domain. By the way he was blowing snot out of his nose, I should have figured out it was that time of year for male sheep to be in some kind of rut or mating mode that makes them feel like King Kong.

Apparently, as I jogged by, I inadvertently provided the catalyst for whatever kind of chemical reaction that takes place in a ram's brain when he is in the mating mode . . . the reaction that makes him jealous and protective of his harem.

Once I passed the huge animal, and without me knowing what was happening, the ram charged, launched himself into the air, and pegged me with the blunt portion of his curled horns slamming into my upper back. I never saw it coming and was knocked forward onto my knees and felt excruciating pain shooting out through my back.

When I realized what had happened and saw my assailant turning toward me for another go at it, I rushed to regain my feet, realizing that if he hit me again while I was on my knees, I might not get back up.

I noticed some two-by-four pieces of lumber Rulon had placed across an empty concrete drain ditch between the road and his house, as a temporary bridge. I sprinted toward that as fast as I could move, but not quite fast enough. As I made it halfway across, I was back-slammed again. I felt myself tottering toward the edge of the boards, as I anticipated impact with the concrete floor of the empty drainage ditch below me. I caught my balance just in time to avert the fall, still reeling from the ram's second lunge.

The realization that the sheep was now pursuing me was frightening. I knew that if he was chasing me over two-by-fours on a drainage ditch, he was serious, and I had nowhere to go.

I limped out onto the road, then ran as fast as I could with what energy I had left, thinking if I distanced myself from his ewes, the ram would stop chasing me. I sprinted down the road, as the pain kept shooting through my spine and up my back.

The ram was right behind me, closing in.

I stopped, picked up the sharpest stick I could find, and turned to face the brute, as he made his third pass at me. I stood my ground until he was within three feet of me, then I quickly stepped to the side and thrust the stick into the animal's neck as he passed by, in a fruitless effort to persuade him that he'd enjoy his time back with the ewes more than with me. It didn't work. Stabbing him with a stick that wouldn't even penetrate his hide just wasn't cutting it. (No pun intended.)

I turned away again, and ran even farther down the road, still trying to distance myself sufficiently that my attacker would lose interest. Fat chance! He charged again, propelling himself at me. I side-stepped him again, but this time, as he brushed by, he bumped me a little on the fly.

I came to grips with the reality of the situation. I wasn't going to outrun this beast, nor did he have any intentions of giving up on me.

He wanted only to get me down on the ground where he could ram me and trample me to death. An avalanche of thoughts rushed into my mind as I prepared for the next assault. *No one's even watching. I could be mince meat before this is over, because I can't outrun him, and I can only play matador so long. Eventually, he will nail me. Once I'm down on the ground, it's all over.*

The sheep swept by again. I stabbed him with a fury this time, as I jumped to the side. I decided if I was going down, I was going to inflict enough pain on this animal, who weighed every bit as much as me, to discourage him from trying to kill me. Maybe he'll go away, I thought, if I can just get this stick through his hide!

Other thoughts began streaming in . . . the proud kind. *I've mixed it up with the Mafia. I've survived a shoot-out. I've been on all kinds of SWAT raids and dangerous arrests. I've brought down some really bad guys. I'd even pinned a bear. How does Judy explain to the kids and the FBI that I was taken out by a sheep?*

The ram made another couple of passes. He just wasn't quitting. I saw another member of my ward, Marvin Richardson, standing in his back yard, taking in the drama and then running back inside his house, hopefully to call Rulin, I thought.

There were other weird thoughts. *What are the members of my ward going to think of Rulin, the honey man, knowing that he let his sheep out, and they killed the bishop?*

The ram had made about eight passes at me and was still blowing snot out of his nose, staring at me through reddened eyes, as he set up on me again. Marvin must have made contact with Rulin, because out of the corner of my eye, I saw Rulin coming from his house, dragging a two-by-four, walking toward me at what seemed a snail's pace, as the ram came at me again. He missed only by inches, as I stabbed him one more time.

Rulin came shuffling over, as though time was not really a factor. I thought, *Come on, Rulin! Come on! You can step it up a little at any time!*

The sheep made another pass. As I spun around again, facing him, I saw Rulin come up behind him, take a round-house swing at him with the two-by-four, and lower the boom directly onto his skull. The ram went down on all fours, kicked his legs around for a few seconds, then slowly got up and meandered back to the ewes.

"Guess I'm going to have to put that one down," Rulin muttered. "Sorry, Bishop!"

"I'd sure appreciate it if you would, Rulin. See you in church." Rulin was still gazing at me, as I limped away.

That night my back was black and blue. I couldn't care less. I was alive!

37

★ ★ ★ ★ ★

SUED BY THE ACLU

DECEMBER 7, 1993

I had not served over a year with the Bureau before realizing that there were two distinct roads to take in the approach to your work. The first was fairly simple: Work just enough each day to put in your time, and then head home without upsetting any apple carts or making any waves. Avoid any gung ho syndromes and adapt a posture of indifference towards any effort that could hurt you politically, endanger a pay raise, or bring down the wrath of a supervisor.

The other road, which I believed was the high road, was this: Walk through a wall for your case when you knew beyond any doubt the subject was guilty, minimize your concerns about criticism, and be action-oriented. Be willing to put in excess overtime and don't be overly-devastated by receiving an occasional letter of censure. Realize that if you are going to do anything at all, you may ruffle some feathers. I had a few letters of censure, one for losing a set of credentials, another for accidentally discharging my weapon (no injury to anyone), and a couple others for rubbing some folks the wrong way. I also had more than five letters of commendation for each letter of censure I received. I believed in the creed inscribed on the work desk of Special Agent Ben Grogan, who I greatly admired, and who was eventually killed in a gunfight in Miami. It stated the following:

> It is not the critic who counts; not the man who points out how the strongman stumbles, or where the doer of deeds could have done them better. The credit belongs to the man who is actually

247

in the arena, whose face is marred by dust and sweat and blood; who strives valiantly; who errs, who comes short again and again, because there is no effort without error and shortcoming; but who does actually strive to do the deeds; who knows great enthusiasms, the great devotions; who spends himself in a worthy cause; who at the best knows in the end the triumph of high achievement, and who at the worst, if he fails, at least fails while daring greatly, so that his place shall never be with those cold and timid souls who know neither victory or defeat.
　　—President Theodore Roosevelt

I discovered that living by this creed sometimes resulted in inadvertently stepping on someone's toes or upsetting people who had chosen a different road. For me, making mistakes and being disciplined for them were fair and justified.

It was unjustified criticism from individuals and outside organizations bent on entrapping and destroying devoted law enforcement officers who were trying to do their work that I became leery of. I believed those people needed to be called to task and held responsible to the American public.

★　★　★　★　★

In November of 1993, the Salt Lake City Police Department obtained an arrest warrant for Raymond Nathaniel Valdez for burglary and theft, and subsequently requested assistance from the FBI's fugitive task force in Salt Lake City to assist in apprehending him. According to information the police had, Valdez was going into Salt Lake on weekends, burglarizing houses, then going back to LaPoint, Utah, on the Northern Ute-Ouray Indian reservation, where he stayed with his protective mother, Rose Valdez.

The FBI task force requested that I attempt to locate and apprehend their fugitive, Valdez, on the reservation, in view of the fact that local authorities had no jurisdiction there since the reservation was considered a sovereign nation.

I called Lieutenant Ed Reynolds, Fort Duchesne Police Department, requesting that he assign an officer to assist me in contacting Raymond Valdez's mother, Rose Valdez, regarding her sons' whereabouts.

Detective Wayne Hollebeke, Uintah County Sheriff's Office, advised me that Rose, historically, had never cooperated with law enforcement where it involved her son, Raymond, and often hid him in her house and in adjacent buildings. Hollebeke believed Rose's hostile attitude toward law enforcement was the catalyst for Raymond's disregard for the law.

Raymond Jr., who had a lengthy rap sheet for flagrant felony violations, was once listed on the State of Utah's "Most Wanted Fugitives" list. He had a girlfriend on the reservation, who was the mother of his two children. On September 27, 1993, Littlewhiteman heard Valdez say he lived with his mother when he was being booked on a drug charge. Littlewhiteman also knew Valdez was unemployed and liked to stay out late at night drinking and abusing hard drugs.

When Officer Littlewhiteman responded to assist me, he was off-duty and had neither his sidearm nor his police vehicle. For his protection, I loaned him my Bureau shotgun, the only other weapon I had available.

We knocked on Rose Valdez's door. She opened the door angrily, casting looks at us that could kill.

I spoke first, displaying my credentials, "Ms. Valdez, I'm from the FBI. This is Officer Greg Littlewhiteman, tribal police. We have a warrant for your son, Raymond Valdez Jr. Is he here?"

"No." The answer was curt and defiant.

I continued, "When did you last see Raymond?"

"He was here a week and a half ago to visit his kids. He hasn't been back since. Is this all you guys have to do is harass us Indian people?" Rose Valdez was instantly on the defensive.

Littlewhiteman chimed in, "I'm Native American, Ms. Valdez. Oglala Sioux."

"Ms. Valdez," I asked, "do you mind if we come in and look around?"

"Come ahead. We've got nothing to hide here." By her facial expressions and countenance, she gave a clear impression that she was lying.

We entered the residence by climbing some wooden steps built in front for entry. Inside the living room was seated an elderly man in his sixties, subsequently identified as Ray Valdez Sr., the fugitive's father. A few other people were also seated, possibly relatives. I kept my revolver holstered, so as not to incite anyone. Littlewhiteman maintained the shotgun close to his body, pointing it down towards the floor at all times. He kept an eye on the occupants of the home, while I quickly searched for Raymond Jr.

I spent no more than two or three minutes searching the residence, and then we began to leave. Rose wasn't content with that. She began screaming at us, commencing a tirade on how white men were always picking on Native Americans, without cause. She pursued us out to our vehicle, screaming at us and attempting to goad us into retaliating.

At one point, Rose came so close to us, while becoming increasingly hysterical, that I asked Littlewhiteman if he had his handcuffs, hoping that if she heard this, she'd back off and leave us alone.

We finally got away without further badgering from Rose and headed into town for lunch. An hour and a half later, we headed for the home of Raymond Jr.'s girlfriend. It was a trailer, similar to Rose Valdez's, but much smaller.

The girlfriend came to the door. We identified ourselves by show of credentials and explained there was a warrant for Raymond, and we were there looking for him. We asked if he was there. His girlfriend advised us she hadn't been in touch with her boyfriend for several days and had no idea where he was. She gave her voluntary consent to search her trailer. We accomplished that in less than two minutes, but with negative results.

As we exited the girlfriend's residence, a friend of hers, Sherman Dubois, was waiting outside her mobile home. He had been standing next to our vehicle. As we entered our car, Dubois quietly volunteered information that he had observed Raymond Jr. at Rose's house just two hours earlier, approximately the same time we had been there listening to Rose deny her son's presence. We immediately returned to Rose's house. Again, we knocked, and she came to the door and opened it. I informed her that we had just developed information that her son had been at her residence the same time she had denied he was there. I advised her of the provisions of the Harboring Statute, making it clear that harboring a fugitive was a felony, punishable by law.

Again, Rose accused us of harassing Indian people; nevertheless, she did grant us verbal permission to search her outbuildings. We found nothing.

As we left Rose's house, we were certain Raymond Jr. was somewhere near, smiling at the ingenuity of his protective mother. On December 27, he surrendered to local authorities, twenty days after our search for him.

★ ★ ★ ★ ★

Several days after the fruitless searches for Raymond Jr., I left my house for a day of ice fishing on the Matt Warner Reservoir, one and a half hours away. I grabbed the daily edition of the *Salt Lake Tribune,* along with my fishing gear, and headed out the door.

Arriving at the lake a couple hours later, I hauled my gear out on the ice, cut a hole in it, started a fire to heat the hot chocolate, baited my hook, and set up a folding chair.

"What a great way to spend the day," I thought, as I picked up the *Tribune* while sipping hot chocolate. There is no way I could have been prepared for what I saw.

On the front page of the *Tribune,* there was a picture in color of Rose and her son, Raymond Jr., looking off into the distance, headlining an article detailing the remarks from a university professor in New Mexico, lamenting the tragedy of Native Americans being historically victimized by the white man and declaring how right in the heart of the state of Utah, the whole process of victimization was being re-enacted by Special Agent Mike McPheters of the FBI and Officer Greg Littlewhiteman of the Fort Duchesne Tribal Police Department. The article detailed Rose Valdez's terrifying experience when the FBI and tribal police entered her home forcefully and without her permission, with guns drawn, pointing them at everyone, ransacking through her home and screaming profanities. The article further described how the incident was being reviewed by the American Civil Liberties Union (ACLU), who would surely see that justice was done in the matter. That article pretty well ruined a good day of fishing.

I returned home that same night and wrote a detailed report on everything that had really happened at the Valdez residence. My supervisor was content with my explanation, and I gave him a heads up that the ACLU was about to make my case one of their pet projects.

Within a couple of days, I was advised by Salt Lake City headquarters that both I and Greg Littlewhiteman were being sued for fifty thousand dollars each by Rose and the ACLU, for violating Rose's Fourth Amendment rights to be protected against illegal search and seizure. She had advised the ACLU that we were never given permission to enter her house, nor to search her outbuildings. She accused us of committing a host of civil rights violations against her and her husband, including using excess profanity, acting violently, and pointing weapons at them. Interestingly enough, none of those who knew me had ever heard me swear or display violence.

As a bishop, serving in that capacity for the fourth time, being referred to on the front page of the state's largest newspaper as a violent individual who pointed guns at everyone, while swearing and rampaging through houses, didn't do a whole lot towards improving my temperament. I asked myself two questions: How can someone get away with that much fabrication and how will all my ward members and my family take this?

Within a week, I was called by a departmental attorney from the U.S. Department of Justice in Washington, D.C., Paul Brown, who advised he was representing me and Littlewhiteman. He indicated, much to my delight, that he specialized in lawsuits against federal officers, resulting from spurious and unfounded allegations.

Over the next three and a half years from 1994 through 1997, Paul Brown traveled back and forth from Washington D.C. to Salt Lake City and Fort Duchesne, Utah, addressing motions by the ACLU, the plaintiff, and presenting motions in favor of myself and Greg Littlewhiteman, the defendants. In addition, he interviewed numerous witnesses and reviewed mountains of testimony. The cost to the government was astronomical.

At one point, the ACLU offered to settle with Greg Littlewhiteman and me for ten thousand dollars. I advised them I wouldn't settle for ten cents, because it would amount to an admission that we had done something wrong. Littlewhiteman was of the same mind-set.

At the court hearings for dismissing the charges for lack of evidence, the federal judge dismissed the allegation of illegal search and allowed the issue of illegal seizure to go to the jury in March 1997.

The trial was a circus. Rose came with her hair completely gray. It had been black when we originally contacted her. She advised the Court her hair had grayed because of the unnecessary trauma she had been subjected to by myself and Littlewhiteman, which caused the acute nervous condition that had taken its toll on her.

Both Greg Littlewhiteman's wife and my wife, Judy, were present for the trial. Judy was accused by the plaintiff of "playing the jury," because one day she wore a bright red dress to the trial.

The evidence that Attorney Paul Brown so effectively presented in our defense was overwhelming and completely vindicated us of any wrongdoing. The coup de gras came when Rose was on the stand and testified that we had forced our way into her home without her permission. She was asked under oath by Paul Brown why she had previously stated in her deposition that she had voluntarily granted us permission to enter. She had no answer. It was obvious she had forgotten what she had said in her deposition. That was when a male juror looked directly at me and grinned from ear to ear. With that telling grin, I knew we'd won the case and had beaten the ACLU.

In April 1999, the ACLU filed an appeal, but lost again.

The case became a landmark in helping to prevent federal law enforcement officers from having ridiculous and unfounded charges lodged against them in the performance of their duties.

Today this case is written into federal law as, "McPheters vs. Valdez" (D.C. No. 94-C-523J).

38

★★★★★

THE MONTANA FREEMEN

MARCH 26, 1996

The barren plains surrounding the little town of Jordan in eastern Montana would be the last place one would think would attract waves of news media, scores of FBI agents, and an excess of citizens-rights celebrities like Bo Gritz and Randy Weaver, but high-profile federal cases seemed to pop up just about anywhere: Waco, Texas; Ruby Ridge, Idaho; and so on.

The Montana Freemen found their "Justus Township" near Jordan the perfect place and opportunity to unleash their off-beat extremism on the country, as they expounded their concept of "individual sovereignty" and rejected the authority of the U.S. Government. In the process of setting up their own government, courts, banking, and credit system, they began issuing bogus checks, based on their twisted concepts of individual freedoms, and ended out in an eighty-one day standoff with the FBI.

The Freemen believed they were protecting the rights of farmers and ranchers from the U.S. Government's propensity to sustain national debt and enter into price manipulations, which they claimed were bankrupting them. Their leader, LeRoy Schweitzer, was adamant in his commitment to defy the federal government, as he violated law after law, committing bank fraud, mail fraud, wire fraud, making false claims to the IRS, interstate transportation of stolen property, threatening public officials, and participating in the armed robbery of a television crew and in firearms violations.

The Freemen even began plowing the fields of the property they were leasing and had no right to work, which infuriated the legal owners and brought great pressure down upon the FBI to act. The Bureau was very cautious, as was the U.S. Attorney General, Janet Reno, who was still recovering from the Waco incident. The government's posture was containment first and aggression last. While the Freemen seemed to be enjoying thumbing their noses at the people who owned the land they were on and at the FBI, some of the local residents were cheering the Bureau on to "Go get 'em!" and others were wanting to avoid bloodshed at all costs.

The FBI became tired of the siege after the first few weeks. Jordan, which had only four hundred residents, eventually became home to one hundred FBI people. The agents from Salt Lake who had first responded found the area covered with melting snow that soon turned the area into a mud bog. It was windy and extremely cold. Agents were living in livestock sheds, spending nights in sleeping bags on straw beds with propane heaters for warmth. The agents were committed to stay until the standoff was resolved.

★　★　★　★　★

APRIL 9, 1996

All agents in the Salt Lake City Division were summoned to do tours at Jordan. I responded and began my twelve-hour shifts, seven days a week, helping to monitor the standoff and being available for whatever response ordered by the Bureau command post. Since no housing was available in Jordan when I first arrived, I stayed at a motel in Miles City and commuted eighty-five miles each way to Jordan to begin my twelve hour shift. The vast deer and antelope herds along the highway were a huge, ever-present traffic hazard. The roads around Jordan were always muddy and unpredictable that time of year. One of our agents assigned to a SWAT team from another division was killed when he lost control of his vehicle.

Our command post was located at the Garfield County Fairgrounds. The Freemen were still holed up in their Justus Township compound about thirty miles from Jordan. I was assigned to a "Search-Interview-Transport" team, tasked with confronting anyone trying to get into the Freemen compound for any reason, including the news media, who were there on a "hit and miss" basis, meaning they would come, tire soon of the conditions, leave, and be replaced by more media. After running out of people to interview, they started interviewing each other for updates on the standoff story. A local store began manufacturing T-shirts for sale that carried the question, "Have you been interviewed yet?"

For me, the living conditions were much better than those for the first responders. I actually shared a room in a small Baptist church, the "Community Bible Center," with four other agents. Beds were at a premium, so I would sleep in one when off my shift, and during my shift, another agent would sleep in the same bed. The meals were served outside and prepared by cook crews who fed Montana's fire fighters during the summer months. Boxes of candy bars of every kind imaginable were on every lunch table with no limit on how many you could eat. We all developed the "Hansel and Gretel" mentality, thinking we had stumbled onto the candy house in the forest.

I marveled at how the Freemen could actually believe they had seceded from the United States of America. I thought, *How can they really believe they can get away with holding their own courts, determining which laws they would obey and disobey, and writing bogus checks to pay off their bills? How could they believe they would get away with threatening federal and state judges?* Yet they must be committed, since they are armed to the teeth and are saying they are ready to die for their beliefs.

I reflected on my church's twelfth article of faith: "We believe in being subject to kings, presidents, rulers, and magistrates, in obeying, honoring, and sustaining the law."

As I considered the vast difference between the position our early prophet, Joseph Smith, took on honoring the laws of the U.S. Constitution, even to the point of submitting himself to being abused and incarcerated by local magistrates and authorities for incidents where he had no guilt, and then considered these outlandish actions by people who sought to blatantly disregard the laws of the land, I was proud to be a member of The Church of Jesus Christ of Latter-day Saints.

While I was there, about twenty of the Freemen subjects were still holed up in the compound. Only three had been arrested. Three minor children were still in the compound. We had them all under constant aerial and land surveillance, but conducted no raids.

Taking such a low-key approach, containing but not confronting, was something new to me. I was not the only one whose patience was wearing thin. I was afraid the lack of aggression and decisiveness might come back to haunt us. The Freemen viewed our reluctance to go after them as a weakness.

At first, only Montana state legislators negotiated with the subjects. The FBI had not yet taken its turn. The reason for that is that the Freemen didn't recognize the FBI as a legitimate entity, since they didn't recognize the U.S. Government. For a long time, the Freemen bottom line seemed to be "We don't negotiate with anyone!"

On my fifty-third birthday, I made the following entry in my journal:

> *This isn't exactly the most wonderful place on Earth to be spending a birthday. Twelve hour shifts. No place to go when off duty. No shops. No television. No one to eat birthday cake with. No birthday cake! Still, I'm glad to be helping with a case that has become the center of focus of FBI concerns in the country today.*
>
> *I feel we are not using the traditional methods of law enforcement that have made us the great agency that we are. We are just sitting tight . . . playing the waiting game. Oh, well!*
>
> *I've seen a beautiful part of the country this week . . . one that I might never have seen were it not for this assignment. There's a silver lining to every cloud. I'm grateful to have a good job and an interesting challenge.*
>
> *Did my laundry today. Got in a nice six-mile run before work. I'll make a birthday out of it yet!*
> *—April 13, 1996*

It seems that when things are tough, it's always children that lighten up the day. This note accompanied a huge pan of freshly-baked rolls delivered to the eating area:

> *Dear FBI People,*
> *Thank you for keeping us safe. We are sorry that you don't get to spend time with your family on Easter. Thank you for what you do.*
>
> *We hope you like the rolls. Thank you for being brave and doing a good job. We want you to know you're not forgotten out there protecting us. We know you must miss your families and loved ones, so we hope these yummy rolls will help you feel better.*
>
> *Wishing you the best,*
> *The Hanson Family*

APRIL 16, 1996

Contrasting with the sweet and supportive nature of the above message was another that was posted by a Freemen supporter for us all to read:

Are you too frightened to read this material, or have you been ordered to discard it?

FBI-ATF, ARE YOU READY TO DIE BECAUSE OF THE CORRUPTION WITHIN?

You joined the Bureau to serve your country. Therefore, you must believe in both. Ours is a Nation of Laws where we expect, and are entitled to, Justice according to Due Process. You may think you are serving that Justice now, but you are really serving Janet Reno and the Justice department who have sent you to Montana for political advantage. The plan is to insure that a very strong and ruthless Anti-Terrorism Bill will pass swiftly. The plan is also the CIA's way of discrediting the FBI. You are being thrown to the wolves of ambition!

You have been set up! Duped! You've been sent into an ambush.

They told you the patriots would not respond. Look around you. It's not the ones you see, but those that remain hidden across America. They are watching every move. They will remember.

If you truly love your country and if your devotion to the Bureau is strong, you will go back home; you will disobey orders to kill the people you have laid siege to. If you stay, and if you attack the Freemen in their home, you may die. And if you do, it will not be for the FBI or for the country, it will be the result of corruption within. Remember Lexington and think about your own family tonight.

SEVEN VERY IMPORTANT QUESTIONS:

1. Do you fully understand the consequences of your actions? There is nowhere to hide. You have been photographed and the documents in Janet Reno's possession identify that you were here. Where will you go if Justus Township turns into another Waco?

2. Do you understand the nature of the alleged crimes

that these people are charged with? Are these alleged white-collar crimes worthy of their continued treatment and eventual death?

3. Do you have the courage to disobey the order to attack? Remember the Russian tank battalion commanders who refused to destroy the freemen (and women and children) in Grozny? Those officers knew right from wrong. Do you?

4. Do you believe that your actions could trigger a civil war in America, which would surely have devastating effects on all of us and our families?

5. Do you fully understand the nature of the war between the CIA and the FBI? The winner will control the country. They will win by discrediting the FBI and by forcing them into no-win situations, such as the one here in Montana. The FBI is being set-up by the CIA and its useful asset, Janet Reno.

6. Do you fully understand that the Nuremberg Defense, "I was only doing what I was ordered," will not protect you from justice?

7. Can you go before God claiming that you killed these humans because it was the right thing to do? Listen to your heart and to God's Spirit. You will be either a villain or a hero depending on what you choose to do.

On April 17 the Freemen began meeting with negotiators again, including a state prosecutor, John Connor. Bo Gritz, a former third-party presidential candidate and Randy Weaver, a subject in Idaho's Ruby Ridge incident, arrived to negotiate, but at first, were not allowed within the inner perimeter. Eventually, however, after a month of trying to negotiate, but with limited success, Gritz, who had some credibility in the patriot movement, was allowed to attempt at negotiating.

On April 27, after talking to the Freemen for seven hours, Gritz felt he was making some headway. After three days of negotiating, however, Gritz soon discovered that his negotiations had failed when the Freemen announced that God was with them, and they were unwilling to budge from their position, even though they had offers on their plate of reduced or dropped charges.

On May 2, the Freemen rejected the FBI's offer to meet under a "flag of truce" to negotiate ending the siege. The subjects continued not to recognize the Bureau as a legitimate entity.

On June 13, the siege finally ended with the surrender of the Free-men. Their charge that the American government was "depriving the people of their property until our posterity wakes up homeless" didn't fly well in the court system.

Eventually their prison sentences ranged from "time served on other matters" to twenty-two years and six months, in the case of their leader, LeRoy M. Schweitzer.

39

★★★★★

THE LAST TRANSFER

AUGUST 20, 1997

After I had twenty-nine years in with the Bureau, and being two and a half years away from mandatory retirement at age fifty-seven, Judy and I were getting itchy feet again. We were seriously considering a new Bureau adventure: working as a legal attaché, specifically in Paris, France, where I could do some of the FBI's bidding on foreign soil. I was semi-fluent in French and had already had experience in conducting investigations in Bolivia and in the Virgin Islands. We had always considered a foreign assignment. There would also be a pay raise that could enhance retirement.

We needed to leave Vernal, Utah. There were limited post-retirement job opportunities there for someone with my background. By fall of 1997, I would be released as bishop, since I would have served five and a half years. The biggest obstacle to foreign assignment would be missing the pitter-patter of the feet of our grandchildren and our sons and daughters.

The transfer came, but not to France. I had determined that foreign assignment would have to follow two years at Bureau headquarters in Washington, D.C. in an administrative capacity, and being that close to retirement, I had no desire to ride a desk. Upon my request, I was transferred to the Riverside California Resident Agency in the Los Angeles Division. It was a good compromise, and I was able to enjoy the association of many agents in a larger office again. Thirty-three agents were assigned to the Riverside office. There was also a cost-of-living enhancement that would count toward retirement. After spending fifteen years in remote one and two-man offices, it was a refreshing and welcome change . . . at first.

We bought a home in Temecula, approximately thirty-five miles south of Riverside. We lived about one hour north of San Diego. Temecula was a newer, well-planned community, tucked into a valley that benefited each afternoon from cool breezes flowing from the west into the valley, from a notch carved into the coastal mountains, bordering the Pacific Ocean. The valley was renowned for its grape orchards and wineries. The natural habitat, although beginning to be over-run with humanity, was still replete with red-tailed hawks, coyotes, deer, rabbits, squirrels, and a few mountain lions.

I was assigned to investigate significant international drug trafficking operations involving Mexican drug cartels and corrupt Mexican military officials who were involved in the trafficking. My new supervisor took full advantage of my experience, assigning me to lead out in planning and executing arrests and in writing affidavits for court approval for wiretapping and other squad operations. I was made a squad relief supervisor again and was sometimes left in charge of the squad when the supervisor was unavailable or out of the office. I also shared the dubious distinction of doing write-ups on our squad operations for the inspectors to pore over in forthcoming office inspections.

Although I enjoyed some of the new challenges I was given, I was missing the hands-on operations I had been involved in for so many years. I began to realize that our squad was for intelligence gathering and for disseminating that intelligence to other local, county, state, and federal agencies. We served a vital and necessary purpose, but totally dissimilar to the overt brand of law enforcement that I had grown to love and enjoy, working the mobs and Cuban car rings in South Florida, timber theft in the forests of Oregon, and the Indian reservations in the far reaches of Oregon and Utah.

Not being computer literate back then, I was overwhelmed with the challenges of searching databases for information I had previously located in file jackets. I found it daunting to learn to word process all my reports on computers that I had previously dictated to stenographers and tape-recorded for transcription from cassettes over the prior three decades.

I was tiring of having to ask first-office agents how to locate basic information in cyberspace that I needed to do my work . . . the same new agent trainees that I led in arrests and on surveillances. The new guys coming out of new agent training with laptops issued to them were a breath of fresh air. Their enthusiasm and zest for the work was contagious, and their garrulous humor was entertaining. Nevertheless, the generation gap separating us was obvious. Even though I enjoyed challenging them in push-ups occasionally or taking in a Padres baseball game with them, there was no older guy on the squad I could identify with. I was pretty oblivious to the social interests of the youngsters and to the nature of things they liked to discuss. I often wondered if any of them could have pictured the J. Edgar Hoover in their minds that I had personally met almost thirty years before.

The handwriting was on the wall. I had become a Bureau dinosaur. It was time for me to go. I knew there would be life beyond the FBI . . . even life beyond being the Agent Bishop.

On October 31, 1998, I retired from the FBI with thirty years and four months service.

40

★★★★★

THE TRANSITION

SEPTEMBER 10, 2001

Judy and I were in Ashburn, Virginia, sitting around the dining room table and visiting with our oldest son, Shad, and his pregnant wife, Tiffany, who was soon to give birth to our thirteenth grandchild. We were trying to decide what activity the next day would make the best use of our time in Washington, D.C., while we waited for Tiffany to give birth.

I asked Judy "So what do you suggest that we do tomorrow?"

She answered "Why don't we go see the Pentagon?"

"Ahhhh . . . the Pentagon's pretty boring, Judy. Why don't we try the White House? We haven't been there for a while." I wasn't crazy about the antiseptic appearance of the Pentagon complex, and with all the military's security measures in place there, I doubted there would be much we could access.

The next morning, Tiffany still wasn't even close to going into labor, so we left early. Shad dropped us off at the metro at about 8:40 AM, and shortly thereafter, we were heading into D.C. We exited at the stop placing us closest to the White House tour. When we reached the gate to the White House at about 9:35 AM, I went into the men's room, while Judy waited out near the front gate. When I exited the bathroom area, people were standing suspiciously still, just gazing toward the roof of the White House, where security personnel were mounting the roof, armed with what appeared to be rifles and rocket-propelled grenade launchers. A highly-excited, authoritative voice began roaring over the public address system.

"Every one get back! Clear the area of the White House immediately.

264

There's been a bomb! Clear the area immediately! I repeat. Leave now!" I later determined security was telling everyone there was a bomb, so they would start moving away. What really had happened was American Airlines Flight 77 had just crashed into the Pentagon.

Still, only a few people were moving. Most were still in a state of shock, thinking more about the White House tour they were missing, and many others probably thinking the whole thing was just a drill.

A security guard approached Judy and I and said, "If you can run, run! We need to get these folks moving."

The crowd was just beginning to move away, as their eyes remain fixed on the roof of the White House, where even more armed security personnel were mounting the roof. There were a couple of men clothed in dark blue FBI raid jackets, some Secret Service officers, and several others attired with black jackets with the words "Bomb Squad" on them.

Once the crowd had cleared the area between the White House and the outer gate and was gradually retreating back towards a park, a short distance away, more security people came running up, shouting "Get back farther! Way back. Fast!"

We continued jogging away from the White House, and when we came to the park, I climbed the stairs towards a monument and looked back for more insight into what was happening. By this time, there were over a dozen officers on the roof of the White House, with their shoulder weapons at the ready, giving the impression the White House was about to be under aerial attack.

As I continued taking in everything from my vantage point, security guards again approached us as they pushed out from the White House in every direction. One came right up to the base of the monument where I was perched and yelled "You'll have to keep moving back, folks!"

Judy and I headed for the Marriott Hotel, just a few blocks away. As we passed a lady in her forties, walking briskly along next to us, she began telling us about the Pentagon just being bombed.

I thought, *Bombed? Who would have bombed the Pentagon? How was it bombed? Did a plane drop a bomb on it? Did someone drive into it with explosives? How many people have died? What's going on here?*

Ten minutes later, we discovered what the lady was talking about, upon our arrival at the Marriott. Everyone there was crowded around some television sets in the main lobby—standing room only. I gasped in amazement, as I observed replays of the American Airlines Flight 11 crash into the north tower of the Worldwide Trade Center in New York City, which had occurred earlier that morning at 8:46 AM, and totally disintegrating, as it sliced off a huge section of that edifice. Then, in another replay, we observed United Airline Flight 175 hit the south tower, and do the same thing seventeen minutes later. The gas tanks on those planes had been filled to capacity for their trips from the east coast to Los Angeles and Seattle, transforming them into giant grenades and enabling them to melt down tons of steel beams upon impact. People were jumping out of windows to their deaths in droves to avoid burning to death.

We also learned that thousands had died and were still dying, including people from countries all over the world, and that the attack planes had been piloted by individuals thought to be Islamic terrorists.

At first, everyone thought the incident involving the first plane was an accident and that the plane inadvertently collided with the gargantuan north tower. All such speculation was erased when the second tower was hit by yet another plane which evaporated into thousands of tiny fragments, leaving a gaping hole of death that would bring that tower, also, down to dormant ash.

Next came the revelation that American Airlines Flight 77 had slammed into the Pentagon at 9:37 AM, just about the time I'd walked out of the men's restroom near the front gate of the White House. Then I recalled the talk of a bomb at the White House and thought, *That was no bomb! That was another plane.* This is where all the "bomb" talk had come from. The bomb was in the shape of a huge commercial airliner.

A few minutes later, Judy and I heard reports of as many as forty or fifty thousand people dying in New York and at the Pentagon. It would be days, even longer, before an accurate inventory of the dead could be completed.

We eventually learned that another commercial airliner, United Airlines Flight 93, had crashed somewhere in Pennsylvania at 10:03 AM. It was rumored this flight was supposed to be flown either into the U.S. Capital Building or into the White House. That would have been near the time we were there.

We tried to call our kids to assure them we were okay. All phone lines were jammed, making it impossible to make either landline or cell calls. Traffic was at a standstill. Everyone was put on alert for suspicious individuals or activities and instructed to call a posted number to alert security in the event something out of the ordinary was discovered. However, that number also was immediately jammed.

Judy and I just looked at one another, incredulously, trying to comprehend the magnitude and the ramifications of the world coming down around us. We were both thinking the same thing. Could all of this be real? No one messes with the United States! After all, we're the most powerful nation on earth. Who would dare do this?

What about those poor people jumping out of windows, dying en masse, even while we were speaking? What about their loved ones? Husbands? Wives? Their children?

What about the firemen and police officers who are putting themselves at risk?

Then, out of the corner of my eye, in the restaurant, I noticed a group of seven people of mid-eastern descent, who were laughing aloud and toasting one another.

"No, this isn't the time or place!" I was telling myself, becoming furious as I looked over at their festivity. What are they so happy about? I thought.

We sat down at a booth near them. I tried to hear, but couldn't discern what they were saying. They continued, acting as though nothing had happened. My blood was beginning to boil, as I repeatedly called the number for reporting suspicious activity, but to no avail. I couldn't get through. I looked everywhere for a police officer or security person. No one was available.

The party was beginning to break up. Of the seven people there, three couples got up and began leaving. A taller man, dark-complected, in his early forties, wearing a nice business suit, was the last to leave, and apparently was handling the bill.

I confronted him, as Judy remained seated.

"You know, I need you to answer a question for me. Thousands of people, mostly my people, are dying today. I noticed everyone at your table seemed pretty happy. Why was that?" The man knew I was demanding an answer.

"Sir! Sir! We were only celebrating a birthday. That was all." He paused, waiting to see if I was going to accept that, or if I would take it further.

I thought quickly. *The man has a strong accent. Probably the reason he was last out with the bill was because the others couldn't speak English. If that's the case, maybe they haven't grasped the full impact of what's going on. I could be jumping to conclusions. On the other hand, could they be celebrating the work of death? I don't have enough to go on here.*

I could do nothing under color of law to detain this man. As he walked away, the pictures I had envisioned in my mind of airliners smashing into the

World Trade Center and the Pentagon were filling my mind. I wanted to pick up a gun and go after someone.

I dialed the number again for reporting suspicious activity. The line was still jammed, as I lost sight of the seven people, fading into the crowd.

For hours, the only transportation available leading out of the city was the highway heading out through Maryland. That would have been three additional hours to get back to Ashburn. The metro finally started running again. By 5:00 PM we were heading back into Ashburn

Shad, Tiffany, and the three children had been on "high alert" all day, since we hadn't been able to establish communication with them. As we knocked at their door and they opened it and saw us, we realized our grandparent stock had soared about five hundred percent that day.

Tiffany had a baby girl three days later. All air transportation was grounded throughout the country, so we were unable to return home. It seemed untimely and inconsiderate, under the circumstances, to even consider any kind of recreation.

On September 13, two days after the attack, I grabbed a metro, headed into Washington D.C., and walked into the entrance to the Pentagon, which was cordoned off and secured by the police. I pulled out my retired FBI credentials and advised I wanted to go in and help with the relief effort. I don't believe the officer was supposed to let me enter, but he did.

From there I worked my way in towards the site where the plane crashed into the Pentagon. The outer perimeter was full of improvised service centers, comprised of huge tents secured by thick one-inch ropes, resembling circus tents. Various church denominations had set up relief centers and eating areas. The Salvation Army was there, as well as most of the major relief organizations chartered in the United States. Most all the federal law enforcement agencies were represented with their contingents of officers, as well as many local, county, and state officials, with their command posts established within the inner perimeter.

I was most impressed with the Red Cross set up. They were tasked with taking in donated food, oceans of it, donated by all the major food chains, and distributing it in some semblance of order, to the corps of emergency medical technicians (EMTs), military personnel, and other specialists, specifically assigned to finding and bringing out any bodies and body parts remaining in the vicinity of the Pentagon crash site, and preserving them for burial, as well as securing any fragments from the air liner that could be preserved as evidence.

I decided to go with the Red Cross, since I wasn't authorized to work in the inner perimeter. I approached a woman who seemed to be in charge of the food distribution unit, identified myself as a retired FBI agent who just wanted to volunteer. I assured her I would do anything at all to help. She started turning me away when I admitted I hadn't yet reported to the local Red Cross center for their half-day orientation.

Just as I began to walk away, somewhat despondent, another lady wearing the Red Cross insignia approached the lady who had turned me away and told her to allow me to work, based upon my background and experience. I was to be allowed to work in food distribution the rest of that day, if I would be willing to be oriented the following morning. I agreed, and was put to work, arranging boxes of packaged food, ready for consumption, along with soft drinks of every kind. There was so much food pouring in, the major challenge we had was preventing spoilage. Runners would come in, pushing empty carts for us to fill, with written orders form different groups working tirelessly inside the inner perimeter, tasked with finding anyone who might still be alive and taking out those who were not.

I was impressed beyond belief with the rescue workers. There were cots set out for them to lie down on when they came out every four hours to eat something and rest, but they wouldn't lie down. They knew if they did, they would go into a sound sleep. That would keep them from doing what they had volunteered to do—work that had to be done on a timely basis. The workers napped in a squatting position with their backs up against the tents. The cots remained empty.

One individual came to us frustrated and upset, saying, "I need this food order right away! Those people haven't been fed all day."

It was almost 7:00 PM . I answered, "You're kidding, right? We've had this food right here all day, just wanting to give it away. And there are people out there who couldn't get any?"

I loaded the man's order, watched him turn the cart away, and gazed pensively, as he jogged back towards the inner perimeter, with the loaded cart.

I soon discovered who it was that had not eaten. It was the group of on-the-scene psychologists that were there, counseling the rescue workers, who for days, had been dragging out bodies and body parts. These dedicated counselors rarely took time to eat.

When I took an occasional break, I noticed so many inspirational scenes that stirred me inside. Military officers, church leaders, all kinds of local officials, law enforcement people, and garden variety volunteers like me were milling around together, getting to know one another, and coming to a recognition that in among those old tents, anchored in dirt and green belts, we were all rising to a purpose far above ourselves.

Stout military men stood unabashedly together, arms and hands linked, offering up their prayers to the Almighty, not caring that all could hear. Bibles were placed on every table, and people were reading them. Children had written and illustrated "Thank you" notes and placed them within view of us volunteers. I copied down a few of them:

I feel safe in America, because it is a good place to be. We Americans are so strong to protect our country.
—Evan

Thank you, firefighters, for all you have done. My dad works in the north wing of the Pentagon, but it could have easily been reversed, and he could have been lost in the Pentagon. You have done your best to find the lost ones, and I just want you all to know you are thanked.
—Brittany Holts, age 12
Seventh grade

I love the flag of America! Thank you for fixing the Pentagon.
—Peggy

You all that did not die in the Pentagon. You are all so lucky, and I am so happy that you did not die in the Pentagon.
—Erin

Don't give up!
—Anonymous

It was a time of unity. President George W. Bush gave a speech, reaching out to the people, that brought tears to my eyes and warmth to my heart. It made me even prouder to be an American and instilled great faith into the future of all Americans. Congress assembled together: Republicans, Democrats, and Independents, and sang "God Bless America!"

The next day, I returned to D.C. for my Red Cross orientation in the morning, and then worked the rest of the day, into the evening.

It was that second day that I met Colonel J. Edgar Wakayama, Ph.D., U.S. Army, the Director of the Operational Test and Evaluation unit of the Office of the Secretary of Defense, Washington, D.C. He was assigned to a special group involved with live fire testing and evaluation. He was a man of Japanese descent, probably in his late forties, obviously in great physical shape, with a commanding appearance, and outfitted in camouflage. He came into the food distribution unit where I was working to handle some business. When he learned I was a retired FBI agent, he took a special interest in me. I thought it may be because he may have been named after Director J. Edgar Hoover. Oddly enough, he advised that was not the case and that he just had a great admiration for the Bureau.

Colonel Wakayama escorted me into the inner perimeter, an area no one could normally enter without special clearance. Here each federal law enforcement agency and military unit had set up their command posts. The colonel accompanied me right up to the fringe of the site where the American Airlines flight had exploded. As I studied the damage, I realized that the crash had occurred near the far end of one wing, but the explosion had flashed out and on through many more rooms and offices further down the line, burning them to a crisp. Much more damage had been sustained to that wing of the Pentagon than the public could see on television.

As I continued staring at the crash site, realizing the plane and all its occupants had disintegrated upon impact, and contemplating the injury and death to so many inside the building, and reflecting upon the thousands who had died in New York City, I sensed a vulnerability that I had never before felt. I was struck with the conviction that America needed God more than ever before.

I will forever relish those two days that I had the privilege of serving in the relief effort. It was a unique, but unfortunately, fleeting, taste of unity and hope for our country that I'd never felt before and that I've never felt since. The twenty hours that I logged in with the Red Cross was a huge honor and privilege. I had seen America at its best!

On September 15th, we returned home with a great appreciation for America and a great love and regard for those who live in it. America: the cradle of our liberty, the cradle of our religion, and the cradle of our hope. And that's what Tiffany named our newly-arrived granddaughter: Hope, to memorialize 9/11. Riley Hope McPheters.

★ ★ ★ ★ ★

As I again contemplated standing in front of those scorched walls of the Pentagon, next to Colonel J. Edgar Wakayama, I realized, deep down inside, that America would never be the same again; neither would the FBI, as it began changing its emphasis and restructuring its priorities in order to preserve the lives of our people.

The era of the FBI of Director J. Edgar Hoover and Special Agents Joe Frechette, Frank Duffin, the White Knight, and Mike McPheters, was gone forever!